COMMONWEALTH OF PENNSYLVANIA
ACT 195

Whodunits,
Farces,
and Fantasies

Whodunits, Farces, and Fantasies

Ten Short Plays

ROBERT W. BOYNTON

and

MAYNARD MACK

Yale University

HAYDEN BOOK COMPANY, INC.

Rochelle Park, New Jersey

Acknowledgments

SHALL WE JOIN THE LADIES? by Sir James M. Barrie is re-
printed by permission of Charles Scribner's Sons. Copyright 1928
Charles Scribner's Sons; renewal copyright © 1956 Lady Cynthia
Asquith, Peter L. Davies, Barclay's Bank Ltd.
SORRY, WRONG NUMBER. Copyright 1952, 1948 by Lucille
Fletcher. Reprinted by permission of the Dramatists Play Service,
Inc. and the author. CAUTION: SORRY, WRONG NUMBER,
being duly copyrighted, is subject to a royalty. The amateur acting rights are controlled exclusively by the Dramatists Play Service, Inc., 440 Park Avenue South, New York, NY 10016. No
amateur production of the play may be given without obtaining in
advance the written permission of the Dramatists Play Service,
Inc., and paying the requisite fee

Library of Congress Cataloging in Publication Data
Main entry under title:

Whodunits, farces, and fantasies.

(Hayden series in literature)
CONTENTS: Barrie, J. M. Shall we join the ladies?—
Fletcher, L. Sorry, wrong number.—Glaspell, S.
Trifles. [etc.]
1. Children's plays. I. Boynton, Robert W.
II. Mack, Maynard, (date)
PN6120.A4W47   822'.041   75-33829
ISBN 0-8104-5503-X

Printed in the United States of America

1	2	3	4	5	6	7	8	9	PRINTING

76	77	78	79	80	81	82	83	YEAR

Preface

The short play, like the short story, is a prominent part of most English curriculums—and for good reason. By definition it is short, and therefore easily digested in one sitting. At the same time it is complete, not just a slice of something larger, and therefore digesting it brings the satisfaction of resolution that any completed action brings.

It's also first-hand, immediately involving, so long as we look on the printed script as an invitation to imaginative production, not simply silent reading and analysis. The ten plays here are not meant to be play scripts (and, for those plays still under copyright protection, formal production must come only with permission), but they are also more than reading matter for a quiet hour at home. The questions at the end of each play suggest considerations to keep in mind in interpreting the scripts in the theater of the classroom or the theater of the mind.

These plays display three of the most popular forms the one-acter has taken: mysteries or thrillers, popularly called *whodunits*, the bread-and-butter fare of radio and television drama; *farces*, wildly exaggerated spoofs of human pomposity and tomfoolery; and *fantasies*, seemingly impossible distortions of reality that are often far too real in terms of what human beings are capable of.

We've included a mixture of recent successfully produced one-acters and older (but still fresh) favorites of the theater, television, and radio. In all our comments and questions we've tried to keep the light touch that makes the dramatic mode in literature so delightful and pleasurable for doer and viewer alike.

Robert W. Boynton
Maynard Mack

Contents

Introduction

i

This is a collection of ten one-act plays that we are confident you will enjoy. We hope you will want to read them, in the first instance, for the interesting people, worlds, and experiences they offer, from hilarious love affairs to bizarre murders, English country houses to San Francisco funeral parlors, and characters named simply Old Man to characters with names you might find in any city telephone book like Lena Grossman, Tony Benedetto, and Sam Smith. We also hope you will want to read them in order to know more than you know now about what it takes to make a good play. For that purpose, you couldn't find better company than that found here—Anton Chekhov, George Bernard Shaw, Sir James Barrie, Susan Glaspell, and half a dozen besides.

Finally, and above all, we hope you will read these plays, and any others you are lucky enough to meet with in your school curriculum, as reminders of the drama that waits to be uncovered in every act and word of ordinary life, including, most emphatically, the classroom.

ii

Consider any classroom for a moment. Though no doubt it lacks a curtain and a stage, it is nevertheless the "setting" every day for acts, thoughts, and feelings, together with confrontations between persons and ideas that generate further acts, thoughts, and feelings, in the manner of a good play. Nothing in the classroom experience, of course, is as highly selective and directive as a playscript has to be; the classroom gives more chance for improvisation and has far more tolerance for mediocre and bad "performances" (otherwise most of us would never get out of Grade 1) than any stage production could possibly permit. Still, the analogy is real. Take a look at your classmates. Already you can probably spot one or more among them who are getting themselves stamped, usually without knowing it, with stock "roles": Tough Guy, Grouser, Grade Grubber, Apple Polisher, Clothes Horse, Sex Pot, Girl Scout, Brain Trust, not to mention certain others too explosive to be named. The labels vary some with the generations and even from school to school, but in the Cast of Characters of the American classroom, most of these "parts" are as durable and predictable as those of Punch and his wife Judy in a Punch-and-Judy show.

Alternatively, take a look at yourself. What makes you so nervous when called on in class? What else but your consciousness of performing before an "audience" of your peers, not necessarily all friendly, to say nothing of that representative of the Establishment, the teacher. And what about the teacher? Have you ever stopped to realize that he or she is required to be "onstage" six or seven hours a day, must assume willy-nilly on entering the class a professional and social role that you and your parents and your community have in some part prescribed, and must therefore preserve a "character" that, if not actually make-believe, like an actor's, is at any rate moulded by the role's demands and will be far less in evidence if you happen to meet him or her on a Saturday night at the bowling alley, drive-in, movie-house, or ballgame?

iii

Inevitably, then, the classroom is a dramatic place, whether anyone wants to make it so or not. Our stand in this book is that everyone should try to make it so, consciously and intensely. The best learning, we are convinced, takes place in situations where you are invited (and are willing) to work with your teacher in bringing an assignment to life in the same manner as a troupe of actors works with its director to bring a playscript to life: the actors profiting from the director's guidelines, but the director, in turn, modifying his guidelines to take account of the actors' unforeseen responses and intuitions. To build this kind of learning environment, no way is more effective, we have found, than the study and practice of drama.

On this account, without suggesting for a moment that your classroom can be made into a theater (a practice that usually inhibits all parties concerned), we propose that the plays in this book be used not merely as a body of literature to be "covered" in some analytical way, but as a fascinating collection of actions, persons, situations, lifestyles, speech idioms, moods, settings, and problems, all to be explored, discussed, threshed out, modified, qualified, ratified, and tried out, so that the texts become a point of departure into life studies rather than a point of reference for literary quizzes. We make the fore-going possible by including among the questions designed to help your understanding of each play a number of presentational suggestions that will call out your powers of imagination and observation simulta-neously, and, if given half a chance, will also generate some lively group discussion and debate, leading both inward to yourself and out-ward to the world.

iv

How, for instance, would you present the young man who comes to the funeral home to mourn Esther's suicide in *Please, No Flowers*? "Not the best looking or the smartest—very poor taste, always dan-druff on his shoulders, but still, I loved him." That much we have from the author himself, speaking through Esther; and then, more directly, through the stage directions: "He is wearing a shapeless tweed suit and carrying a bouquet of mixed flowers." But none of this is very much to go on, once you start thinking about the part. Will you have him short or tall, heavy-set or slim, blond or dark? And his shapeless suit—what color? And why? To explain why, and also why the girl or boy in the next seat disagrees with you completely, will take you both far into in-terpreting both the play and your own individual tastes and the sorts of personal association you each have with certain physical and color characteristics.

Even the bouquet the young man carries will demand some re-search, or at least a good memory. What should be its general charac-ter and appearance? What flowers will you have recognizable in it—apart from the yellow rose that is pulled from it for Lena later on? Should it indicate a specific season? Are there any signs that the play is supposed to take place at a specific season? If so, what flowers are in order? How much do you know, in fact, about which flowers belong to which season? On the other hand, if the play gives no indications of season, could it be argued that the director should import some for at-mospheric effect? What season would you choose, and for what effect? Whatever you decide about the season, how would you go about mak-ing the young man's bouquet express something about his personality and his feelings for Esther?

As he stands before Esther's coffin, the young man weeps, and later on she reciprocates. This is the toughest challenge of all. How *do* people weep? You have many times seen and heard them do so, either in real life or in the films or on TV, and surely on occasion you have done some weeping yourself. Why is it, then, that you have never really *registered* any part of it? Can you mime, even superficially, the movements of the face, convulsions of the body, fluctuations of the voice? Try it. Get a classmate to try it. Then the next time it happens on TV or in a film, don't just let it wash over you: *look.* One of the special dividends from working seriously with plays is that you begin to use your eyes and ears as they were meant to be used, and to see and hear the lives around you as they deserve to be seen and heard.

v

We could continue at some length about the virtues of working and playing with plays, not the least of which is the fact that work in this kind of context soon becomes indistinguishable from play and the play becomes undistinguished unless there is work. But we think we have said enough to persuade the venturesome. All that you need to bear in mind as you approach this book is the reason angels can fly: They take themselves lightly, if seriously.

Part I
Three
Whodunits

Shall We Join the Ladies?

JAMES M. BARRIE

Sorry, Wrong Number

LUCILLE FLETCHER

Trifles

SUSAN GLASPELL

This play is a whodunit—with a fresh twist. A rich man whose brother has been murdered invites all the suspects to a dinner party and then assures them that before the evening is over one of them will reveal himself or herself to be the murderer. One of them does so, but just who it is will puzzle you even after you have read the play, once or a number of times.

Shall We Join the Ladies?

JAMES M. BARRIE

Characters

SAM SMITH   *The host. He is a little old bachelor, who beams on his guests like an elderly cupid. That is how his guests regard him, but they are to be undeceived.*

LADY JANE RAYE   *Young and very beautiful.*

SIR JOSEPH WRATHIE   *An elderly and arrogant financier.*

MRS. PREEN   *Middle-aged and somewhat neurotic.*

MR. VAILE   *About forty, and a perfect little gentleman, if socks and spats can do it.*

MR. GOURLAY   *An artist, but not a very attractive one.*

MRS. CASTRO   *A mysterious widow from Buenos Aires. In the late thirties.*

MISS ISIT   *Younger than the widow, but her name obviously needs to be queried.*

CAPTAIN JENNINGS   *A typical young officer, probably in the guards.*

MRS. BLAND   *In her thirties. We hear nothing of a Mr. Bland. She is inclined to be gushing, especially to her host.*

MISS VAILE   *Vaile's sister, so she says. But there is something wrong here.*

MR. PREEN   *Of middle age, self-indulgent, but well liked by the rest.*

LADY WRATHIE   *Sir Joseph's wife. She probably has ambitions of her own to match those of her husband.*

DOLPHIN   *A silent and incredibly efficient butler.*

LUCY   *A maid.*

A POLICEMAN.

SCENE: *The dining room of Sam Smith's country house. The time is late evening. It is a spacious, dark-panelled room, the furniture is very fine and solid, the lighting discreet. In the center is a large mahogany table. The silver and glass are very beautiful. The windows in the right wall are heavily curtained. There is a door down left, and double doors back stage to the left of center. There is a massive sideboard against the left wall, and a serving table up right. On each are the wines, glasses, and other details ready for appropriate moments.*

When the curtain rises, dessert is being served, by Dolphin and Lucy, to Sam Smith and his twelve guests who are seated around the table. There is hilarious laughter over some quip we are just too late to catch. But we notice that Lady Jane is not laughing, for she is scanning the table and counting the company. As the laughter subsides:

LADY JANE   *(Appalled; rising)*   We are thirteen at table!

GOURLAY   What's that?

(Many fingers begin to count.)

LADY JANE   We are thirteen.   *(She looks down at Smith.)*

LADY WRATHIE   Fourteen

CAPTAIN JENNINGS   Twelve.   *(Almost together)*

PREEN   Surely not!

LADY JANE   *(To Smith)*   We are thirteen.

SMITH   Oh dear, how careless of me. Is there anything I can do?

SIR JOSEPH   *(As at a board meeting)*   Leave this to me. All keep your seats.   *(He rises.)*

MRS. PREEN   I am afraid Lady Jane has risen.   *(Lady Jane sits.)*

LADY WRATHIE   Joseph, you have risen yourself.   *(Sir Joseph sits.)*

MRS. CASTRO   *(With an air of mystery)*   Were we thirteen all those other nights?

MRS. PREEN   (*Reassuring herself and the company*)   We always had a guest or two from outside, you remember.

MISS ISIT   (*Brightly*)   All we have got to do is to make our number fourteen.

VAILE   (*Leaning forward*)   But how, Miss Isit?

MISS ISIT   Why, Dolphin, of course!

MRS. PREEN   It's too clever of you, Miss Isit. (*To her host*)   Mr. Smith, Dolphin may sit down with us, mayn't he?

LADY JANE   Please, dear Mr. Smith; just for a moment. That breaks the spell.

SIR JOSEPH   (*With a look at Dolphin who is behind and just below him.*)   We won't eat you, Dolphin. (*But he has crunched some similar ones.*)

SMITH   Let me explain to him. (*To Dolphin who turns to Smith respectfully*)   You see, Dolphin, there is a superstition that if thirteen people sit down at table, something staggering will happen to one of them before the night is out. (*To the others*)   That is it, isn't it?

MRS. BLAND   (*Darkly*)   Namely, death.

SMITH   (*Brightly*)   Yes, namely, death.

LADY JANE   But not before the night is out, you dear; before the year is out.

SMITH   I thought it was before the night was out.

GOURLAY   (*Making to shift his chair*)   Sit here, Dolphin.

(*Dolphin makes a reluctant movement.*)

MISS VAILE   No, I want him.

MISS ISIT   It was my idea, and I insist on having him.

MRS. CASTRO   (*Moving her chair towards Gourlay*)   Yes, here between us.

(*Dolphin moves down. The maid smoothly slides a chair between Mrs. Castro and Miss Isit. Dolphin sits, so that he is now facing Smith. The maid retires to left.*)

MRS. PREEN   (*With childish abandon*)   Saved!

SMITH   As we are saved, and he does not seem happy, may he resume his duties?

(*Dolphin rises and is checked by*)

LADY WRATHIE   Yes, yes; and now we ladies may withdraw.

PREEN   First, a glass of wine with you, Dolphin.

VAILE   (*Ever seeking to undermine Preen's popularity*)   Is this wise?

PREEN   (*Ignoring him*)   To the health of our friend, Dolphin.

(*The company drink Dolphin's health without rising. He gives a slight stiff bow and goes up left. A moment later he is discreetly noting who needs a glass refilled. There is a slight stir among the ladies who would now rise but for a detaining gesture from Sir Joseph, who stands.*)

SIR JOSEPH   One moment. Another toast. Fellow-guests, tomorrow morning, alas, this party has to break up, and I am sure you will all agree with me that we have had a delightful week. It has not been an eventful week; it has been too happy for that.

CAPTAIN JENNINGS   (*Rising, with a smile at Lady Jane*)   I rise to protest. When I came here a week ago I had never met Lady Jane. Now, as you know, we are engaged. (*The maid commences an ecstatic sigh which is quelled by a glance from Dolphin.*)   I certainly call it an eventful week.

LADY JANE   (*Very prettily*)   Yes, please, Sir Joseph.

SIR JOSEPH   I stand corrected. And now we are in the last evening of it. We are drawing to the end of a perfect day—

PREEN   (*Who is also an orator*)   In seconding this motion—

VAILE   Pooh!

(*His lack of good manners checks Preen, and Sir Joseph continues, addressing Smith.*)

SIR JOSEPH   Though I have known you intimately but for a short time, I already find it impossible to call you anything but Sam Smith.

MRS. CASTRO   (*With a dazzling smile*)   In our hearts, Mr. Smith, that is what we ladies call you also.

(*Smith gives a little smile and bows in her direction.*)

PREEN   If I might say a word—

VAILE   Tuts.

(*Preen is speechless.*)

SIR JOSEPH   (*Ignoring all this, and indicating their host with an expansive gesture*)   Ladies and gentlemen, is he not like a pocket edition of Mr. Pickwick?

GOURLAY   Exactly. This is how I should like to paint him.

MRS. BLAND   (*Leaning in his direction—very gushing*)   Mr. Smith, you love, we think that if you were married you could not be so nice.

SIR JOSEPH   At any rate, he could not be so simple. (*This amuses everybody at the table.*)   For you are a very simple soul, Sam Smith. Well, we esteem you the more for your simplicity. (*He *picks up his glass.*) Friends all, I give you the toast of—Sam Smith.

(*The toast is drunk with acclamation. Dolphin, who has been quite impassive throughout the speech, refills Preen's glass. The maid is busy for a moment at the sideboard, then returns to her place. There are cries of "Sam Smith!" and "Speech!"*)

SMITH   (*Rising; with his Pickwickian smile*) Ladies and gentlemen, you are very kind, and I don't pretend that it isn't pleasant to me to be praised. Tell me,   (*a tiny pause*)   have you wondered why I invited you here?

MISS ISIT   Because you like us, of course, you muddle-headed old darling.

SMITH   (*Blandly*) Was that the reason?

SIR JOSEPH   (*Inclined to be playful*) Take care, Sammy, you are not saying what you mean!

(*The guests all display great interest.*)

SMITH   Am I not? Kindly excuse. I dare say I am as simple as Sir Joseph says. And yet, do you really know me? Does any person ever know another absolutely? Has not the simplest of us a secret drawer inside him with—with a lock to it?

MISS ISIT   If you have, Mr. Smith, be a dear and open it to us.

MRS. CASTRO   (*This is to Miss Isit.*) How delicious! He is going to tell us of his first and only love.

SMITH   Ah, Mrs. Castro, I think I had one once—very nice—but I have forgotten her name. The person I loved best was—my brother.

PREEN   I never knew you had a brother.

SMITH   I suppose none of you knew. He died two years ago.

SIR JOSEPH   Sorry, Sam Smith.

MRS. PREEN   (*Drawing the chocolates nearer her*) We should like to hear about him if it isn't too sad.

SMITH   Would you? (*There is a murmur of assent, and he continues.*) He was many years my junior and as attractive as I am commonplace. (*A murmur of deprecation*) He died in a foreign land. (*Gravely*) Natural causes were certified. But—there were suspicious circumstances, and I went out there to probe the matter to the full. (*To Mrs. Bland*) I did, too.

PREEN   You didn't say where the place was.

(*Miss Isit drinks.*)

SMITH   It was—Monte Carlo. (*He pauses. As Miss Isit's glass is lowered it slips from her hand to the floor. No one notes it, apparent-*

ly, but Smith and Dolphin, and the maid, who instantly removes the pieces.)   Dolphin, another glass for Miss Isit.

(*Almost before the request is made, Dolphin is gliding smoothly to Miss Isit with another glass. He fills it without the slightest expression on his face.*)

LADY JANE   Do go on.

(*Everybody is most intent.*)

SMITH   My inquiries were slow, but I became convinced that my brother had been poisoned.

MRS. BLAND   How dreadful. You poor man.

GOURLAY   I hope, Sam Smith, you got on the track of the criminals.

SMITH   (*Blandly*) Oh, yes. (*A chair creaks.*) Did you speak, Miss Isit?

MISS ISIT   Did I? I think not. What did you say about the criminals?

SMITH   Not criminals; there was only one.

PREEN   Man or woman?

SMITH   We are not yet certain. (*Preen nods understandingly, and empties his glass.*) What we do know is that my brother was visited in his room that night by someone who must have been the murderer. It was someone who spoke English and who certainly dressed as a man, but it may have been a woman. There is proof that it was someone who had been to the tables that night. I got in touch with every "possible," though I had to follow some of them to distant parts.

(*Dolphin quietly refills Preen's glass.*)

LADY WRATHIE   It is extraordinarily interesting.

SMITH   (*Replying direct to her*) Outwardly, many of them seemed to be quite respectable people.

SIR JOSEPH   Ah, one can't go by that, Sam Smith.

SMITH   I didn't. I made the most exhaustive inquiries into their private lives. (*Smoothly*) I did it so cunningly that not one of them suspected why I was so anxious to make his or her acquaintance; and then—when I was ready for them, I invited them to my house for a week, and— (*with a gentle, embracing sweep of the hands*) they are all sitting round my table this evening. (*For a moment a horrified silence; then a low murmur of indignation which dies down as he resumes.*) You wanted to know why I had asked you here, and I am afraid that in consequence I have wandered a little from the toast; but I thank you, Sir Joseph, I thank you all, for the too kind way in which you have drunk my health.

(He sits down as modestly as he had risen, but it is noted that the smile has gone from his face and that he is licking his lips. A confused babel breaks out, during which Dolphin, who has displayed no emotion whatever, goes about refilling glasses.)

PREEN   In the name of every one of us, Mr. Smith, I tell you that this is an outrage.

SMITH   I was afraid you wouldn't like it.

SIR JOSEPH   May I ask, sir, whether all this week you have been surreptitiously ferreting into our private affairs, perhaps even rummaging our trunks?

SMITH   *(Brightening)*   That was it. You remember how I pressed you all to show your prowess on the tennis courts and the golf links while I stayed at home? That was my time for the trunks.   *(He sips his wine.)*

LADY JANE   *(Braving it out)*   Was there ever such a man? Did you open our letters?

(The company is now very still.)

SMITH   *(To Lady Jane)*   Every one of them.   *(Dolphin refils his glass and retires to up right.)*   And there were some very queer things in them.   *(Speaking to the company generally)*   There was one about a luncheon at the Ritz. "You will know me," the man wrote, "by the gardenia I shall carry in my hand." Perhaps I shouldn't have mentioned that. But the lady who got that letter needn't be frightened. She is married, and her husband is here with her, but I won't tell you any more.

MISS ISIT   *(Resentfully)*   I think he should be compelled to tell.

PREEN   Wrathie, there are only two ladies here with their husbands.

SIR JOSEPH   *(Meeting the challenge)*   Yours and mine, Preen.

LADY WRATHIE   *(In a tone brooking no further argument)*   Joseph, I don't need to tell you it wasn't your wife.

MRS. PREEN   *(For Lady Wrathie's benefit)*   It certainly wasn't yours, Willie.

PREEN   Of that I am well assured.

SIR JOSEPH   Take care what you say, Preen. That is very like a reflection on my wife.   *(His voice rises in cold anger.)*

GOURLAY   *(Contemptuous of these anxieties)*   Let that pass. The other is the serious thing—so serious that it is a nightmare.   *(To Smith)*   Whom do you accuse of doing away with your brother, sir? Out with it.

SMITH   *(Looking around at his guests)*   You are not all turning against me, are you? I assure you I don't accuse any of you—yet. I know that one of you did it, but I am not sure which one. I shall know soon.

VAILE   Soon? How soon?

SMITH   Soon after the men join the ladies tonight. I ought to tell you that I am to try a little experiment tonight, something I have thought out which I have every confidence will make the guilty person fall into my hands, like a—ripe plum. (*His right hand closes slowly, and rather horribly.*)

LADY JANE   (*Hitting the hand*)   Don't do that.

(*Vaile empties his glass. There is a disturbed murmur and restless movement. Dolphin, during this, comes down and refills Vaile's glass.*)

SIR JOSEPH   We insist, Smith, on hearing what this experiment is to be.

SMITH   That would spoil it. But I can tell you this. My speech had a little pit in it, and all the time I was talking I was watching whether any of you would fall into that pit.

MRS. PREEN   (*Rising; nervously*)   I didn't notice any pit.

(*Sir Joseph and Lady Wrathie exchange a contemptuous smile of triumph.*)

SMITH   (*Courteously*)   You weren't meant to, Mrs. Preen.

(*Mrs. Preen sits rather suddenly. Dolphin moves up to right.*)

PREEN   May I ask, without pressing the personal note, did anyone fall into your pit?

SMITH   (*With a private smile*)   I think so.

(*The maid makes a slight movement. She is watching Mrs. Preen very anxiously.*)

CAPTAIN JENNINGS   Smith, we must have the name of this person.

LADY WRATHIE   Mrs. Preen has fainted!

(*There is instant commotion. Mrs. Preen is lying back in her chair. Sir Joseph and Vaile are attentive but futile. Preen hurries round to up right, and takes a glass of water from Dolphin who has brought it from the table up stage. Lady Jane has risen. But Mrs. Preen recovers very quickly. Sir Joseph puts down the napkin with which he had fanned her. Lady Jane sits.*)

MRS. PREEN   Why—what—who—I am all right now. Willie, go back to your seat. Why are you all staring at me so?

MISS ISIT   (*Insincerely*)   Dear Mrs. Preen, we are so glad you are better. I wonder what upset you? (*She exchanges a smile with Mrs. Castro.*)

PREEN   (*To the company, returning to his place*)   I never knew her to faint before. (*He instantly regrets his words.*)

MISS ISIT   (*As before*)   I expect it was the heat.

PREEN   (*From behind his chair*)   Say it was the heat, Emily.

MRS. PREEN   No, it wasn't the heat, Miss Isit. It was Mr. Smith's talk of a pit.

PREEN   (*Distressed*)   My dear— (*He sits.*)

MRS. PREEN   (*In a curious tone*)   I suddenly remembered how, as that man mentioned that the place of the crime was Monte Carlo, some lady let her wineglass fall. That was why I fainted. (*With assumed vagueness*)   I can't remember who she was.

LADY WRATHIE   It was Miss Isit.

MRS. PREEN   (*Casually*)   Really?

MISS ISIT   There is a thing called the law of libel. If Lady Wrathie and Mrs. Preen will kindly formulate their charges—

GOURLAY   Oh, come, let us keep our heads.

SMITH   That's what I say.

GOURLAY   What about a motive? Scotland Yard always seeks for that first.

SMITH   I see two possible motives. If a woman did it—well, they tended to run after my brother, and you all know of what a woman scorned is capable.

PREEN   (*Reminiscently*)   Rather. (*Then he is confused.*)

SMITH   Then again, my brother had a large sum of money with him, which disappeared.

SIR JOSEPH   If you could trace that money it might be a help.

SMITH   (*Leaning forward keenly*)   All sorts of things are a help. The way you are all pretending to know nothing about the matter is a help. It might be a help if I could find out which of you has a clammy hand that at this moment wants to creep beneath the table. (*Not a hand creeps, but several glance at others' hands.*)   I'll tell you something more. (*Mrs. Castro stiffens. The maid glances at her.*)   Murderers' hearts beat differently from other hearts. (*Raising a finger*)   Listen! (*There is complete stillness. He almost whispers.*)   Whose was it?

(*A cry from Miss Vaile. All look at her, and she shows confusion.*)

MISS VAILE   I thought I heard it. It seemed to come from across the table. (*A resentful murmur*)   Please don't think because this man made me scream that I did it. I never was on a yacht in my life, at Monte Carlo or anywhere else.

(*The murmur assumes a triumphant tone.*)

VAILE   (*Sharply*)   Bella!

MISS VAILE   (*Still more confused*)   Have I said—anything odd?

GOURLAY   (*Very pleased*)   A yacht? There has been no talk of a yacht.

(*Vaile suppresses fury.*)

MISS VAILE   (*Shrinking back*)   Hasn't there?

SMITH   (*Indulgently*)   Perhaps there should have been. It was on his yacht my brother died.

MRS. CASTRO   You said "in his rooms."

SMITH   Yes, that is what I *said*. I wanted to find out which of you knew better.

LADY JANE   And Miss Vaile—

MISS VAILE   I can explain it all if—if—

MISS ISIT   (*Sneering*)   Yes, give her a little time.

SMITH   Perhaps you would all like to take a few minutes.

MISS VAILE   I admit I was at Monte Carlo—with my brother—when an Englishman died there rather mysteriously on a yacht. When Mr. Smith told us of his brother's death, I concluded that it was probably the same person.

VAILE   I presume that you accept my sister's statement?

MISS ISIT   Ab—so—lute—ly.

SMITH   She is not the only one of you who knew that yacht. You all admit having been at Monte Carlo two years ago, I suppose?

CAPTAIN JENNINGS   One of us wasn't. Lady Jane was never there.

SMITH   (*His eyes gleaming*)   What do you say to that, Lady Jane?

(*Lady Jane falters.*)

CAPTAIN JENNINGS   Tell him, Jane.

SMITH   Yes, tell me.

CAPTAIN JENNINGS   You were never there; say so.

LADY JANE   (*With a touch of defiance*)   Why shouldn't I have been there?

CAPTAIN JENNINGS   No reason. But when I happened to mention Monte Carlo to you the other day I certainly understood—Jane, I never forget a word you say, and you did say you had never been there.

LADY JANE   So you—you, Jack—you accuse me—you—me—

CAPTAIN JENNINGS   I haven't—I haven't!

LADY JANE   (*Suddenly very cold*)   You have all heard that Captain Jennings and I are engaged. I want you to understand that we are so no longer.

CAPTAIN JENNINGS   Jane!

(*Lady Jane has removed her engagement ring as he speaks. For a moment she holds it, hesitant; but by this time Dolphin has come smoothly to her right, with a salver on which she deposits the ring. In silence he conveys it up and across to the captain, who takes it sullenly. There is an audible gurgle of sympathy from the maid. This is a breach of etiquette, and Dolphin, with stony disapproval, opens the door down left, and the maid makes a shameful exit. Dolphin then refills Captain Jennings' glass.*)

SMITH   (*In a kindly tone*)   Take comfort, Captain. If Lady Jane should prove to be the person wanted—mind you, perhaps she isn't—why then, the ring is a matter of small importance, because you would be parted in any case. I mean by the handcuffs. I forgot to say that I have them here. (*He gropes at his feet, and brings to light the handcuffs. Dolphin is instantly at his left with the salver, on which they are deposited.*)   Pass them round, Dolphin. (*To the guests*)   Perhaps some of you have never seen them before.

(*Dolphin moves from Smith with the salver going around the table clockwise, displaying the handcuffs to each as if proffering some dish. It is coldly rejected by all.*)

PREEN   (*As this is in progress*)   A pocket edition of Pickwick we called him; he is more like a pocket edition of the devil.

SMITH   (*In mild and smiling reproof*)   Please, a little courtesy. After all, I am your host. (*Dolphin has reached Miss Vaile.*)   Do take a look at them, Miss Vaile; they are an adjustable pair in case they should be needed for small wrists. (*Miss Vaile is furious. Mrs. Bland smiles at the handcuffs. Dolphin passes on to Captain Jennings who ignores them. Miss Isit gives them a brief look.*)   Would you like to try them on, Mrs. Castro? They close with a click—a click.

(*Mrs. Castro sits rigid.*)

SIR JOSEPH   We quite understand.

(*Dolphin shows the handcuffs to Gourley, who smiles at them sardonically. Vaile will not look at them. Dolphin passes on.*)

MRS. BLAND   (*Rising*)   How stupid of us. We have all forgotten that he said the murderer may have been a woman in man's clothes, and I have just remembered that when we played the charade on Wednesday he wanted the ladies to dress up as men. Was it to see whether one of us looked as if she could have passed for a man that night at Monte Carlo?

SMITH   You've got it, Mrs. Bland.

SIR JOSEPH   Well, none of you did dress up, at any rate.

MRS. BLAND   (*Distressed*)   Oh, Sir Joseph. Some of us did dress up, in private, and we all agreed that—of course, there's nothing in it, but we all agreed that the only figure which might have deceived a careless eye was Lady Wrathie's.

PREEN   I say!

LADY WRATHIE   Joseph, do you sit there and permit this?

(*Dolphin replenishes her glass.*)

SMITH   Now, now! There is nothing to be touchy about. Have I not been considerate?

SIR JOSEPH   Smith, I hold you to be an impudent scoundrel.

SMITH   (*Mildly*)   May not I, who lost a brother in circumstances so painful, appeal for a little kindly consideration from those of you who are innocent—shady characters though you be?

PREEN   I must say that rather touches me. Some of us might have reasons for being reluctant to have our past at Monte inquired into, without being the person you are asking for.

SMITH   (*Glass in hand and sitting back*)   Precisely. I am presuming that to be the position of eleven of you.

LADY WRATHIE   (*Rising; imperiously*)   Joseph, I must ask you to come upstairs with me to pack our things.

MISS ISIT   For my part, after poor Mr. Smith's appeal I think it would be rather heartless not to stay and see the thing out. Especially, Mr. Smith, if you would give us just an inkling of what your—little experiment—in the drawing-room—is to be?

SMITH   (*Gravely, twirling the glass in his fingers*)   I can't say anything about it except that it isn't to take place in the drawing-room. (*He sets down the glass.*)   You ladies are to go this evening to Dolphin's room, where we shall join you presently.

(*For the first time, Dolphin displays a reaction. In moving, at that moment, to the service table up right, he halts, looking at his master's back. He then completes his first intention.*)

MRS. PREEN   Why should we go there?

SMITH   (*Gently; leaning towards her*)   Because I tell you to, Mrs. Preen.

LADY WRATHIE   I go to no such room. I leave this house at once.

MRS. PREEN   (*Rising*)   I also.

LADY JANE   (*Rising also*)   All of us. I want to go home.

(*The men rise, stepping back from the chairs.*)

LADY WRATHIE   (*Moving from the table*)   Joseph, come.

MRS. PREEN   Willie, I am ready. I wish you a long good-bye, Mr. Smith.

(*The rest of the ladies, having risen, move up to the door up left with dignity. Dolphin has reached the door in time to open it. The ladies stop, and some move back a pace or two, for a policeman is standing just beyond the threshold. The ladies all turn and glare at Smith.*)

SMITH   (*Without looking at them*) The ladies will now adjourn—to Dolphin's room.

LADY WRATHIE   I say no.

MRS. CASTRO   Let us. (*Smith stands, as she advances to him.*) Why shouldn't the innocent ones help him? (*She gives him her hand with a disarming smile.*)

SMITH   (*Pressing her fingers, retaining them*) I knew you would be on my side, Mrs. Castro. (*Confidentially*) Cold hand—warm heart. That's the saying, isn't it?

(*Mrs. Castro shrinks back, withdrawing her hand.*)

LADY WRATHIE   Those who wish to leave this man's house, follow me.

SMITH   (*After a glance in her direction, raising his voice*) My brother's cigarette case was of faded green leather, and a hole had been burned in the back of it.

(*For some reason this takes the fight out of Lady Wrathie. She tosses her head and departs for Dolphin's room. The other ladies follow: first Mrs. Preen, Lady Jane, Mrs. Castro, then Miss Vaile. As Miss Vaile passes Smith, he whispers a word or two to her. She is rigid for a moment and then hurries out, followed by Mrs. Bland.*)

VAILE   (*As these are leaving*) What did you say to my sister?

SMITH   I only said to her that she isn't your sister. (*Vaile clenches his hands at his sides. Checking Miss Isit, the last to leave.*) So you never met my brother, Miss Isit?

MISS ISIT   (*Coolly*) Not that I know of, Mr. Smith.

SMITH   I have a photograph of him that I should like to show you.

MISS ISIT   I don't care to see it.

SMITH   You are going to see it. (*He whips a small photograph from his pocket and puts it before her eyes.*)

MISS ISIT   (*Surprised*) That is not—

(*She checks herself. Smith smiles dangerously.*)

SMITH   No, that is not my brother. That is someone you have never seen. But how did you know it wasn't my brother? (*Miss Isit is silent.*) I rather think you knew Dick, Miss Isit.

MISS ISIT   (*Having recovered, drops a curtsy*)   I rather think I did, Mr. Sam. What then?

(*She goes out impudently. Dolphin closes the door. The men stare uncertainly at Smith, who with a secret smile turns away from the door. He takes up a decanter and a box of cigarettes and toddles down to the chair exactly opposite his original place. He is now with his back to the audience.*)

SMITH   Draw up closer, won't you?   (*He sits. They all drift, very reluctantly, to the chairs nearest him on either side. The sole exception is Vaile who is studying a picture near the door. One fancies he would go out if Smith were not looking.*)   You are not leaving us, Vaile?

VAILE   (*Startled*)   I thought—

SMITH   (*Sharply*)   Sit down.

VAILE   Oh, quite.

(*He sits on the left on the chair previously occupied by Miss Vaile. At his right are Preen and then Jennings. Mrs. Bland's chair is empty. Gourlay is in his original seat, and Sir Joseph in that occupied by Mrs. Preen. Vaile's original chair is left empty.*)

SMITH   You are not drinking anything, Gourlay. Captain, the port is with you.

(*The wine revolves, but no one partakes.*)

PREEN   (*Heavily*)   Smith, there are a few words that I think it my duty to say. This is a very unusual situation.

SMITH   Yes. You'll have a cigarette, Preen?

(*The cigarettes are passed round but are not accepted.*)

GOURLAY   I wonder why Mrs. Bland—she is the only one of them there seems nothing against.

VAILE   A bit fishy, that.

PREEN   (*Murmuring*)   It was rather odd, my wife fainting.

CAPTAIN JENNINGS   (*Gloomily*)   I dare say the ladies are saying the same sort of thing about us. (*He lights one of his own cigarettes.*)

(*Dolphin is offering them liqueurs.*)

PREEN   (*Sulkily*)   No, thanks.   (*But he takes one*)   Smith, I am sure I speak for all of us when I say we would esteem it a favor if you ask Dolphin to withdraw.

(*Jennings refuses a liqueur with a shake of the head.*)

SMITH (*Accepting a liqueur*) He has his duties.

(*Dolphin passes below Smith to Gourlay.*)

GOURLAY (*Pettishly*) No thanks. (*Dolphin moves on to Sir Joseph.*) He gets on my nerves. Can nothing disturb this man?

CAPTAIN JENNINGS Evidently nothing.

SIR JOSEPH (*Having waved Dolphin irritably away*) Everything seems to point to its being a woman—wouldn't you say, Smith?

SMITH I wouldn't say anything, Sir Joseph. Dolphin thinks it was a man.

SIR JOSEPH One of us here?

(*Smith nods. The men all regard Dolphin with great distaste. He, as impassive as ever, is now at the sideboard, his back to the company.*)

GOURLAY Did he know your brother?

(*All listen intently.*)

SMITH He was my brother's servant out there.

VAILE (*Rising instantly*) What? He wasn't the fellow who—?

SMITH (*Leaning forward*) Who what, Vaile?

PREEN I say! (*He gives a significant grin to Gourlay and Sir Joseph.*)

VAILE (*Hotly*) What do you say?

PREEN (*Doggedly*) Nothing. (*He looks up at him amused.*) But— I say—

(*Vaile looks venomously at Dolphin's back. Preen turns and looks in the same direction. The other two men are also watching Dolphin, who is busy setting liqueurs back, and arranging glasses.*)

GOURLAY Are we to understand that you have had Dolphin spying on us here?

SMITH That was the idea. And he helped me by taking your fingerprints.

(*Dolphin crosses back to up right.*)

VAILE (*Throwing himself back in his chair*) How can that help?

SMITH He sent them to Scotland Yard.

SIR JOSEPH (*Vindictively*) Oh, he did, did he? (*His napkin falls unheeded.*)

PREEN What shows fingermarks best?

SMITH Glass, I believe.

PREEN   (*Putting down his glass*)   Now I see why the Americans went dry.°

(*Dolphin moves down the side of the table, attentive.*)

SIR JOSEPH   Smith, how can you be sure that Dolphin wasn't the man himself?

(*Smith makes no answer or sign. Dolphin imperturbably picks up Sir Joseph's napkin and returns it to him.*)

PREEN   Somehow I still cling to the hope that it was a woman.

VAILE   (*Trying to keep the anxiety from his voice*)   If it is a woman, Smith, what will you do?

SMITH   (*In a cold dry voice*)   She shall hang by the neck until she is dead.   (*Almost genially*)   You won't try the Benedictine, Vaile?

VAILE   (*In a hoarse whisper*)   No, thanks.

(*The maid enters from up left with the coffee tray, which she presents under Dolphin's superintendence. Most of the men accept. The cups are already full.*)

SIR JOSEPH   (*In his lighter manner*)   Did you notice what the ladies are doing in Dolphin's room, Lucy?

(*The maid, at Sir Joseph's elbow, gives a scared glance at Smith.*)

MAID   (*Trembling*)   Yes, Sir Joseph, they are wondering, Sir Joseph, which of you it was that did it.   (*She passes on to Gourlay.*)

PREEN   How like women!

GOURLAY   (*Accepting coffee*)   By the way, Smith, do you know how the poison was administered?

(*The maid passes on to Smith.*)

SMITH   (*About to take a cup*)   Yes, in coffee.

MAID   You are to take the *yellow* cup, sir.

SMITH   (*Pausing*)   Who said so?

MAID   The lady who poured out this evening, sir.

PREEN   Aha, who was she?

MAID   Lady Jane Raye, sir.

(*Smith takes the yellow cup. As the maid passes on to above Jennings:*)

PREEN   I don't like it.

(*Smith is about to raise his cup.*)

°"went dry," that is, passed the Eighteenth Amendment to the Constitution in 1919 forbidding the manufacture, sale, and export and import of liquor.

GOURLAY   Smith, don't drink that coffee!

(*Smith withdraws his hand.*)

JENNINGS   (*In wrath*)   Why shouldn't he drink it?

(*A gesture of dismissal to the maid who goes to above Vaile.*)

GOURLAY   Well, if it was she—a desperate woman—it was given in coffee the other time, remember? But stop, she wouldn't be likely to do it in the same way a second time.

VAILE   (*Takes the coffee*)   I'm not so sure. Perhaps she doesn't suspect that Smith knows how it was given the first time. We didn't know till the ladies had left the room.

PREEN   (*Admiring him at last*)   I say, Vaile, that's good.

(*The maid replaces the tray on the buffet and stands ready for further instructions. Dolphin stands above the table, silent and impassive.*)

JENNINGS   (*During the above*)   I have no doubt she merely meant that she had sugared it to his taste.

VAILE   (*Smiling and leaning forward*)   Sugar!

PREEN   Sugar!

GOURLAY   Couldn't we analyze it?

JENNINGS   (*Pushing his chair back; angrily*)   Smith, I insist on your drinking that coffee.

(*Smith gives no sign or movement.*)

VAILE   Lady Jane! Who would have thought it?

PREEN   Lady Jane! Who would have thought it?

JENNINGS   (*Reaching for the cup*)   Give me the yellow cup.   (*He drains it.*)

(*The maid presses her hand to her mouth.*)

SIR JOSEPH   (*After a tense moment*)   Nobly done, in any case.   (*He leans forward to Jennings.*)   Look here, Jennings—you are among friends—it hadn't an odd taste, had it?

JENNINGS   (*Harshly*)   Not a bit.

VAILE   He wouldn't feel the effects yet.

PREEN   (*With confidence in Vaile*)   He wouldn't feel them yet.

(*The maid sways slightly and recovers.*)

SMITH   Vaile ought to know.

PREEN   (*As before*)   Vaile knows.

SIR JOSEPH   Why ought Vaile to know, Smith?

SMITH   He used to practice as a doctor.

(Vaile reacts.)

SIR JOSEPH   You never mentioned that to me, Vaile.
VAILE   *(Defiantly)*   Why should I?
SMITH   Why should he? He is not allowed to practice now.

(Vaile shows his teeth viciously.)

PREEN   A doctor—poison—ease of access—

(His confidence in Vaile destroyed, he casts him an unpleasant glance, rises, and wanders despondently to the above table.)

SIR JOSEPH   We are where we were again.

(The maid shows signs of collapse. Dolphin is instantly at her side and escorts her from the room by doors up left center.)

JENNINGS   At any rate, that fellow has gone.

(Gourlay gives a short laugh. All look at him.)

GOURLAY   Excuse me. I suddenly remembered that Wrathie had called this the end of a perfect day.
SMITH   It isn't ended yet.

(Preen, now at the top end of the buffet, pours himself some brandy, swirling it thoughtfully.)

PREEN   *(As if to himself)*   I feel I am not my old bright self.   *(He sips.)*   I can't believe for a moment it was my wife.   *(He sips.)*   And yet—   *(he sips)*   —that fainting, you know.   *(He sips.)*   I should go away for a bit until it blew over.   *(He sips.)*   I don't think I should ever marry again.   *(He finishes the brandy cheerfully.)*
GOURLAY   There is something shocking about sitting here, suspecting each other in this way. Let us go to that room and have it out.
SMITH   I am quite ready.   *(Looking around)*   Nothing more to drink, anyone? Bring your cigarette, Captain.
SIR JOSEPH   *(Hoarsely)*   Smith—Sam—before we go, can I have a word with you alone?
SMITH   *(Shaking his head slowly)*   Sorry, Joseph. And now—   *(he rises)*   —shall we join the ladies?

(They all rise. As they do so, a dreadful scream is heard from the direction of Dolphin's room—a woman's scream. The men stand tense and horrified. The next moment, Dolphin appears in the doorway up left center. He is no longer the imperturbable butler. He is livid. He tries to speak, but no words will come. He stands

transfixed as the guests, led by Captain Jennings, dash past him and out. Dolphin looks at his master with mingled horror and appeal. There is no response, and Dolphin goes out blindly. Smith sits slowly. He pours and drinks a small glass of brandy deliberately. He sets down the glass and commences to rise as—)

(Curtain Falls Very Slowly.)

Questions

1. We begin at a jovial moment toward the close of dinner; then the joviality is suddenly interrupted by Lady Jane's noticing that there are thirteen at table. What does the playwright reveal to us in this way about her? Is this characteristic of hers important as a clue, or is it one of the many false clues that the author everywhere places in our way? How does Sam Smith account to his guests for there being thirteen at table?

2. What sort of man would it take to do what Smith has done to bring these guests together? In fact, what *has* he done to bring them together? What has he done during their week in his house? What does he let happen this very evening as part of his plan? What direct hints does the author give us of his nature? (Consider especially the stage directions as he explains to his guests why he has brought them there).

3. What parts do the butler and the maid play except as waiters at dinner? What reasons can you assign for Dolphin's being made to sit down to break the number thirteen? For the women being adjourned to *his* room for coffee? For the maid's showing "signs of collapse"? For his actions and state as described in the last stage direction? What might cause the "horror" with which he looks at his master? And the "appeal" in that look?

4. Make a list of the clues or false clues by which the author directs our attention to each of the following as the guilty party: (a) Lady Jane, (b) Miss Isit, (c) Mrs. Preen, (d) Miss Vaile, (e) Mrs. Castro, (f) Mr. Vaile, (g) Lady Wrathie, (h) Mr. Gourlay, (i) Mr. Preen, (j) Sir Joseph Wrathie, (k) Mrs. Bland, (l) Captain Jennings. (Do not be surprised if in some instances the clues are few and ambiguous). When you have decided which person actually is the guilty one, draw up an airtight account of your case against him or her. Since not all of your classmates may agree with you, you will need to be prepared for debate.

5. Write a short paper arguing that from the evidence the play provides, the guilty person can never be *known for sure.*

6. *Shall We Join the Ladies?* is an exciting play to give a reading of in the classroom. Which role would *you* choose to read? Why? Which role do you think your teacher would choose you to read? Why? Does this suggest that there is a "real me" inside you that you have not succeeded in making known? Do you in the classroom, like an actor, put on a face to meet the faces that you meet—play a role? Do you do this likewise in sports? In what way does your sports role differ? How about your parents—what are you like with them? And the members of the other sex—do you strive to give them the same image you give your teacher and your parents? Why or why not?

7. What did Shakespeare mean when he said that "all the world's a stage, and all the men and women merely players"? Do the people at Sam Smith's dinner party illustrate the truth of that view? Does Sam Smith? Do you? How?

T his is a murder play like *Shall We Join the Ladies?* but rather different in effect. Here the killing is not two years in the past but about to occur. Furthermore, in place of a table of twelve dinner guests suddenly startled from a mood of festivity to one of alarm, we begin in this play with a nervous lone woman in her bedroom, graduating from peevishness to terror as her efforts to "communicate" fail. As in Barrie's play, the person responsible for the murder remains unnamed and unidentified, the thugs who carry out his plan referring to him only as "our client"; but this likeness is more apparent than real, for here we are never in serious doubt as to who the murderer is or what the motives are. The two plays are curiously alike, however, in one particular: each has a strong close in which the passion of a woman's scream is set off against another voice speaking with the utmost coolness and detachment.

Sorry, Wrong Number

LUCILLE FLETCHER

Characters

MRS. STEVENSON
1ST OPERATOR
1ST MAN
2ND MAN
CHIEF OPERATOR
2ND OPERATOR
3RD OPERATOR
4TH OPERATOR
5TH OPERATOR
INFORMATION
HOSPITAL RECEPTIONIST
WESTERN UNION
SERGEANT DUFFY
A LUNCH ROOM COUNTER ATTENDANT

SCENE: *As curtain rises, we see a divided stage, only the center part of which is lighted and furnished as Mrs. Stevenson's bedroom. Expensive, rather fussy furnishings. A large bed, on which Mrs. Stevenson, clad in bed-jacket, is lying. A night-table close by, with phone, lighted lamp, and pill bottles. A mantel, with clock, right. A closed door, right. A window, with curtains closed, rear. The set is lit by one lamp on night-table. It is enclosed by three flats. Beyond this central set, the stage, on either side, is in darkness.*

Mrs. Stevenson is dialling a number on phone, as curtain rises. She listens to phone, slams down receiver in irritation. As she does so, we hear sound of a train roaring by in the distance. She reaches for her pill bottle, pours herself a glass of water, shakes out pill, swallows it, then reaches for phone again, dials number nervously. SOUND: *Number being dialled on phone: Busy signal.*

MRS. STEVENSON   (*A querulous, self-centered neurotic*) Oh—dear! (*Slams down receiver. Dials Operator*) (*Scene: A spotlight, left of side flat, picks up, out of peripheral darkness, figure of 1st Operator, sitting with headphones at small table. If spotlight not available, use flashlight, clicked on by 1st operator, illumining her face.*)

OPERATOR   Your call, please?

MRS. STEVENSON   Operator? I have been dialling Murray Hill 4-0098 now for the last three-quarters of an hour, and the line is always busy. But I don't see how it *could* be busy that long. Will you try it for me, please?

OPERATOR   Murray Hill 4-0098? One moment, please.

(*Scene: She makes gesture of plugging in call through a switchboard.*)

MRS. STEVENSON   I don't see how it could be busy all this time. It's my husband's office. He's working late tonight, and I'm all alone here in the house. My health is very poor—and I've been feeling so nervous all day. . . .

OPERATOR   Ringing Murray Hill 4-0098. . . .   (*Sound: Phone buzz. It rings three times. Receiver is picked up at other end.*) (*Scene: Spotlight picks up figure of a heavy-set man, seated at desk with phone on right side of dark periphery of stage. He is wearing a hat. Picks up phone, which rings three times.*)

MAN   Hello.

MRS. STEVENSON   Hello . . . ?   (*A little puzzled*)   Hello. Is Mr. Stevenson there?

MAN   (*Into phone, as though he had not heard*) Hello. . . . (*Louder*) Hello. (*Scene: Spotlight on left now moves from Operator to another man, George. A killer type, also wearing hat, but standing as in a phone booth. A three-sided screen may be used to suggest this*).

2ND MAN   (*Slow heavy quality, faintly foreign accent*)   Hello.

1ST MAN   Hello, George?

GEORGE   Yes, sir.

MRS. STEVENSON   (*Louder and more imperious, to phone*)   Hello. Who's this? What number am I calling, please?

1ST MAN   We have heard from our client. He says the coast is clear for tonight.

GEORGE   Yes, sir.

1ST MAN   Where are you now?

GEORGE   In a phone booth.

1ST MAN   Okay. You know the address. At eleven o'clock the private patrolman goes around to the bar on Second Avenue for a beer. Be sure that all the lights downstairs are out. There should be only one light visible from the street. At eleven-fifteen a subway train crosses the bridge. It makes a noise in case her window is open, and she should scream.

MRS. STEVENSON   (*Shocked*)   Oh—HELLO! What number is this, please?

GEORGE   Okay. I understand.

1ST MAN   Make it quick. As little blood as possible. Our client does not wish to make her suffer long.

GEORGE   A knife okay, sir?

1ST MAN   Yes. A knife will be okay. And remember—remove the rings and bracelets, and the jewelry in the bureau drawer. Our client wishes it to look like simple robbery.

GEORGE   Okay—I get— (*Scene: Spotlight suddenly goes out on George.*) (*Sound: A bland buzzing signal*) (*Scene: Spotlight goes off on 1st Man.*)

MRS. STEVENSON   (*Clicking phone*) Oh . . . ! (*Bland buzzing signal continues. She hangs up.*) How awful! How unspeakably . . . (*Scene: She lies back on her pillows, overcome for a few seconds, then suddenly pulls herself together, reaches for phone.*) (*Sound: Dialling. Phone buzz*) (*Scene: Spotlight goes on at 1st Operator's switchboard. 1st and 2nd Man exit as unobtrusively as possible, in darkness.*)

OPERATOR   Your call, please?

MRS. STEVENSON   (*Unnerved and breathless, into phone*)   Operator. I
—I've just been cut off.
OPERATOR   I'm sorry, madam. What number were you calling?
MRS. STEVENSON   Why—it was supposed to be Murray Hill 4-0098, but
it wasn't. Some wires must have crossed—I was cut into a wrong
number—and—I've just heard the most dreadful thing—a—a
murder—and—(*imperiously*)   Operator, you'll simply have to re-
trace that call at once.
OPERATOR   I beg your pardon, madam—I don't quite—
MRS. STEVENSON   Oh—I know it was a wrong number, and I had no
business listening—but these two men—they were cold-blooded
fiends—and they were going to murder somebody—some poor innocent woman—who was all alone—in a house near a bridge. And
we've got to stop them—we've got to—
OPERATOR   (*Patiently*)   What number were you calling, madam?
MRS. STEVENSON   That doesn't matter. This was a *wrong* number. And
you dialled it. And we've got to find out what it was—immediately!
OPERATOR   But—madam—
MRS. STEVENSON   Oh—why are you so stupid? Look—it was obviously
a case of some little slip of the finger. I told you to try Murray
Hill 4-0098 for me—you dialled it but your finger must have
slipped—and I was connected with some other number—and I
could hear them, but they couldn't hear me. Now, I simply fail to
see why you couldn't make that same mistake again—on purpose
—why you couldn't *try* to dial Murray Hill 4-0098 in the same
careless sort of way. . . .
OPERATOR   (*Quickly*)   Murray Hill 4-0098? I will try to get it for you,
madam.
MRS. STEVENSON   (*Sarcastically*)   Thank you. (*Scene: She bridles,
adjusts herself on her pillows, reaches for handkerchief, wipes
forehead, glancing uneasily for a moment toward window, while
still holding phone.*)   (*Sound of ringing: Busy signal*)
OPERATOR   I am sorry. Murray Hill 4-0098 is busy.
MRS. STEVENSON   (*Frantically clicking receiver*)   Operator. Operator.
OPERATOR   Yes, madam.
MRS. STEVENSON   (*Angrily*)   You *didn't* try to get that wrong number
at all. I asked explicitly. And all you did was dial correctly.
OPERATOR   I am sorry. What number were you calling?
MRS. STEVENSON   Can't you, for once, forget what number I was calling
and do something specific? Now I want to trace that call. It's my
civic duty—it's *your* civic duty—to trace that call . . . and to
apprehend those dangerous killers—and if *you* won't . . .

OPERATOR   (*Glancing around wearily*)   I will connect you with the Chief Operator.

MRS. STEVENSON   *Please!*   (*Sound of ringing*) (*Scene: Operator puts hand over mouthpiece of phone, gestures into darkness. A half whisper:*

OPERATOR   Miss Curtis. Will you pick up on 17, please? (*Miss Curtis, Chief Operator, enters. Middle-aged, efficient type, pleasant. Wearing headphones.*)

MISS CURTIS   Yes, dear. What's the trouble?

OPERATOR   Somebody wanting a call traced. I can't make head nor tail of it. . . .

MISS CURTIS   (*Sitting down at desk, as Operator gets up*)   Sure, dear. 17? (*She makes gesture of plugging in her headphone, coolly and professionally.*)   This is the Chief Operator.

MRS. STEVENSON   Chief Operator? I want you to trace a call. A telephone call. Immediately. I don't know where it came from, or who was making it, but it's absolutely necessary that it be tracked down. Because it was about a murder. Yes, a terrible, cold-blooded murder of a poor innocent woman—tonight—at eleven-fifteen.

CHIEF OPERATOR   I see.

MRS. STEVENSON   (*High-strung, demanding*)   Can you trace it for me? Can you track down those men?

CHIEF OPERATOR   It depends, madam.

MRS. STEVENSON   Depends on what?

CHIEF OPERATOR   If the parties have stopped talking to each other.

MRS. STEVENSON   Oh—but—but of course they must have stopped talking to each other by *now*. That was at least five minutes ago —and they didn't sound like the type who would make a long call.

CHIEF OPERATOR   Well, I can try tracing it. (*Scene: She takes pencil out of her hair-do.*)   Now—what is your name, madam?

MRS. STEVENSON   Mrs. Stevenson. Mrs. Elbert Stevenson. But—listen—

CHIEF OPERATOR   (*Writing it down*)   And your telephone number?

MRS. STEVENSON   (*More irritated*)   Plaza 4-2295. But if you go on wasting all this time—   (*Scene: She glances at clock on mantel.*)

CHIEF OPERATOR   And what is your reason for wanting this call traced?

MRS. STEVENSON   My reason? Well—for heaven's sake—isn't it obvious? I overhear two men—they're killers—they're planning to murder this woman—it's a matter for the police.

CHIEF OPERATOR   Have you told the police?

MRS. STEVENSON   No. How could I?

CHIEF OPERATOR   Well, Mrs. Stevenson—I seriously doubt whether we

could make this check for you at this time just on your say-so as a
private individual. We'd have to have something more official.

MRS. STEVENSON   Oh—for heaven's sake! You mean to tell me I can't
report a murder without getting tied up in all this red tape? Why
—it's perfectly idiotic. All right, then. I *will* call the police. (*She
slams down receiver.*) (*Scene: Spotlight goes off on two Operators.*) Ridiculous! (*Sound of dialling*) (*Scene: Mrs. Stevenson
dials numbers on phone, as two Operators exit unobtrusively in
darkness.*) (*On right of stage, spotlight picks up a 2nd Operator,
seated like first, with headphones at table [same one vacated by
1st Man].*)

2ND OPERATOR   Your call, please?

MRS. STEVENSON   (*Very annoyed*)   The Police Department—*please.*

2ND OPERATOR   Ringing the Police Department. (*Ring twice. Phone is
picked up.*) (*Scene: Left stage, at table vacated by 1st and Chief
Operator, spotlight now picks up Sergeant Duffy, seated in a
relaxed position. Just entering beside him is a young man in cap
and apron, carrying a large brown paper parcel, delivery boy for a
local lunch counter. Phone is ringing.*)

YOUNG MAN   Here's your lunch, Sarge. They didn't have no jelly
doughnuts, so I give you French crullers. Okay, Sarge?

S. DUFFY   French crullers. I got ulcers. Whyn't you make it apple
pie? (*Picks up phone, which has rung twice*) Police department. Precinct 43. Duffy speaking. (*Scene: Lunch Room Attendant, anxiously.* We don't have no apple pie, either, Sarge—)

MRS. STEVENSON   Police Department? Oh. This is Mrs. Stevenson—
Mrs. Elbert Smythe Stevenson of 53 North Sutton Place. I'm
calling up to report a murder. (*Scene: Duffy has been examining
lunch, but double-takes suddenly on above.*)

DUFFY   Eh?

MRS. STEVENSON   I mean—the murder hasn't been committed yet. I
just overheard plans for it over the telephone . . . over a wrong
number that the operator gave me. (*Scene: Duffy relaxes, sighs,
starts taking lunch from bag.*)   I've been trying to trace down the
call myself, but everybody is so stupid—and I guess in the end
you're the only people who could *do* anything.

DUFFY   (*Not too impressed*) (*Scene: Attendant, who exits*) Yes,
ma'am.

MRS. STEVENSON   (*Trying to impress him*)   It was a perfectly *definite*
murder. I heard their plans distinctly. (*Scene: Duffy begins to
eat sandwich, phone at his ear.*)   Two men were talking, and
they were going to murder some woman at eleven-fifteen tonight
—she lived in a house near a bridge.

DUFFY Yes, ma'am.

MRS. STEVENSON And there was a private patrolman on the street. He was going to go around for a beer on Second Avenue. And there was some third man—a client, who was paying to have this poor woman murdered—they were going to take her rings and bracelets—and use a knife . . . well, it's unnerved me dreadfully—and I'm not well. . . .

DUFFY I see. (*Scene: Having finished sandwich, he wipes mouth with paper napkin.*) When was all this, ma'am?

MRS. STEVENSON About eight minutes ago. Oh . . . (*Relieved*) Then you *can* do something? You *do* understand—

DUFFY And what is your name, ma'am? (*Scene: He reaches for pad.*)

MRS. STEVENSON (*Impatiently*) Mrs. Stevenson. Mrs. Elbert Stevenson.

DUFFY And your address?

MRS. STEVENSON 53 North Sutton Place. *That's* near a bridge. The Queensboro Bridge, you know—and *we* have a private patrolman on *our* street—and Second Avenue—

DUFFY And what was that number you were calling?

MRS. STEVENSON Murray Hill 4-0098. (*Scene: Duffy writes it down.*) But—that wasn't the number I overheard. I mean Murray Hill 4-0098 is my husband's office. (*Scene: Duffy, in exasperation, holds pencil poised.*) He's working late tonight, and I was trying to reach him to ask him to come home. I'm an invalid, you know—and it's the maid's night off—and I *hate* to be alone—even though he says I'm perfectly safe as long as I have the telephone right beside my bed.

DUFFY (*Stolidly*) (*Scene: He has put pencil down, pushes pad away.*) Well—we'll look into it, Mrs. Stevenson—and see if we can check it with the telephone company.

MRS. STEVENSON (*Getting impatient*) But the telephone company said they couldn't check the call if the parties had stopped talking. I've already taken care of *that*.

DUFFY Oh—yes? (*Scene: He yawns slightly.*)

MRS. STEVENSON (*High-handed*) Personally I feel you ought to do something far more immediate and drastic than just check the call. What good does checking the call do, if they've stopped talking? By the time you track it down, they'll already have committed the murder.

DUFFY (*Scene: He reaches for paper cup of coffee.*) Well—we'll take care of it, lady. Don't worry. (*Scene: He begins to take off paper top of coffee container.*)

MRS. STEVENSON   I'd say the whole thing calls for a search—a complete
and thorough search of the whole city. (*Scene: Duffy puts down
phone for a moment, to work on cup, as her voice continues.*) I'm very near a bridge, and I'm not far from Second Avenue. And I know *I'd* feel a whole lot better if you sent around a
radio car to *this* neighborhood at once.

DUFFY   (*Scene: Picks up phone again, drinks coffee.*)   And what
makes you think the murder's going to be committed in your
neighborhood, ma'am?

MRS. STEVENSON   Oh—I don't know. The coincidence is so horrible.
Second Avenue—the patrolman—the bridge. . . .

DUFFY   (*Scene: He sips coffee.*)   Second Avenue is a very long street,
ma'am. And do you happen to know how many bridges there are
in the city of New York alone? Not to mention Brooklyn, Staten
Island, Queens, and the Bronx? And how do you know there isn't
some little house out on Staten Island—on some little Second Avenue you never heard about? (*Scene: A long gulp of coffee*)   How do you know they were even talking about New York
at all?

MRS. STEVENSON   But I heard the call on the New York dialling system.

DUFFY   How do you know it wasn't a long distance call you overheard?
Telephones are funny things. (*Scene: He sets down coffee.*)   Look, lady, why don't you look at it this way? Supposing
you hadn't broken in on that telephone call? Supposing you'd got
your husband the way you always do? Would this murder have
made any difference to you then?

MRS. STEVENSON   I suppose not. But it's so inhuman—so cold-blooded. . . .

DUFFY   A lot of murders are committed in this city every day, ma'am.
If we could do something to stop 'em, we would. But a clue of this
kind that's so vague isn't much more use to us than no clue at all.

MRS. STEVENSON   But, surely—

DUFFY   Unless, of course, you have some reason for thinking this call
is phoney—and that someone may be planning to murder *you?*

MRS. STEVENSON   *Me?* Oh—no—I hardly think so. I—I mean—why
should anybody? I'm alone all day and night—I see nobody except my maid Eloise—she's a big two-hundred-pounder—she's
too lazy to bring up my breakfast tray—and the only other person
is my husband Elbert—he's crazy about me—adores me—waits
on me hand and foot—he's scarcely left my side since I took sick
twelve years ago—

DUFFY   Well—then—there's nothing for you to worry about, is there? (*Scene: Lunch Counter Attendant has entered. He is carrying a piece of apple pie on a plate. Points it out to Duffy triumphantly.*) And now—if you'll just leave the rest of this to us—

MRS. STEVENSON But what will you *do*? It's so late—it's nearly eleven o'clock.

DUFFY (*Firmly*) (*Scene: He nods to Attendant, pleased*) We'll take care of it, lady.

MRS. STEVENSON Will you broadcast it all over the city? And send out squads? And warn your radio cars to watch out—especially in suspicious neighborhoods like mine? (*Scene: Attendant, in triumph, has put pie down in front of Duffy. Takes fork out of his pocket, stands at attention, waiting.*)

DUFFY (*More firmly*) Lady, I *said* we'd take care of it. (*Scene: Glances at pie.*) Just now I've got a couple of other matters here on my desk that require my immediate—

MRS. STEVENSON Oh! (*She slams down receiver.*) Idiot. (*Scene: Duffy, listening at phone, hangs up. Shrugs. Winks at Attendant as though to say, "What a crazy character!" Attacks his pie as spotlight fades out.*) (*Mrs. Stevenson, in bed, looking at phone nervously*) Now—why did I do that? Now—he'll think I *am* a fool. (*Scene: She sits there tensely, then throws herself back against pillows, lies there a moment, whimpering with self-pity.*) Oh— why doesn't Elbert come home? *Why* doesn't he? (*Scene: We hear sound of train roaring by in the distance. She sits up reaching for phone.*) (*Sound of dialling operator*) (*Scene: Spotlight picks up 2nd Operator, seated right.*)

OPERATOR Your call, please?

MRS. STEVENSON Operator—for Heaven's sake—will you ring that Murray Hill 4-0098 number again? I can't think what's keeping him so long.

OPERATOR Ringing Murray Hill 4-0098. (*Rings; busy signal*) The line is busy. Shall I—

MRS. STEVENSON (*Nastily*) I can hear it. You don't have to tell me. I know it's busy. (*Slams down receiver*) (*Scene: Spotlight fades off on 2nd Operator.*) (*Scene: Mrs. Stevenson sinks back against pillows again, whimpering to herself fretfully. She glances at clock, then turning, punches her pillows up, trying to make herself comfortable. But she isn't. Whimpers to herself as she squirms restlessly in bed.*) If I could only get out of this bed for a little while. If I could get a breath of fresh air—or just lean out the window—and see the street. . . . (*Scene: She sighs, reaches for pill bottle, shakes out a pill. As she does so, the phone rings. She darts for it instantly.*) Hello, Elbert? Hello. Hello. Hello.

Oh—what's the *matter* with this phone? HELLO? HEL-
LO? (*Slams down the receiver*) (Scene: She stares at it, tense-
ly.) (*The phone rings again. Once. She picks it up.*) Hello?
Hello. . . . Oh—for Heaven's sake—who *is* this? Hello. HEL-
LO. (*Slams down receiver. Dials operator.*) (*Scene: Spotlight
comes on left, showing 3rd Operator, at spot vacated by Duffy.*)

3RD OPERATOR   Your call, please?

MRS. STEVENSON   (*Very annoyed and imperious*) Hello. Operator. I
don't know what's the matter with this telephone tonight, but it's
positively driving me crazy. I've never seen such inefficient, miserable service. Now, look. I'm an invalid, and I'm very nervous,
and I'm *not* supposed to be annoyed. But if this keeps on much
longer. . . .

3RD OPERATOR   (*A young sweet type*) What seems to be the trouble,
madam?

MRS. STEVENSON   Well—everything's wrong. The whole world could be
murdered, for all you people care. And now—my phone keeps
ringing. . . .

OPERATOR   Yes, madam?

MRS. STEVENSON   Ringing and ringing and ringing every five seconds or
so, and when I pick it up, there's no one there.

OPERATOR   I am sorry, madam. If you will hang up, I will test it for
you.

MRS. STEVENSON   I don't want you to test it for me. I want you to put
through that call—whatever it is—at once.

OPERATOR   (*Gently*) I am afraid that is not possible, madam.

MRS. STEVENSON   (*Storming*) Not possible? And why—may I ask?

OPERATOR   The system is automatic, madam. If someone is trying to
dial your number, there is no way to check whether the call is
coming through the system or not—unless the person who is trying to reach you complains to his particular operator—

MRS. STEVENSON   Well, of all the stupid, complicated . . . ! And
meanwhile *I've* got to sit here in my bed, *suffering* every time that
phone rings—imagining everything. . . .

OPERATOR   I will try to check it for you, madam.

MRS. STEVENSON   Check it! Check it! That's all anybody can do. Of all
the stupid, idiotic . . . ! (*She hangs up.*) Oh—what's the
use. . . . (*Scene: 3rd Operator fades out of spotlight, as instantly Mrs. Stevenson's phone rings again. She picks up receiver. Wildly.*) Hello. HELLO. Stop ringing, do you hear me?
Answer me? What do you want? Do you realize you're driving me
crazy? (*Scene: Spotlight goes on right. We see a man in eye-
shade and shirt-sleeves, at desk with phone and tele-
grams.*) Stark, staring. . . .

MAN   (*Dull flat voice*)   Hello. Is this Plaza 4-2295?

MRS. STEVENSON   (*Catching her breath*)   Yes. Yes. This is Plaza 4-2295.

WESTERN UNION   This is Western Union. I have a telegram here for Mrs. Elbert Stevenson. Is there anyone there to receive the message?

MRS. STEVENSON   (*Trying to calm herself*)   I am Mrs. Stevenson.

WESTERN UNION   (*Reading flatly*)   The telegram is as follows: "Mrs. Elbert Stevenson. 53 North Sutton Place, New York, New York. Darling. Terribly sorry. Tried to get you for last hour, but line busy. Leaving for Boston eleven PM tonight on urgent business. Back tomorrow afternoon. Keep happy. Love. Signed. Elbert."

MRS. STEVENSON   (*Breathlessly, aghast, to herself*)   Oh . . . no. . . .

WESTERN UNION   That is all, madam. Do you wish us to deliver a copy of the message?

MRS. STEVENSON   No—no, thank you.

WESTERN UNION   Thank you, madam. Good night. (*He hangs up phone.*) (*Scene: Spotlight on Western Union immediately out*)

MRS. STEVENSON   (*Mechanically, to phone*)   Good night. (*She hangs up slowly. Suddenly bursting into*)   No—no—it isn't true! He couldn't do it! Not when he knows I'll be all alone. It's some trick—some fiendish. . . . (*Scene: We hear sound of train roaring by outside. She half rises in bed, in panic, glaring toward curtains. Her movements are frenzied. She beats with her knuckles on bed, then suddenly stops, and reaches for phone.*) (*She dials operator.*) (*Scene: Spotlight picks up 4th Operator, seated left.*)

OPERATOR   (*Coolly*)   Your call, please?

MRS. STEVENSON   Operator—try that Murray Hill 4-0098 number for me just once more, please.

OPERATOR   Ringing Murray Hill 4-0098. (*Call goes through. We hear ringing at other end. Ring after ring.*) (*Scene: If telephone noises are not used audibly, have Operator say after a brief pause: "They do not answer."*)

MRS. STEVENSON   He's gone. Oh—Elbert, how could you? How could you . . . ? (*She hangs up phone, sobbing pityingly to herself, turning restlessly.*) (*Scene: Spotlight goes out on 4th Operator.*)   But I can't be alone tonight. I can't. If I'm alone one more second . . . (*Scene: She runs hands wildly through hair.*)   I don't care what he says—or what the expense is—I'm a sick woman—I'm entitled . . . (*Scene: With trembling fingers she picks up receiver again.*) (*She dials Information.*) (*Scene: The spotlight picks up Information Operator, seated right.*)

INFORMATION   This is Information.

MRS. STEVENSON   I want the telephone number of Henchley Hospital.

INFORMATION   Henchley Hospital? Do you have the address, madam?

MRS. STEVENSON   No. It's somewhere in the 70's, though. It's a very small, private and exclusive hospital where I had my appendix out two years ago. Henchley. H-E-N-C—

INFORMATION   One moment, please.

MRS. STEVENSON   Please—hurry. And please—what *is* the time?

INFORMATION   I do not know, madam. You may find out the time by dialling Meridian 7-1212.

MRS. STEVENSON   (*Irritated*) Oh—for heaven's sake! Couldn't you—?

INFORMATION   The number of Henchley Hospital is Butterfield 7-0105, madam.

MRS. STEVENSON   Butterfield 7-0105. (*She hangs up before she finishes speaking, and immediately dials number as she repeats it.*) (*Scene: Spotlight goes out on Information.*) (*Phone rings.*) (*Scene: Spotlight picks up woman in nurse's uniform, seated at desk, left.*)

WOMAN   (*Middle-aged, solid, firm, practical*) Henchley Hospital, good evening.

MRS. STEVENSON   Nurses' Registry.

WOMAN   Who was it you wished to speak to, please?

MRS. STEVENSON   (*High-handed*) I want the Nurses' Registry at once. I want a trained nurse. I want to hire her immediately. For the night.

WOMAN   I see. And what is the nature of the case, madam?

MRS. STEVENSON   Nerves. I'm very nervous. I need soothing—and companionship. My husband is away—and I'm—

WOMAN   Have you been recommended to us by any doctor in particular, madam?

MRS. STEVENSON   No. But I really don't see why all this catechizing is necessary. I want a trained nurse. I was a patient in your hospital two years ago. And after all, I *do* expect to *pay* this person—

WOMAN   We quite understand that, madam. But registered nurses are very scarce just now—and our superintendent has asked us to send people out only on cases where the physician in charge feels it is absolutely necessary.

MRS. STEVENSON   (*Growing hysterical*) Well—it *is* absolutely necessary. I'm a sick woman. I—I'm very upset. Very. I'm alone in this house—and I'm an invalid—and tonight I overheard a telephone conversation that upset me dreadfully. About a murder—a poor woman who was going to be murdered at eleven-fifteen tonight— in fact, if someone doesn't come at once—I'm afraid I'll go out of my mind. . . . (*Almost off handle by now*)

WOMAN   (*Calmly*) I see. Well—I'll speak to Miss Phillips as soon as she comes in. And what is your name, madam?

MRS. STEVENSON   Miss Phillips. And when do you expect her in?

WOMAN   I really don't know, madam. She went out to supper at eleven o'clock.

MRS. STEVENSON   Eleven o'clock. But it's not eleven yet. (*She cries out.*) Oh, my clock *has* stopped. I thought it was running down. What time is it? (*Scene: Woman glances at wristwatch.*)

WOMAN   Just fourteen minutes past eleven. . . . (*Sound of phone receiver being lifted on same line as Mrs. Stevenson's. A click.*)

MRS. STEVENSON   (*Crying out*) What's *that?*

WOMAN   What was what, madam?

MRS. STEVENSON   That—that click just now—in my own telephone? As though someone had lifted the receiver off the hook of the extension phone downstairs. . . .

WOMAN   I didn't hear it, madam. Now—about this . . .

MRS. STEVENSON   (*Scared*) But I *did.* There's someone in this house. Someone downstairs in the kitchen. And they're listening to me now. They're. . . . (*Scene: She puts hand over her mouth, hangs up phone.*) (*Scene: She sits there, in terror, frozen, listening.*) (*In a suffocated voice*) I won't pick it up, I won't let them hear me. I'll be quiet—and they'll think . . . (*With growing terror*) But if I don't call someone now—while they're still down there—there'll be no time. . . . (*She picks up receiver. Bland buzzing signal. She dials operator. Ring twice.*) (Scene: *On second ring, spotlight goes on right. We see 5th Operator.*)

OPERATOR   (*Fat and lethargic*) Your call, please?

MRS. STEVENSON   (*A desperate whisper*) Operator—I—I'm in desperate trouble . . . I—

OPERATOR   I cannot hear you, madam. Please speak louder.

MRS. STEVENSON   (*Still whispering*) I don't dare. I—there's someone listening. Can you hear me now?

OPERATOR   Your call, please? What number are you calling, madam?

MRS. STEVENSON   (*Desperately*) You've got to hear me. Oh—please. You've got to help me. There's someone in this house. Someone who's going to murder me. And you've got to get in touch with the . . . (*Click of receiver being put down on Mrs. Stevenson's line. Bursting out wildly*) Oh—there it is . . . he's put it down . . . he's coming . . . (*She screams.*) he's coming up the stairs . . . (*Scene: She thrashes in bed, phone cord catching in lamp wire, lamp topples, goes out. Darkness.*) (*Hoarsely*) Give me the Police Department. . . . (*Scene: We see on the dark center stage, the shadow of door opening.*) (*Screaming*) The police! . . . (*Scene: On stage, swift rush of a shadow, advancing to bed—sound of her voice is choked out, as*)

OPERATOR   Ringing the Police Department. (*Phone is rung. We hear*

sound of a train beginning to fade in. On second ring, Mrs. Ste-
venson screams again, but roaring of train drowns out her voice.
For a few seconds we hear nothing but roaring of train, then dying
away, phone at police headquarters ringing.) (Scene: Spotlight
goes on Duffy, left stage.)

DUFFY   Police Department. Precincts 43. Duffy speaking. (*Pause*)
(*Scene: Nothing visible but darkness on center stage.*) Police Department. Duffy speaking. (*Scene: A flashlight goes on, illuminat-*
ing open phone to one side of Mrs. Stevenson's bed. Nearby, hang-
ing down, is her lifeless hand. We see the second man, George, in
black gloves, reach down and pick up phone. He is breathing
hard.)

GEORGE   Sorry. Wrong number. (*Hangs up*) (*Scene: He replaces*
receiver on hook quietly, exits, as Duffy hangs up with a shrug,
and Curtain Falls.)

Questions

1. (a) At what point in the play did you first suspect who "the client"
   was? At what point were you sure? Trace your process of discovery,
   point by point, clue by clue. (b) Make a time schedule of the client's
   evening activities as the play indicates them or implies them. What
   signs are there that the crime has been carefully prepared? (c) What do
   you take the client's "motives" to be? How fair is it to say that they
   are implied in the play's characterization of Mrs. Stevenson? Do these
   motives justify the client's action or merely explain it?

2. The play's setting is a big city. How would you know this, even if there
   were no other evidence, from the words and actions of the telephone
   operators? Of the policeman? Of the hospital? From the life Mrs. Stevenson leads? From the nature of the murder plan? In what way would
   you expect these to differ if this were a small country town? The setting here, however, is not simply vaguely urban or metropolitan; it is a
   precise New York address. Show how this is necessary to the plot.

3. The play was written for radio. Therefore, we were meant to hear it,
   not to see it—except in our imaginations. Looking carefully at Mrs.
   Stevenson's words and the stage directions, what qualities do you think
   should be present in the voice of the actress who speaks the part? In
   the voice of the actor who speaks the part of Duffy? How should the

voices of the two thugs differ? Account as well as you can for the fact that the author gives the real perpetrator of the murder no words to speak and hence no "voice" in a play made up of "voices." How does this intensify the horror of the murder?

4. Though the play's main effect is to produce excitement, suspense, and terror, it manages at the same time to communicate a vivid sense of the impersonality and anonymity, the intense concern for self and apathy toward others, that are well known characteristics today of the societies our twentieth-century technologies have built. What aspects of these conditions appear in the illness of Mrs. Stevenson? In the routines of her husband? In the police sergeant? In the hospital administrator? In the telephone service? To what extent are the attitudes that are shown justified by the circumstances? To what extent are they not?

5. (a) When the reader or the spectator of a play is enabled by the playwright to know more about the meaning of a situation than the person actually involved in it—as we do in the case of Mrs. Stevenson, since she goes to her death without suspecting who "the client" is—we have an effect that is called *dramatic irony.* (b) This effect occurs also when a character speaks words that have more or different meanings for us in the audience than they do for the speaker. For examples of this, consider the first and third speeches of Mrs. Stevenson after the Western Union man hangs up. What does she assume? What do we? (c) Dramatic irony occurs likewise when a character interprets what is said to him by others in a more limited or different way than we do in the audience. Consider here the telegram itself. How does she interpret it? How do we?

6. The more ordinary kinds of irony—those which involve some sort of incongruity between expectation and outcome, as when exercises undertaken by a man to keep his health bring on a heart attack—also occur in drama. Irony of this sort may be seen here in the fact that a person can be more isolated and helpless in a vast city teeming with other people than in a remote village. Could you describe a further irony of this sort in *Sorry, Wrong Number* with the phrase: "The Connection That Did Not Connect"? To what would you be referring if you did?

7. Set down in a list the "voices" needed for acting this play. Opposite each voice put the name of a classmate that you think could best handle the part, and beside the name, enter your reasons for that particular choice. Compare your list and reasons with those of one or two friends—and if possible, with those of everyone in the class. The effort to "cast" a play, to fit each part as written to an appropriate actor (here to one particular actor's "voice") will enable you to uncover the play's distinctive qualities far more effectively than a simple reading.

8. The same truth holds for the effort to act out a play—or even a piece of it. For example, read aloud with a friend the last episode of *Sorry, Wrong Number*, beginning where Mrs. Stevenson dials Henchley Hospital. When you speak the lines of the hospital Woman, try to imply with your voice as many of the following circumstances as possible: that it is late at night; that you belong to a hospital staff accustomed to putting "facts" ahead of "feelings"; that as part of your job you have been exposed to the night fancies of neurotics, psychos, kooks, and so are more than a little bored with them; that hospital bureaucracies do not encourage decision-making by any but authorized persons —which you are not. Likewise, when you shift to the part of Mrs. Stevenson, try to suggest with your voice both the qualities that make her tiresome and also the loneliness, fear, and hysteria that justifiably beset her as she realizes her predicament. Do not forget in interpreting her character the feelings of outrage and pity that motivate her first attempts to report and thwart the plot she has overheard.

Here we have another murder play. A farmer is found strangled beside his own bed; the natural suspect is his wife, yet there appears to be no motive. At least there appears to be no motive to the three men involved—the sheriff, the county attorney, and a neighboring farmer. To the two women, things are clearer.

Trifles

SUSAN GLASPELL

SCENE: *The kitchen in the now abandoned farmhouse of John Wright, a gloomy kitchen, and left without having been put in order—the walls covered with a faded wallpaper. Down right is a door leading to the parlor. On the right wall above this door is a built-in kitchen cupboard with shelves in the upper portion and drawers below. In the rear wall at right, up two steps is a door opening onto stairs leading to the second floor. In the rear wall at left is a door to the shed and from there to the outside. Between these two doors is an old-fashioned black iron stove. Running along the left wall from the shed door is an old iron sink and sink shelf, in which is set a hand pump. Downstage of the sink is an uncurtained window. Near the window is an old wooden rocker. Center stage is an unpainted wooden kitchen table with straight chairs on either side. There is a small chair down right. Unwashed pans under the sink, a loaf of bread outside the breadbox, a dish towel on the table—other signs of incompleted work. At the rear the shed door opens and the Sheriff comes in followed by the County Attorney and Hale. The Sheriff and Hale are men in middle life, the County Attorney is a young man; all are much bun-*

dled up and go at once to the stove. They are followed by the two
women—the Sheriff's wife, Mrs. Peters, first; she is a slight wiry
woman, a thin nervous face. Mrs. Hale is larger and would or-
dinarily be called more comfortable looking, but she is disturbed
now and looks fearfully about as she enters. The women have
come in slowly, and stand close together near the door.

COUNTY ATTORNEY   (*At stove rubbing his hands*)   This feels good.
  Come up to the fire, ladies.
MRS. PETERS   (*After taking a step forward*)   I'm not—cold.
SHERIFF   (*Unbuttoning his overcoat and stepping away from the stove*
  to right of table as if to mark the beginning of official busi-
  ness) Now, Mr. Hale, before we move things about, you explain to
  Mr. Henderson just what you saw when you came here yesterday
  morning.
COUNTY ATTORNEY   (*Crossing down to left of the table*)   By the way,
  has anything been moved? Are things just as you left them yesterday?
SHERIFF   (*Looking about*)   It's just the same. When it dropped below
  zero last night I thought I'd better send Frank out this morning to
  make a fire for us—((*Sits right of center table*)   no use getting
  pneumonia with a big case on, but I told him not to touch anything except the stove—and you know Frank.
COUNTY ATTORNEY   Somebody should have been left here yesterday.
SHERIFF   Oh—yesterday. When I had to send Frank to Morris Center
  for that man who went crazy—I want you to know I had my
  hands full yesterday. I knew you could get back from Omaha by
  today and as long as I went over everything here myself—
COUNTY ATTORNEY   Well, Mr. Hale, tell just what happened when you
  came here yesterday morning.
HALE   (*Crossing down to above table*)   Harry and I had started to
  town with a load of potatoes. We came along the road from my
  place and as I got here I said, "I'm going to see if I can't get John
  Wright to go in with me on a party telephone." I spoke to Wright
  about it once before and he put me off, saying folks talked too
  much anyway, and all he asked was peace and quiet—I guess you
  know about how much he talked himself; but I thought maybe if I
  went to the house and talked about it before his wife, though I
  said to Harry that I didn't know as what his wife wanted made
  much difference to John—
COUNTY ATTORNEY   Let's talk about that later, Mr. Hale. I do want to
  talk about that, but tell now just what happened when you got to
  the house.

HALE   I didn't hear or see anything; I knocked at the door, and still it was all quiet inside. I knew they must be up, it was past eight o'clock. So I knocked again, and I thought I heard somebody say, "Come in." I wasn't sure, I'm not sure yet, but I opened the door —this door (*Indicating the door by which the two women are still standing*) and there in that rocker— (*Pointing to it*) sat Mrs. Wright. (*They all look at the rocker down left.*)

COUNTY ATTORNEY   What—was she doing?

HALE   She was rockin' back and forth. She had her apron in her hand and was kind of—pleating it.

COUNTY ATTORNEY   And how did she—look?

HALE   Well, she looked queer.

COUNTY ATTORNEY   How do you mean—queer?

HALE   Well, as if she didn't know what she was going to do next. And kind of done up.

COUNTY ATTORNEY   (*Takes out notebook and pencil and sits left of center table*) How did she seem to feel about your coming?

HALE   Why, I don't think she minded—one way or other. She didn't pay much attention. I said, "How do, Mrs. Wright, it's cold, ain't it?" And she said, "Is it?"—and went on kind of pleating at her apron. Well, I was surprised; she didn't ask me to come up to the stove, or to set down, but just sat there, not even looking at me, so I said, "I want to see John." And then she—laughed. I guess you would call it a laugh. I thought of Harry and the team outside, so I said a little sharp: "Can't I see John?" "No," she says, kind o' dull like. "Ain't he home?" says I. "Yes," says she, "he's home." "Then why can't I see him?" I asked her, out of patience. " 'Cause he's dead," says she. *"Dead?"* says I. She just nodded her head, not getting a bit excited, but rockin' back and forth. "Why—where is he?" says I, not knowing what to say. She just pointed upstairs—like that. (*Himself pointing to the room above*) I started for the stairs, with the idea of going up there. I walked from there to here—then I says, "Why, what did he die of?" "He died of a rope round his neck," says she, and just went on pleatin' at her apron. Well, I went out and called Harry. I thought I might—need help. We went upstairs and there he was lyin'—

COUNTY ATTORNEY   I think I'd rather have you go into that upstairs, where you can point it all out. Just go on now with the rest of the story.

HALE   Well, my first thought was to get that rope off. It looked . . . (*Stops, his face twitches*) . . . but Harry, he went up to him, and he said, "No, he's dead all right, and we'd better not touch anything." So we went back downstairs. She was still sitting that same way. "Has anybody been notified?" I asked. "No," says she, unconcerned. "Who did this, Mrs. Wright?" said Harry. He said it business-like—and she stopped pleatin' of her apron. "I don't know," she says. "You don't *know?*" says Harry. "No," says she. "Weren't you sleepin' in the bed with him?" says Harry. "Yes," says she, "but I was on the inside." "Somebody slipped a rope round his neck and strangled him and you didn't wake up?" says Harry. "I didn't wake up," she said after him. We must 'a' looked as if we didn't see how that could be, for after a minute she said, "I sleep sound." Harry was going to ask her more questions but I said maybe we ought to let her tell her story first to the coroner, or the sheriff, so Harry went fast as he could to Rivers' place, where there's a telephone.

COUNTY ATTORNEY   And what did Mrs. Wright do when she knew that you had gone for the coroner?

HALE   She moved from the rocker to that chair over there   (*Pointing to a small chair in the down right corner*)   and just sat there with her hands held together and looking down. I got a feeling that I ought to make some conversation, so I said I had come in to see if John wanted to put in a telephone, and at that she started to laugh, and then she stopped and looked at me—scared. (*The County Attorney, who has had his notebook out, makes a note.*)   I dunno, maybe it wasn't scared. I wouldn't like to say it was. Soon Harry got back, and then Dr. Lloyd came, and you, Mr. Peters, and so I guess that's all I know that you don't.

COUNTY ATTORNEY   (*Rising and looking around*)   I guess we'll go up-stairs first—and then out to the barn and around there. (*To the Sheriff*)   You're convinced that there was nothing important here —nothing that would point to any motive?

SHERIFF   Nothing here but kitchen things. (*The County Attorney, after again looking around the kitchen, opens the door of a cup-board closet in right wall. He brings a small chair from right— gets up on it and looks on a shelf. Pulls his hand away, sticky.*)

COUNTY ATTORNEY   Here's a nice mess. (*The women draw nearer up center.*)

MRS. PETERS   (*To the other woman*)   Oh, her fruit; it did freeze. (*To the Lawyer*)   She worried about that when it turned so cold. She said the fire'd go out and her jars would break.

SHERIFF   (*Rises*)   Well, can you beat the women! Held for murder and worryin' about her preserves.

COUNTY ATTORNEY   (*Getting down from chair*)   I guess before we're through she may have something more serious than preserves to worry about. (*Crosses down right center*)

HALE   Well, women are used to worrying over trifles. (*The two women move a little closer together.*)

COUNTY ATTORNEY   (*With the gallantry of a young politician*) And yet, for all their worries, what would we do without the ladies? (*The women do not unbend. He goes below the center table to the sink, takes a dipperful of water from the pail and pouring it into a basin, washes his hands. While he is doing this the Sheriff and Hale cross to cupboard, which they inspect. The County Attorney starts to wipe his hands on the roller towel, turns it for a cleaner place.*) Dirty towels! (*Kicks his foot against the pans under the sink*) Not much of a housekeeper, would you say, ladies?

MRS. HALE   (*Stiffly*) There's a great deal of work to be done on a farm.

COUNTY ATTORNEY   To be sure. And yet (*With a little bow to her*) I know there are some Dickson County farmhouses which do not have such roller towels. (*He gives it a pull to expose its full length again.*)

MRS. HALE   Those towels get dirty awful quick. Men's hands aren't always as clean as they might be.

COUNTY ATTORNEY   Ah, loyal to your sex, I see. But you and Mrs. Wright were neighbors. I suppose you were friends, too.

MRS. HALE   (*Shaking her head*) I've not seen much of her of late years. I've not been in this house—it's more than a year.

COUNTY ATTORNEY   (*Crossing to women up center*) And why was that? You didn't like her?

MRS. HALE   I liked her all well enough. Farmers' wives have their hands full, Mr. Henderson. And then—

COUNTY ATTORNEY   Yes—?

MRS. HALE   (*Looking about*) It never seemed a very cheerful place.

COUNTY ATTORNEY   No—it's not cheerful. I shouldn't say she had the homemaking instinct.

MRS. HALE   Well, I don't know as Wright had, either.

COUNTY ATTORNEY   You mean that they didn't get on very well?

MRS. HALE   No, I don't mean anything. But I don't think a place'd be any cheerfuller for John Wright's being in it.

COUNTY ATTORNEY   I'd like to talk more of that a little later. I want to get the lay of things upstairs now. (*He goes past the women to up right where steps lead to a stair door.*)

SHERIFF   I suppose anything Mrs. Peters does'll be all right. She was to take in some clothes for her, you know, and a few little things. We left in such a hurry yesterday.

COUNTY ATTORNEY   Yes, but I would like to see what you take, Mrs.

Peters, and keep an eye out for anything that might be of use to us.

MRS. PETERS   Yes, Mr. Henderson. (*The men leave by up right door to stairs. The women listen to the men's steps on the stairs, then look about the kitchen.*)

MRS. HALE   (*Crossing left to sink*) I'd hate to have men coming into my kitchen, snooping around and criticizing. (*She arranges the pans under sink which the Lawyer had shoved out of place.*)

MRS. PETERS   Of course it's no more than their duty. (*Crosses to cupboard up right*)

MRS. HALE   Duty's all right, but I guess that deputy sheriff that came out to make the fire might have got a little of this on. (*Gives the roller towel a pull*) Wish I'd thought of that sooner. Seems mean to talk about her for not having things slicked up when she had to come away in such a hurry. (*Crosses right to Mrs. Peters at cupboard*)

MRS. PETERS   (*Who has been looking through cupboard, lifts one end of a towel that covers a pan*) She had bread set. (*Stands still*)

MRS. HALE   (*Eyes fixed on a loaf of bread beside the breadbox, which is on a low shelf of the cupboard*) She was going to put this in there. (*Picks up loaf, then abruptly drops it. In a manner of returning to familiar things*) It's a shame about her fruit. I wonder if it's all gone. (*Gets up on the chair and looks*) I think there's some here that's all right, Mrs. Peters. Yes—here; (*Holding it toward the window*) this is cherries, too. (*Looking again*) I declare I believe that's the only one. (*Gets down, jar in her hand. Goes to the sink and wipes it off on the outside*) She'll feel awful bad after all her hard work in the hot weather. I remember the afternoon I put up my cherries last summer. (*She puts the jar on the big kitchen table, center of the room. With a sigh, is about to sit down in the rocking chair. Before she is seated realizes what chair it is; with a slow look at it, steps back. The chair which she has touched rocks back and forth. Mrs. Peters moves to center table and they both watch the chair rock for a moment or two.*)

MRS. PETERS   (*Shaking off the mood which the empty rocking chair has evoked. Now in a businesslike manner she speaks*) Well, I must get those things from the front room closet. (*She goes to the door at the right, but, after looking into the other room, steps back*) You coming with me, Mrs. Hale? You could help me carry them. (*They go in the other room; reappear, Mrs. Peters carrying a dress, petticoat and skirt, Mrs. Hale following with a pair of shoes.*) My, it's cold in there. (*She puts the clothes on the big table, and hurries to the stove.*)

MRS. HALE   (*Right of center table examining the skirt*)   Wright was close. I think maybe that's why she kept so much to herself. She didn't even belong to the Ladies' Aid. I suppose she felt she couldn't do her part, and then you don't enjoy things when you feel shabby. I heard she used to wear pretty clothes and be lively, when she was Minnie Foster, one of the town girls singing in the choir. But that—oh, that was thirty years ago. This all you was to take in?

MRS. PETERS   She said she wanted an apron. Funny thing to want, for there isn't much to get you dirty in jail, goodness knows. But I suppose just to make her feel more natural. (*Crosses to cupboard*)   She said they was in the top drawer in this cupboard. Yes, here. And then her little shawl that always hung behind the door. (*Opens stair door and looks*)   Yes, here it is. (*Quickly shuts door leading upstairs*)

MRS. HALE   (*Abruptly moving toward her*)   Mrs. Peters?

MRS. PETERS   Yes, Mrs. Hale? (*At up right door*)

MRS. HALE   Do you think she did it?

MRS. PETERS   (*In a frightened voice*)   Oh, I don't know.

MRS. HALE   Well, I don't think she did. Asking for an apron and her little shawl. Worrying about her fruit.

MRS. PETERS   (*Starts to speak, glances up, where footsteps are heard in the room above. In a low voice*)   Mr. Peters says it looks bad for her. Mr. Henderson is awful sarcastic in a speech and he'll make fun of her sayin' she didn't wake up.

MRS. HALE   Well, I guess John Wright didn't wake when they was slipping that rope under his neck.

MRS. PETERS   (*Crossing slowly to table and placing shawl and apron on table with other clothing*)   No, it's strange. It must have been done awful crafty and still. They say it was such a—funny way to kill a man, rigging it all up like that.

MRS. HALE   (*Crossing to left of Mrs. Peters at table*)   That's just what Mr. Hale said. There was a gun in the house. He says that's what he can't understand.

MRS. PETERS   Mr. Henderson said coming out that what was needed for the case was a motive; something to show anger, or—sudden feeling.

MRS. HALE   (*Who is standing by the table*)   Well, I don't see any signs of anger around here. (*She puts her hand on the dish towel which lies on the table, stands looking down at table, one-half of which is clean, the other half messy.*)   It's wiped to here. (*Makes a move as if to finish work, then turns and looks at loaf of bread outside the breadbox. Drops towel. In that voice of coming back to familiar things*)   Wonder how they are finding things upstairs. (*Crossing below table to down right*) I hope she had it a little more red-up up there. You know, it seems kind of sneaking. Locking her up in town and then coming out here and trying to get her own house to turn against her!

MRS. PETERS   But, Mrs. Hale, the law is the law.

MRS. HALE   I s'pose 'tis. (*Unbuttoning her coat*) Better loosen up your things, Mrs. Peters. You won't feel them when you go out. (*Mrs. Peters takes off her fur tippet, goes to hang it on chair back left of table, stands looking at the work basket on floor near down left window.*)

MRS. PETERS   She was piecing a quilt. (*She brings the large sewing basket to the center table and they look at the bright pieces, Mrs. Hale above the table and Mrs. Peters left of it.*)

MRS. HALE   It's a log cabin pattern. Pretty, isn't it? I wonder if she was goin' to quilt it or just knot it? (*Footsteps have been heard coming down the stairs. The Sheriff enters followed by Hale and the County Attorney.*)

SHERIFF   They wonder if she was going to quilt it or just knot it! (*The men laugh, the women look abashed.*)

COUNTY ATTORNEY   (*Rubbing his hands over the stove*) Frank's fire didn't do much up there, did it? Well, let's go out to the barn and get that cleared up. (*The men go outside by up left door.*)

MRS. HALE   (*Resentfully*) I don't know as there's anything so strange, our takin' up our time with little things while we're waiting for them to get the evidence. (*She sits in chair right of table smoothing out a block with decision.*) I don't see as it's anything to laugh about.

MRS. PETERS   (*Apologetically*) Of course they've got awful important things on their minds. (*Pulls up a chair and joins Mrs. Hale at the left of the table.*)

MRS. HALE   (*Examining another block*) Mrs. Peters, look at this one. Here, this is the one she was working on, and look at the sewing! All the rest of it has been so nice and even. And look at this! It's all over the place! Why, it looks as if she didn't know what she was about! (*After she has said this they look at each other, then start to glance back at the door. After an instant Mrs. Hale has pulled at a knot and ripped the sewing.*)

MRS. PETERS   Oh, what are you doing, Mrs. Hale?

MRS. HALE   (*Mildly*) Just pulling out a stitch or two that's not sewed very good. (*Threading a needle*) Bad sewing always made me fidgety.

MRS. PETERS   (*With a glance at door, nervously*) I don't think we ought to touch things.

MRS. HALE   I'll just finish up this end. (*Suddenly stopping and leaning forward*)   Mrs. Peters?

MRS. PETERS   Yes, Mrs. Hale?

MRS. HALE   What do you suppose she was so nervous about?

MRS. PETERS   Oh—I don't know. I don't know as she was nervous. I sometimes sew awful queer when I'm just tired. (*Mrs. Hale starts to say something, looks at Mrs. Peters, then goes on sewing.*)   Well, I must get these things wrapped up. They may be through sooner than we think. (*Putting apron and other things together*)   I wonder where I can find a piece of paper, and string. (*Rises*)

MRS. HALE   In that cupboard, maybe.

MRS. PETERS   (*Crosses right looking in cupboard*)   Why, here's a birdcage. (*Holds it up*)   Did she have a bird, Mrs. Hale?

MRS. HALE   Why, I don't know whether she did or not—I've not been here for so long. There was a man around last year selling canaries cheap, but I don't know as she took one; maybe she did. She used to sing real pretty herself.

MRS. PETERS   (*Glancing around*)   Seems funny to think of a bird here. But she must have had one, or why would she have a cage? I wonder what happened to it?

MRS. HALE   I s'pose maybe the cat got it.

MRS. PETERS   No, she didn't have a cat. She's got that feeling some people have about cats—being afraid of them. My cat got in her room and she was real upset and asked me to take it out.

MRS. HALE   My sister Bessie was like that. Queer, ain't it?

MRS. PETERS   (*Examining the cage*)   Why, look at this door. It's broke. One hinge is pulled apart. (*Takes a step down to Mrs. Hale's right*)

MRS. HALE   (*Looking too*)   Looks as if someone must have been rough with it.

MRS. PETERS   Why, yes. (*She brings the cage forward and puts it on the table.*)

MRS. HALE   (*Glancing toward up left door*)   I wish if they're going to find any evidence they'd be about it. I don't like this place.

MRS. PETERS   But I'm awful glad you came with me, Mrs. Hale. It would be lonesome for me sitting here alone.

MRS. HALE   It would, wouldn't it? (*Dropping her sewing*)   But I tell you what I do wish, Mrs. Peters. I wish I had come over sometimes when *she* was here. I— (*looking around the room*) — wish I had.

MRS. PETERS   But of course you were awful busy, Mrs. Hale—your house and your children.

MRS. HALE   (*Rises and crosses left*) I could've come. I stayed away
because it weren't cheerful—and that's why I ought to have come.
I— (*Looking out left window*) —I've never liked this place.
Maybe because it's down in a hollow and you don't see the road. I
dunno what it is, but it's a lonesome place and always was. I wish
I had come over to see Minnie Foster sometimes. I can see now—
(*Shakes her head*)

MRS. PETERS   (*Left of table and above it*) Well, you mustn't reproach
yourself, Mrs. Hale. Somehow we just don't see how it is with
other folks until—something turns up.

MRS. HALE   Not having children makes less work—but it makes a
quiet house, and Wright out to work all day, and no company
when he did come in. (*Turning from window*) Did you know
John Wright. Mrs. Peters?

MRS. PETERS   Not to know him; I've seen him in town. They say he
was a good man.

MRS. HALE   Yes—good; he didn't drink, and kept his word as well as
most, I guess, and paid his debts. But he was a hard man, Mrs.
Peters. Just to pass the time of day with him— (*Shivers*) Like
a raw wind that gets to the bone. (*Pauses, her eye falling on the
cage*) I should think she would 'a' wanted a bird. But what do
you suppose went with it?

MRS. PETERS   I don't know, unless it got sick and died. (*She reaches
over and swings the broken door, swings it again, both women
watch it.*)

MRS. HALE   You weren't raised round here, were you? (*Mrs. Peters
shakes her head.*) You didn't know—her?

MRS. PETERS   Not till they brought her yesterday.

MRS. HALE   She—come to think of it, she was kind of like a bird herself—real sweet and pretty, but kind of timid and—fluttery. How
—she—did—change. (*Silence; then as if struck by a happy
thought and relieved to get back to everyday things. Crosses right
above Mrs. Peters to cupboard, replaces small chair used to stand
on to its original place down right*) Tell you what, Mrs. Peters,
why don't you take the quilt in with you? It might take up her
mind.

MRS. PETERS   Why, I think that's a real nice idea, Mrs. Hale. There
couldn't possibly be any objection to it, could there? Now, just
what would I take? I wonder if her patches are in here—and her
things. (*They look in the sewing basket.*)

MRS. HALE   (*Crosses to right of table*) Here's some red. I expect this
has got sewing things in it. (*Brings out a fancy box*) What a
pretty box. Looks like something somebody would give you.

Maybe her scissors are in here. (*Opens box. Suddenly puts her hand to her nose*) Why— (*Mrs. Peters bends nearer, then turns her face away.*) There's something wrapped up in this piece of silk.

MRS. PETERS   Why, this isn't her scissors.

MRS. HALE   (*Lifting the silk*) Oh, Mrs. Peters—it's— (*Mrs. Peters bends closer.*)

MRS. PETERS   It's the bird.

MRS. HALE   But, Mrs. Peters—look at it! Its neck! Look at its neck! It's all—other side to.

MRS. PETERS   Somebody—wrung—its—neck. (*Their eyes meet. A look of growing comprehension, of horror. Steps are heard outside. Mrs. Hale slips box under quilt pieces, and sinks into her chair. Enter Sheriff and County Attorney. Mrs. Peters steps down left and stands looking out of window.*)

COUNTY ATTORNEY   (*As one turning from serious things to little pleasantries*) Well, ladies, have you decided whether she was going to quilt it or knot it? (*Crosses to center above table.*)

MRS. PETERS   We think she was going to—knot it. (*Sheriff crosses to right of stove, lifts stove lid and glances at fire, then stands warming hands at stove.*)

COUNTY ATTORNEY   Well, that's interesting, I'm sure. (*Seeing the birdcage*) Has the bird flown?

MRS. HALE   (*Putting more quilt pieces over the box*) We think the—cat got it.

COUNTY ATTORNEY   (*Preoccupied*) Is there a cat? (*Mrs. Hale glances in a quick covert way at Mrs. Peters.*)

MRS. PETERS   (*Turning from window, takes a step in*) Well, not now. They're superstitious, you know. They leave.

COUNTY ATTORNEY   (*To Sheriff Peters, continuing an interrupted conversation* No sign at all of anyone having come from the outside. Their own rope. Now let's go up again and go over it piece by piece. (*They start upstairs*) It would have to have been someone who knew just the— (*Mrs. Peters sits down left of table. The two women sit there not looking at one another, but as if peering into something and at the same time holding back. When they talk now it is in the manner of feeling their way over strange ground, as if afraid of what they are saying, but as if they cannot help saying it.*)

MRS. HALE   (*Hesitatively and in hushed voice*) She liked the bird. She was going to bury it in that pretty box.

MRS. PETERS   (*In a whisper*) When I was a girl—my kitten—there was a boy took a hatchet, and before my eyes—and before I could get there— (*Covers her face an instant*)　If they hadn't held me back I would have— (*Catches herself, looks upstairs where steps are heard, falters weakly*)　—hurt him.

MRS. HALE　(*With a slow look around her*)　I wonder how it would seem never to have had any children around. (*Pause*) No, Wright wouldn't like the bird—a thing that sang. She used to sing. He killed that, too.

MRS. PETERS　(*Moving uneasily*)　We don't know who killed the bird.

MRS. HALE　I knew John Wright.

MRS. PETERS　It was an awful thing was done in this house that night, Mrs. Hale. Killing a man while he slept, slipping a rope around his neck that choked the life out of him.

MRS. HALE　His neck. Choked the life out of him. (*Her hand goes out and rests on the birdcage.*)

MRS. PETERS　(*With rising voice*)　We don't know who killed him. We don't know.

MRS. HALE　(*Her own feeling not interrupted*)　If there'd been years and years of nothing, then a bird to sing to you, it would be awful —still, after the bird was still.

MRS. PETERS　(*Something within her speaking*)　I know what stillness is. When we homesteaded in Dakota, and my first baby died— after he was two years old, and me with no other then—

MRS. HALE　(*Moving*)　How soon do you suppose they'll be through looking for the evidence?

MRS. PETERS.　I know what stillness is. (*Pulling herself back*)　The law has got to punish crime, Mrs. Hale.

MRS. HALE　(*Not as if answering that*)　I wish you'd seen Minnie Foster when she wore a white dress with blue ribbons and stood up there in the choir and sang. (*A look around the room*)　Oh, I wish I'd come over here once in a while! That was a crime! That was a crime! Who's going to punish that?

MRS. PETERS　(*Looking upstairs*)　We mustn't—take on.

MRS. HALE　I might have known she needed help! I know how things can be—for women. I tell you, it's queer, Mrs. Peters. We live close together and we live far apart. We all go through the same things—it's all just a different kind of the same thing. (*Brushes her eyes, noticing the jar of fruit, reaches out for it*)　If I was you I wouldn't tell her her fruit was gone. Tell her it *ain't*. Tell her it's all right. Take this in to prove it to her. She—may never know whether it was broke or not.

MRS. PETERS　(*Takes the jar, looks about for something to wrap it in; takes petticoat from the clothes brought from the other room, very nervously begins winding this around the jar. In a false voice)* My, it's a good thing the men couldn't hear us. Wouldn't they just laugh! Getting all stirred up over a little thing like a— dead canary. As if that could have anything to do with—with— wouldn't they *laugh! (The men are heard coming downstairs.)*

MRS. HALE *(Under her breath)* Maybe they would—maybe they wouldn't.

COUNTY ATTORNEY No, Peters, it's all perfectly clear except a reason for doing it. But you know juries when it comes to women. If there was some definite thing. *(Crosses slowly to above table. Sheriff crosses down right. Mrs. Hale and Mrs. Peters remain seated at either side of table.)* Something to show—something to make a story about—a thing that would connect up with this strange way of doing it— *(The women's eyes meet for an instant. Enter Hale from outer door.)*

HALE *(Remaining up left by door)* Well, I've got the team around. Pretty cold out there.

COUNTY ATTORNEY I'm going to stay awhile by myself. *(To the Sheriff)* You can send Frank out for me, can't you? I want to go over everything. I'm not satisfied that we can't do better.

SHERIFF Do you want to see what Mrs. Peters is going to take in? *(The Lawyer picks up the apron, laughs.)*

COUNTY ATTORNEY Oh, I guess they're not very dangerous things the ladies have picked out. *(Moves a few things about, disturbing the quilt pieces which cover the box. Steps back)* No, Mrs. Peters doesn't need supervising. For that matter a sheriff's wife is married to the law. Ever think of it that way, Mrs. Peters?

MRS. PETERS Not—just that way.

SHERIFF *(Chuckling)* Married to the law. *(Moves to down right door to the other room)* I just want you to come in here a minute, George. We ought to take a look at these windows.

COUNTY ATTORNEY *(Scoffingly)* Oh, windows!

SHERIFF We'll be right out, Mr. Hale. *(Hale goes outside. The Sheriff follows the County Attorney into the other room. Then Mrs. Hale rises, hands tight together, looking intensely at Mrs. Peters, whose eyes make a slow turn, finally meeting Mrs. Hale's. A moment Mrs. Hale holds her, then her own eyes point the way to where the box is concealed. Suddenly Mrs. Peters throws back quilt pieces and tries to put the box in the bag she is carrying. It is too big. She opens box, starts to take bird out, cannot touch it. goes to pieces, stands there helpless. Sound of a knob turning in the other room. Mrs. Hale snatches the box and puts it in the pocket of her big coat. Enter County Attorney and Sheriff, who remains down right.)*

COUNTY ATTORNEY   (*Crosses to up left door facetiously*)   Well, Henry,
   at least we found out that she was not going to quilt it. She was
   going to—what is it you call it, ladies?
MRS. HALE   (*Standing center below table facing front, her hand
   against her.pocket*)   We call it—knot it, Mr. Henderson.

CURTAIN

Questions

1. How does the death of John Wright become known? How does Mrs.
   Wright explain it? How does the Attorney propose to explain it? Why
   does he set so much value on finding a "motive"?
2. Though Mrs. Wright never appears, we learn a great deal about her.
   Write a brief background and character sketch of her from the evidence
   in the play. We also learn a great deal about Mr. Wright. What kind of
   man was he? Is it understandable that he was killed? Is it justified?
   Why or why not?
3. Distinguish Mrs. Peters and Mrs. Hale from each other: (a) in appearance, (b) in social position, (c) in knowledge of Mrs. Wright, and (d) in
   reaction to the men and their activities. List the clues that the women
   turn up which might incriminate Mrs. Wright. How do they neutralize
   each of them? What past experiences that the women themselves have
   had help determine their attitude toward what Mrs. Wright may have
   done? At what point do we know for sure that they will say nothing to
   the men of what they have found?
4. How do the women view the men? How do the men view the women?
   Do the men's attitudes toward the women in any way influence the
   outcome? What is ironical about Mrs. Hale's last remark? What is
   ironical about the play's title? What larger irony in the play as a whole
   could be summed up in the phrase: "The humble shall be lifted up and
   the proud shall be abased."
5. In *Sorry, Wrong Number* a murder is the central event and takes place
   in the play itself. In *Shall We Join the Ladies?* a murder is still the
   central event in that the dinner party has no purpose except to find out
   the guilty party. In *Trifles*, the murder seems less prominent, even less
   important, among the concerns of the play. Why? What else is *Trifles*
   about besides the murder of John Wright?

6. (a) The women come on stage at the beginning of the play with the men, but between Mrs. Peters' disclaimer that she's not cold and her remark about Mrs. Wright's fruit having frozen, they have no lines and nothing is indicated about their behavior. If you were directing the play, would you have the women keep themselves as unobtrusive as possible during this time? Or would you have them exhibit some sort of visible reaction to parts of farmer Hale's narrative? Defend your decision. (b) If your choice is that the women exhibit a reaction, at what point would you have them do so? And what form would you have their reaction take?

7. Read aloud with a friend the episode beginning when Mrs. Peters puts the birdcage on the table and ending when they both realize what happened to the bird. Try to capture the personality differences of the two women in the way you make each talk. When you come to the lines about the bird's neck, speak them with an emphasis suitable to their significance in the play. (In order to do this, you will need to decide first what their significance is. One clue: could it be argued that John Wright settled in advance without knowing it the method of his own death?)

8. Do you regard what the women do as right or wrong? What would you do yourself in their situation? Why?

Part II
Four Farces

The Bear
ANTON CHEKHOV

How He Lied to Her Husband
GEORGE BERNARD SHAW

The Ugly Duckling
A. A. MILNE

Strictly Matrimony
ERROL HILL

A favorite theme of comedy is the triumph of reality, of common sense—life as it sanely is—over someone's crackpot effort to deny it, warp it, keep it at bay, or smother it with unimportant matters. In *The Bear*, a handsome and marriageable widow with everything to live for has taken a wildly romantic decision to spend the rest of her days mourning her husband. But life, in the form of a "bear," intrudes, kindles, and conquers.

The Bear

ANTON CHEKHOV

Characters

ELENA IVANOVNA POPOVA   (*a young widow with dimpled cheeks, and a landowner*)
GRIGORY STEPANOVICH SMIRNOV   (*a middle-aged landowner*)
LUKA   (*Popova's old servant*)

The drawing room of Popova's country home.

(*Popova, in deep mourning, does not remove her eyes from a photograph.*)

LUKA   It isn't right, madam . . . you're only destroying yourself . . . the chambermaid and the cook have gone off berry picking, every living being is rejoicing; even the cat knows how to be content, walking around the yard catching birdies, and you sit in your room all day as if it were a convent, and you don't take pleasure in anything. Yes, really! Almost a year has passed since you've gone out of the house!

POPOVA   And I shall never go out. . . . What for? My life is already ended. He lies in his grave; I have buried myself in these four walls . . . we are both dead.

LUKA   There you go again! Nikolai Mikhailovich is dead, that's as it was meant to be, it's the will of God, may he rest in peace. . . . You've done your mourning and that will do. You can't go on weeping and mourning forever. My wife died when her time came, too. . . . Well? I grieved, I wept for a month, and that was enough for her; and if I had to weep like Lazarus, for four days, well, the old lady just wasn't worth it. (*Sighs*) You've forgotten all your neighbors. You don't go anywhere or accept any calls. We live, so to speak, like spiders. We never see the light. The mice have eaten my livery. It isn't as if there weren't any nice neighbors—the district is full of them . . . there's a regiment stationed at Riblov, such officers—they're like bonbons—you'll never get your fill of them! And in the barracks, never a Friday goes by without a ball; and, if you please, the military band plays music every day. . . . Yes, madam, my dear lady: you're young, beautiful, in the full bloom of youth—if only you took a little pleasure in life . . . beauty doesn't last forever, you know! In ten years' time, you'll be wanting to spread your tail like a peahen in front of the officers—and it will be too late.

POPOVA   (*Determined*)   I must ask you never to talk to me like that! You know that when Nikolai Mikhailovich died, life lost all its salt for me. It may seem to you that I am alive, but that's only conjecture! I vowed to wear mourning to my grave and not to see the light of day. . . . Do you hear me? May his departed spirit see how much I love him. . . . Yes, I know, it's no mystery to you that he was often mean to me, cruel . . . and even unfaithful, but I shall remain true to the grave and show him I know how to love. There, beyond the grave, he will see me as I was before his death. . . .

LUKA   Instead of talking like that, you should be taking a walk in the garden or have Toby or Giant harnessed and go visit some of the neighbors . . .

POPOVA   Ai! (*She weeps.*)

LUKA   Madam! Dear lady! What's the matter with you! Christ be with you!

POPOVA   Oh, how he loved Toby! He always used to ride on him to

visit the Korchagins or the Vlasovs. How wonderfully he rode!
How graceful he was when he pulled at the reins with all his
strength! Do you remember? Toby, Toby! Tell them to give him
an extra bag of oats today.

LUKA   Yes, madam.

(*Sound of loud ringing*)

POPOVA   (*Shudders*)   Who's that? Tell them I'm not at home!

LUKA   Of course, madam.   (*He exits.*)

POPOVA   (*Alone. Looks at the photograph*)   You will see, Nicholas,
how much I can love and forgive . . . my love will die only when I
do, when my poor heart stops beating. (*Laughing through her
tears*)   Have you no shame? I'm a good girl, a virtuous little wife.
I've locked myself in and I'll be true to you to the grave, and you
. . . aren't you ashamed, you chubby cheeks? You deceived me,
you made scenes, for weeks on end you left me alone. . . .

LUKA   (*Enters, alarmed*)   Madam, somebody is asking for you. He
wants to see you. . . .

POPOVA   But didn't you tell them that since the death of my husband,
I don't see anybody?

LUKA   I did, but he didn't want to listen; he spoke about some very
important business.

POPOVA   I am *not at home*!

LUKA   That's what I told him . . . but . . . the devil . . . he cursed
and pushed past me right into the room . . . he's in the dining
room right now.

POPOVA   (*Losing her temper*)   Very well, let him come in . . . such
manners! (*Sighs*)   But it's obvious I'll have to go live in a convent. . . . (*Thoughtfully*)   Yes, a convent. . . .

SMIRNOV   (*To Luka*)   You idiot, you talk too much. . . . Ass! (*Sees
Popova and changes to dignified speech.*)   Madam, may I introduce myself: retired lieutenant of the artillery and landowner,
Grigory Stepanovich Smirnov! I feel the necessity of troubling
you about a highly important matter. . . .

POPOVA   (*Refusing her hand*)   What do you want?

SMIRNOV   Your late husband, whom I had the pleasure of knowing, has
remained in my debt for two twelve-hundred-ruble notes. Since I
must pay the interest at the agricultural bank tomorrow, I have
come to ask you, madam, to pay me the money today.

POPOVA   One thousand two hundred. . . . And why was my husband
in debt to you?

SMIRNOV   He used to buy oats from me.

POPOVA   (*Sighing, to Luka*)   So, Luka, don't you forget to tell them to give Toby an extra bag of oats.

(*Luka goes out.*)

(*To Smirnov*)   If Nikolai Mikhailovich was in debt to you, then it goes without saying that I'll pay; but please excuse me today. I haven't any spare cash. The day after tomorrow, my steward will be back from town and I will give him instructions to pay you what is owed; until then I cannot comply with your wishes. . . . Besides, today is the anniversary—exactly seven months ago my husband died, and I'm in such a mood that I'm not quite disposed to occupy myself with money matters.

SMIRNOV   And I'm in such a mood that if I don't pay the interest tomorrow, I'll be owing so much that my troubles will drown me. They'll take away my estate!

POPOVA   You'll receive your money the day after tomorrow.

SMIRNOV   I don't want the money the day after tomorrow. I want it today.

POPOVA   You must excuse me. I can't pay you today.

SMIRNOV   And I can't wait until after tomorrow.

POPOVA   What can I do, if I don't have it now?

SMIRNOV   You mean to say you can't pay?

POPOVA   I can't pay. . . .

SMIRNOV   Hm! Is that your last word?

POPOVA   That is my last word.

SMIRNOV   Positively the last?

POPOVA   Positively.

SMIRNOV   Thank you very much. We'll make a note of that.   (*Shrugs his shoulders*)   And people want me to be calm and collected! Just now, on the way here, I met a tax officer and he asked me: why are you always so angry, Grigory Stepanovich? Goodness' sake, how can I be anything but angry? I need money desperately . . . I rode out yesterday early in the morning, at daybreak, and went to see all my debtors; and if only one of them had paid his debt . . . I was dog-tired, spent the night God knows where—a Jewish tavern beside a barrel of vodka. . . . Finally I got here, fifty miles from home, hoping to be paid, and you treat me to a "mood." How can I help being angry?

POPOVA   It seems to me that I clearly said: My steward will return from the country and then you will be paid.

SMIRNOV   I didn't come to your steward, but to you! What the hell, if you'll pardon the expression, would I do with your steward?

POPOVA   Excuse me, my dear sir, I am not accustomed to such unusual expressions nor to such a tone. I'm not listening to you any more. (*Goes out quickly*)

SMIRNOV (*Alone*) Well, how do you like that? "A mood." . . . "Husband died seven months ago"! Must I pay the interest or mustn't I? I ask you: Must I pay, or must I not? So, your husband's dead, and you're in a mood and all that finicky stuff . . . and your steward's away somewhere, may he drop dead. What do you want me to do? Do you think I can fly away from my creditors in a balloon or something? Or should I run and bash my head against the wall? I go to Gruzdev—and he's not at home; Yaroshevich is hiding; with Kuritsin it's a quarrel to the death and I almost throw him out the window; Mazutov has diarrhea; and this one is in a "mood." Not one of these swine wants to pay me! And all because I'm too nice to them. I'm a sniveling idiot, I'm spineless, I'm an old lady! I'm too delicate with them! So, just you wait! You'll find out what I'm like! I won't let you play around with me, you devils! I'll stay and stick it out until she pays. Brr! . . . How furious I am today, how furious! I'm shaking inside from rage and I can hardly catch my breath. . . . Damn it! My God, I even feel sick! (*He shouts*) Hey you!

LUKA (*Enters*) What do you want?

SMIRNOV Give me some kvass or some water! (*Luka exits.*) What logic is there in this! A man needs money desperately, it's like a noose around his neck—and she won't pay because, you see, she's not disposed to occupy herself with money matters! . . . That's the logic of a woman! That's why I never did like and do not like to talk to women. I'd rather sit on a keg of gunpowder than talk to a woman. Brr! . . . I even have goose pimples, this skirt has put me in such a rage! All I have to do is see one of those poetical creatures from a distance, and I get so angry it gives me a cramp in the leg. I just want to shout for help.

LUKA (*Entering with water*) Madam is sick and won't see anyone.

SMIRNOV Get out! (*Luka goes.*) Sick and won't see anyone! No need to see me . . . I'll stay and sit here until you give me the money. You can stay sick for a week, and I'll stay for a week . . . if you're sick for a year, I'll stay a year. . . . I'll get my own back, dear lady! You can't impress me with your widow's weeds and your dimpled cheeks . . . we know all about those dimples! (*Shouts through the window*) Semyon, unharness the horses! We're not going away quite yet! I'm staying here! Tell them in the stable to give the horses some oats! You brute, you let the horse on the left side get all tangled up in the reins again! (*Teasing*) "Never mind" . . . I'll give you a never mind! (*Goes away from the window*) The heat is unbearable and nobody pays up. I slept badly last night and on top of everything else this skirt in mourning is "in a mood" . . . my head aches . . . should I have some vodka? I wonder, should I? (*Shouts*) Hey, you!

LUKA   (*Enters*) What is it?

SMIRNOV   Give me a glass of vodka. (*Luka goes out.*) Oof! (*Sits down and examines himself*) Nobody would say I was looking well! Dusty all over, boots dirty, unwashed, unkempt, straw on my waistcoat. . . . The dear lady probably took me for a robber. (*Yawns*) It's not very polite to present myself in a drawing room looking like this; oh well, who cares? . . . I'm not here as a visitor but as a creditor, and there's no official costume for creditors. . . .

LUKA   (*Enters with vodka*) You're taking liberties, my good man. . . .

SMIRNOV   (*Angrily*) What?

LUKA   I . . . nothing . . . I only . . .

SMIRNOV   Who are you talking to? Shut up!

LUKA   (*Aside*) The devil sent this leech. An ill wind brought him. . . . (*Luka goes out.*)

SMIRNOV   Oh how furious I am! I'm so mad I could crush the whole world into a powder! I even feel faint! (*Shouts*) Hey, you!

POPOVA   (*Enters, eyes downcast*) My dear sir, in my solitude, I have long ago grown unaccustomed to the masculine voice and I cannot bear shouting. I must request you not to disturb my peace and quiet!

SMIRNOV   Pay me my money and I'll go.

POPOVA   I told you in plain language: I haven't any spare cash now; wait until the day after tomorrow.

SMIRNOV   And I also told you respectfully, in plain language: I don't need the money the day after tomorrow, but today. If you don't pay me today, then tomorrow I'll have to hang myself.

POPOVA   But what can I do if I don't have the money? You're so strange!

SMIRNOV   Then you won't pay me now? No?

POPOVA   I can't. . . .

SMIRNOV   In that case, I can stay here and wait until you pay. . . . (*Sits down*) You'll pay the day after tomorrow? Excellent! In that case I'll stay here until the day after tomorrow. I'll sit here all that time . . . (*Jumps up*) I ask you: Have I got to pay the interest tomorrow, or not? Or do you think I'm joking?

POPOVA   My dear sir, I ask you not to shout! This isn't a stable!

SMIRNOV   I wasn't asking you about a stable but about this: do I have to pay the interest tomorrow or not?

POPOVA   You don't know how to behave in the company of a lady!

SMIRNOV   No, I don't know how to behave in the company of a lady!

POPOVA   No, you don't! You are an ill-bred, rude man! Respectable people don't talk to a woman like that!

SMIRNOV   Ach, it's astonishing! How would you like me to talk to you? In French, perhaps? (*Lisps in anger*) *Madame, je vous prie* . . . Ah, pardon, I've made you uneasy! Such lovely weather we're having today! And you look so becoming in your mourning dress. (*Bows and scrapes*)

POPOVA   That's rude and not very clever!

SMIRNOV   (*Teasing*) Rude and not very clever! I don't know how to behave in the company of ladies. Madam, in my time I've seen far more women than you've seen sparrows. Three times I've fought duels over women; I've jilted twelve women, nine have jilted me! Yes! There was a time when I played the fool; I became sentimental over women, used honeyed words, fawned on them, bowed and scraped. . . . I loved, suffered, sighed at the moon; I became limp, melted, shivered . . . I loved passionately, madly, every which way, devil take me, I chattered away like a magpie about the emancipation of women, ran through half my fortune as a result of my tender feelings; but now, if you will excuse me, I'm on to your ways! I've had enough! Dark eyes, passionate eyes, ruby lips, dimpled cheeks; the moon, whispers, bated breath—for all that I wouldn't give a good goddamn. Present company excepted, of course, but all women, young and old alike, are affected clowns, gossips, hateful, consummate liars to the marrow of their bones, vain, trivial, ruthless, outrageously illogical, and as far as this is concerned   (*Taps on his forehead*)   well, excuse my frankness, any sparrow could give pointers to a philosopher in petticoats! Look at one of those poetical creatures: muslin, ethereal demigoddess, a thousand raptures, and you look into her soul —a common crocodile! (*Grips the back of a chair; the chair cracks and breaks.*)   But the most revolting part of it all is that this crocodile imagines that she has a chef d'oeuvre, her own privilege, a monopoly on tender feelings. The hell with it—you can hang me upside down by that nail if a woman is capable of loving anything besides a lapdog. All she can do when she's in love is slobber! While the man suffers and sacrifices, all her love is expressed in playing with her skirt and trying to lead him around firmly by the nose. You have the misfortune of being a woman, you know yourself what the nature of a woman is like.

Tell me honestly: have you ever in your life seen a woman who is sincere, faithful, and constant? You never have! Only old and ugly ladies are faithful and constant! You're more liable to meet a horned cat or a white woodcock than a faithful woman!

POPOVA   Pardon me, but in your opinion, who is faithful and constant in love? The man?

SMIRNOV   Yes, the man!

POPOVA   The man! (*Malicious laugh*) Men are faithful and constant in love! That's news! (*Heatedly*) What right have you to say that? Men are faithful and constant! For that matter, as far as I know, of all the men I have known and now know, my late husband was the best. . . . I loved him passionately, with all my being, as only a young intellectual woman can love; I gave him my youth, my happiness, my life, my fortune; he was my life's breath; I worshiped him as if I were a heathen, and . . . and, what good did it do—this best of men himself deceived me shamelessly at every step of the way. After his death, I found his desk full of love letters; and when he was alive—it's terrible to remember—he used to leave me alone for weeks at a time, and before my very eyes he paid court to other women and deceived me. He . . . and, in spite of all that, I loved him and was true to him . . . and besides, now that he is dead, I am still faithful and constant. I have shut myself up in these four walls forever and I won't remove these widow's weeds until my dying day. . . .

SMIRNOV   (*Laughs contemptuously*) Widow's weeds! . . . I don't know what you take me for! As if I didn't know why you wear that black domino and bury yourself in these four walls! Well, well! It's so secret, so poetic! When a Junker° or some fool of a poet passes by this country house, he'll look up at your window and think: "Here lives the mysterious Tamara, who, for the love of her husband, buried herself in these four walls." We know these tricks!

POPOVA   (*Flaring*) What? How dare you say that to me?

SMIRNOV   You may have buried yourself alive, but you haven't forgotten to powder yourself!

POPOVA   How dare you use such expressions with me?

SMIRNOV   Please don't shout. I'm not your steward! You must allow me to call a spade a spade. I'm not a woman and I'm used to saying what's on my mind! Don't you shout at me!

POPOVA   I'm not shouting, you are! Please leave me in peace!

SMIRNOV   Pay me my money and I'll go.

POPOVA   I won't give you any money!

°*Junker:* Prussian aristocrat

SMIRNOV   Yes, you will.

POPOVA   To spite you, I won't pay you anything. You can leave me in peace!

SMIRNOV   I don't have the pleasure of being either your husband or your fiancé, so please don't make scenes! (*Sits down*) I don't like it.

POPOVA   (*Choking with rage*)   You're sitting down?

SMIRNOV   Yes, I am.

POPOVA   I ask you to get out!

SMIRNOV   Give me my money . . . (*Aside*)   Oh, I'm so furious! Furious!

POPOVA   I don't want to talk to impudent people! Get out of here! (*Pause*)   You're not going? No?

SMIRNOV   No.

POPOVA   No?

SMIRNOV   No!

POPOVA   Good for you! (*Rings*)

(*Luka enters.*)

Luka, show the gentleman out!

LUKA   (*Goes up to Smirnov*)   Sir, will you please leave, as you have been asked. You mustn't . . .

SMIRNOV   (*Jumping up*)   Shut up! Who do you think you're talking to? I'll make mincemeat out of you!

LUKA   (*His hand to his heart*)   Oh my God! Saints above! (*Falls into chair*)   Oh, I feel ill! I feel ill! I can't catch my breath!

POPOVA   Where's Dasha? Dasha! (*She shouts*)   Dasha! Pelagea! (*She rings*)

LUKA   Oh! They've all gone berry picking . . . there's nobody at home . . . I'm ill! Water!

POPOVA   Will you please get out!

SMIRNOV   Will you please be more polite?

POPOVA   (*Clenches her fist and stamps her feet*)   You're a muzhik!° You're a crude bear! A brute! A monster!

SMIRNOV   What? What did you say?

POPOVA   I said that you were a bear, a monster!

SMIRNOV   (*Advancing toward her*)   Excuse me, but what right do you have to insult me?

POPOVA   Yes, I am insulting you . . . so what? Do you think I'm afraid of you?

SMIRNOV   And do you think just because you're one of those poetical

°*muzhik:* peasant

creatures, that you have the right to insult me with impunity? Yes? I challenge you!

LUKA   Lord in Heaven! Saints above! . . . Water!

SMIRNOV   Pistols!

POPOVA   Do you think just because you have big fists and you can bellow like a bull, that I'm afraid of you? You're such a bully!

SMIRNOV   I challenge you! I'm not going to let anybody insult me, and I don't care if you are a woman, a fragile creature!

POPOVA   (*Trying to get a word in edgewise*) Bear! Bear! Bear!

SMIRNOV   It's about time we got rid of the prejudice that only men must pay for their insults! Devil take it, if women want to be equal, they should behave as equals! Let's fight!

POPOVA   You want to fight! By all means!

SMIRNOV   This minute!

POPOVA   This minute! My husband had some pistols . . . I'll go and get them right away. (*Goes out hurriedly and then returns*) What pleasure I'll have putting a bullet through that thick head of yours! The hell with you! (*She goes out.*)

SMIRNOV   I'll shoot her down like a chicken! I'm not a little boy or a sentimental puppy. Fragile creatures don't exist for me.

LUKA   Kind sir! Holy father! (*Kneels*) Have pity on a poor old man and go away from here! You've frightened her to death and now you're going to shoot her?

SMIRNOV   (*Not listening to him*) If she fights, then it means she believes in equality of rights and the emancipation of women. Here the sexes are equal! I'll shoot her like a chicken! But what a woman! (*Imitates her*) "The hell with you! . . . I'll put a bullet through that thick head of yours! . . ." What a woman! How she blushed, her eyes shone . . . she accepted my challenge! To tell the truth, it was the first time in my life I've seen a woman like that. . . .

LUKA   Dear sir, please go away! I'll pray to God on your behalf as long as I live!

SMIRNOV   That's a woman for you! A woman like that I can understand! A real woman! Not a sour-faced nincompoop but fiery, gunpowder! Fireworks! I'm even sorry to have to kill her!

LUKA   (*Weeps*) Dear sir . . . go away!

SMIRNOV   I positively like her! Positively! Even though she has dimpled cheeks, I like her! I'm almost ready to forget about the debt. . . . My fury has diminished. Wonderful woman!

POPOVA   (*Enters with pistols*) Here they are, the pistols. Before we fight, you must show me how to fire. . . . I've never had a pistol in my hands before . . .

LUKA Oh dear Lord, for pity's sake. . . . I'll go and find the gardener and the coachman. . . . What did we do to deserve such trouble? (*Exits.*)

SMIRNOV (*Examining the pistols*) You see, there are several sorts of pistols . . . there are special dueling pistols, the Mortimer with primers. Then there are Smith and Wesson revolvers, triple action with extractors . . . excellent pistols! . . . they cost a minimum of ninety rubles a pair. . . . You must hold the revolver like this . . . (*Aside*) What eyes, what eyes! A woman to set you on fire!

POPOVA Like this?

SMIRNOV Yes, like this . . . then you cock the pistol . . . take aim . . . put your head back a little . . . stretch your arm out all the way . . . that's right . . . then with this finger press on this little piece of goods . . . and that's all there is to do . . . but the most important thing is not to get excited and aim without hurrying . . . try to keep your arm from shaking.

POPOVA Good . . . it's not comfortable to shoot indoors. Let's go into the garden.

SMIRNOV Let's go. But I'm giving you advance notice that I'm going to fire into the air.

POPOVA That's the last straw! Why?

SMIRNOV Why? . . . Why . . . because it's my business, that's why.

POPOVA Are you afraid? Yes? Aahhh! No, sir. You're not going to get out of it that easily! Be so good as to follow me! I will not rest until I've put a hole through your forehead . . . that forehead I hate so much! Are you afraid?

SMIRNOV Yes, I'm afraid.

POPOVA You're lying! Why don't you want to fight?

SMIRNOV Because . . . because you . . . because I like you.

POPOVA (*Laughs angrily*) He likes me! He dares say that he likes me! (*Points to the door*) Out!

SMIRNOV (*Loads the revolver in silence, takes cap and goes; at the door, stops for half a minute while they look at each other in silence; then he approaches Popova hesitantly*) Listen. . . . Are you still angry? I'm extremely irritated, but, do you understand me, how can I express it . . . the fact is, that, you see, strictly speaking . . . (*He shouts*) Is it my fault, really, for liking you? (*Grabs the back of a chair; chair cracks and breaks.*) Why the hell do you have such fragile furniture! I like you! Do you understand? I . . . I'm almost in love with you!

POPOVA Get away from me—I hate you!

SMIRNOV God, what a woman! I've never in my life seen anything like her! I'm lost! I'm done for! I'm caught like a mouse in a trap!

POPOVA   Stand back or I'll shoot!

SMIRNOV   Shoot! You could never understand what happiness it would be to die under the gaze of those wonderful eyes, to be shot by a revolver which was held by those little velvet hands. . . . I've gone out of my mind! Think about it and decide right away, because if I leave here, then we'll never see each other again! Decide . . . I'm a nobleman, a respectable gentleman, of good family. I have an income of ten thousand a year. . . . I can put a bullet through a coin tossed in the air . . . I have some fine horses. . . . Will you be my wife?

POPOVA   (*Indignantly brandishes her revolver*)   Let's fight! I challenge you!

SMIRNOV   I'm out of my mind . . . I don't understand anything . . . (*Shouts*) Hey, you, water!

POPOVA   (*Shouts*)   Let's fight!

SMIRNOV   I've gone out of my mind. I'm in love like a boy, like an idiot! (*He grabs her hand, she screams with pain.*) I love you! (*Kneels*) I love you as I've never loved before! I've jilted twelve women, nine women have jilted me, but I've never loved one of them as I love you. . . . I'm weak, I'm a limp rag . . . I'm on my knees like a fool, offering you my hand. . . . Shame, shame! I haven't been in love for five years, I vowed I wouldn't; and suddenly I'm in love, like a fish out of water. I'm offering my hand in marriage. Yes or no? You don't want to? You don't need to! (*Gets up and quickly goes to the door*)

POPOVA   Wait!

SMIRNOV   (*Stops*)   Well?

POPOVA   Nothing . . . you can go . . . go away . . . wait. . . . No, get out, get out! I hate you! But— Don't go! Oh, if you only knew how furious I am, how angry! (*Throws revolver on table*) My fingers are swollen from that nasty thing. . . . (*Tears her handkerchief furiously*)   What are you waiting for? Get out!

SMIRNOV   Farewell!

POPOVA   Yes, yes, go away! (*Shouts*) Where are you going? Stop. . . . Oh, go away! Oh, how furious I am! Don't come near me! Don't come near me!

SMIRNOV   (*Approaching her*)   How angry I am with myself! I'm in love like a student, I've been on my knees. . . . It gives me the shivers. (*Rudely*)   I love you! A lot of good it will do me to fall in love with you! Tomorrow I've got to pay the interest, begin the mowing of the hay. (*Puts his arm around her waist*) I'll never forgive myself for this. . . .

POPOVA   Get away from me! Get your hands away! I . . . hate you! I
    . . . challenge you!

*(Prolonged kiss. Luka enters with an ax, the Gardener with a rake,
the Coachman with a pitchfork, and Workmen with cudgels.)*

LUKA   *(Catches sight of the pair kissing)* Lord in heaven! *(Pause)*
POPOVA   *(Lowering her eyes)*   Luka, tell them in the stable not to give
    Toby any oats today.

CURTAIN

Questions

1. How does Popova justify her decision to wall herself away from the
   world? What hints does the playwright give us of other motives of
   which she herself is perhaps unconscious? Consider carefully her second and fifth speeches. If you were directing the play, would you cast
   her as a woman who is tall and powerful or delicate and small? Refined
   looking or coarse looking? Soft-voiced or noisy? Why?
2. Luka is obviously a spokesman for common sense. List half a dozen
   specific details from his first two speeches that show him to be such.
   What comic function does he have? What are his activities during most
   of the play with respect to Smirnov? Would the ending be as funny
   without Luka's entrance at that point? Why not? How would you
   "cast" the part of Luka in view of his comic functions? What should be
   his age? Stature? Mannerisms? Voice? Give reasons for your answers.
3. What evidence can you find that Smirnov *is* a bear? We are told that
   he has a reputation in the neighborhood for being "always" in a certain
   frame of mind—what frame of mind? In what words and actions does
   this frame of mind show itself in his behavior while Popova is with
   Luka? With Popova herself? How would you cast him as to age, stature, mannerisms?
4. Trace the process by which Smirnov moves from (a) his obsession with
   his debt, to (b) an interest in Popova as a woman, to (c) a proposal of
   marriage. How much experience has he had with women? What opinions of them does he express to Popova? What opinions of her does he
   express? Write a brief character sketch of Smirnov in which you try to

account for his contradictory actions. Why do you think Popova accepts him? What is the meaning of her final remark in the play?

5. Cite three moments when the play seems to you particularly comical and describe as precisely as you can where the humor lies.

6. Chekhov tells us nothing about the setting of *The Bear* apart from the fact that it is in the drawing room in Popova's country house. For best stage effect, in what style do you think the room should be furnished? How many chairs does the text require? What kind? What other furniture is called for? What properties besides furniture? Make a complete list. Though the text does not specify, a room of such a house would certainly have pictures of some sort on the walls. What sort of pictures would seem to express best the play's spirit?

A n idealistic adolescent imagines himself in love with an honorable woman considerably older than he. He writes poems to her and makes himself useful by occasionally taking her to the theater, all with the approval of her husband, who knows that the affair is perfectly innocent, despite the young man's romantic illusions about carrying his beloved away to a new life of their own. When the woman suddenly discovers that the young man's poems are missing from her workbox, she realizes that they have probably fallen into her husband's hands; she persuades the young man to lie to her husband if he is confronted with them. He dutifully does lie, but with results that neither he nor she could possibly have foreseen.

How He Lied to Her Husband

GEORGE BERNARD SHAW

Characters

HER LOVER   (*Apjohn*)
HER HUSBAND   (*Bompas*)
HERSELF   (*Aurora Bompas*)

It is eight o'clock in the evening. The curtains are drawn and the lamps lighted in the drawing room of Her flat in Cromwell Road. Her lover, a beautiful youth of eighteen, in evening dress and cape, comes in alone. The door is near the corner; and as he appears in the doorway, he has the fireplace on the nearest wall to

75

his right. Near the fireplace a small ornamental table has on it a hand mirror, a fan, a pair of long white gloves, and a little white woollen cloud to wrap a woman's head in. On the other side of the room, near the piano, is a broad, square, softly upholstered stool. The room is furnished in the most approved South Kensington fashion: that is, it is as like a shop window as possible, and is intended to demonstrate the social position and spending powers of its owners, and not in the least to make them comfortable.

He is, be it repeated, a very beautiful youth, moving as in a dream, walking as on air. He puts his flowers down carefully on the table beside the fan; takes off his cape, and, as there is no room on the table for it, takes it to the piano; puts his hat on the cape; crosses to the hearth; looks at his watch; puts it up again; notices the things on the table; lights up as if he saw heaven opening before him; goes to the table and takes the cloud in both hands, nestling his nose into its softness and kissing it; kisses the gloves one after another; kisses the fan; gasps a long shuddering sigh of ecstasy; sits down on the stool and presses his hands to his eyes to shut out reality and dream a little; takes his hands down and shakes his head with a little smile of rebuke for his folly; catches sight of a speck of dust on his shoes and hastily and carefully brushes it off with his handkerchief; rises and takes the hand mirror from the table to make sure of his tie with the gravest anxiety; and is looking at his watch again when She comes in, much flustered. As she is dressed for the theater; has spoilt, petted ways; and wears many diamonds, she has an air of being a young and beautiful woman; but as a matter of hard fact, she is, dress and pretensions apart, a very ordinary South Kensington female of about thirty-seven, hopelessly inferior in physical and spiritual distinction to the beautiful youth, who hastily puts down the mirror as she enters.

in factuation w/ older woman / look at description!
seen thru opening lines!

HE   (*Kissing her hand*)   At last!

SHE   Henry: something dreadful has happened.

HE   What's the matter?

SHE   I have lost your poems.

HE   They were unworthy of you. I will write you some more.

SHE   No, thank you. Never any more poems for me. Oh, how could I have been so mad! so rash! so imprudent!

HE   Thank heaven for your madness, your rashness, your imprudence!

imprudent

SHE (*Impatiently*) Oh, be sensible, Henry. Can't you see what a terrible thing this is for me? Suppose anybody finds these poems! What will they think?

HE They will think that a man once loved a woman more devotedly than ever man loved woman before. But they will not know what man it was.

SHE What good is that to me if everybody will know what woman it was?

HE But how will they know?

SHE How will they know! Why, my name is all over them: my silly, unhappy name. Oh, if I had only been christened Mary Jane, or Gladys Muriel, or Beatrice, or Francesca, or Guinevere, or something quite common! But Aurora! Aurora! I'm the only Aurora in London; and everybody knows it. I believe I'm the only Aurora in the world. And it's so horribly easy to rhyme to it! Oh, Henry, why didn't you try to restrain your feelings a little in common consideration for me? Why didn't you write with some little reserve?

[handwritten: Why did she let poetry go on?]

HE Write poems to you with reserve! You ask me that!

SHE (*With perfunctory tenderness*) Yes, dear, of course it was very nice of you; and I know it was my own fault as much as yours. I ought to have noticed that your verses ought never to have been addressed to a married woman.

HE Ah, how I wish they had been addressed to an unmarried woman! How I wish they had!

SHE Indeed you have no right to wish anything of the sort. They are quite unfit for anybody but a married woman. That's just the difficulty. What will my sisters-in-law think of them?

HE (*Painfully jarred*) Have you got sisters-in-law? *[handwritten: in fact naked.]*

SHE Yes, of course I have. Do you suppose I am an angel?

HE (*Biting his lips*) I do. Heaven help me, I do—or I did—or (*He almost chokes a sob*)

SHE (*Softening and putting her hand caressingly on his shoulder*) Listen to me, dear. It's very nice of you to live with me in a dream, and to love me, and so on; but I can't help my husband having disagreeable relatives, can I?

HE (*Brightening up*) Ah, of course they are your husband's relatives: I forgot that. Forgive me, Aurora. (*He takes her hand from his shoulder and kisses it. She sits down on the stool. He remains near the table, with his back to it, smiling fatuously down at her.*)

SHE The fact is, Teddy's got nothing but relatives. *[handwritten: husband]* He has eight sisters and six half-sisters, and ever so many brothers—but I don't

[handwritten: Do you think Aurora romantically attracted to Henry? Fatuously]

mind his brothers. Now if you only knew the least little thing about the world, Henry, you'd know that in a large family, though the sisters quarrel with one another like mad all the time, yet let one of the brothers marry, and they all turn on their unfortunate sister-in-law and devote the rest of their lives with perfect unanimity to persuading him that his wife is unworthy of him. They can do it to her very face without her knowing it, because they always have a lot of stupid low family jokes that nobody understands but themselves. Half the time you can't tell what they're talking about: it just drives you wild. There ought to be a law against a man's sister ever entering his house after he's married. I'm as certain as that I'm sitting here that Georgina stole those poems out of my workbox.

HE   She will not understand them, I think.

SHE   Oh, won't she! She'll understand them only too well. She'll understand more harm than ever was in them: nasty vulgar-minded cat!

HE   (*Going to her*) Oh don't, don't think of people in that way. Don't think of her at all. (*He takes her hand and sits down on the carpet at her feet.*) Aurora: do you remember the evening when I sat here at your feet and read you those poems for the first time?

SHE   I shouldn't have let you: I see that now. When I think of Georgina sitting there at Teddy's feet and reading them to him for the first time, I feel I shall just go distracted.

HE   Yes, you are right. It will be a profanation.

SHE   Oh, I don't care about the profanation; but what will Teddy think? What will he do? (*Suddenly throwing his head away from her knee*) You don't seem to think a bit about Teddy. (*She jumps up, more and more agitated.*)

HE   (*Supine on the floor; for she has thrown him off his balance*) To me Teddy is nothing, and Georgina less than nothing.

SHE   You'll soon find out how much less than nothing she is. If you think a woman can't do any harm because she's only a scandal-mongering dowdy ragbag, you're greatly mistaken. (*She flounces about the room. He gets up slowly and dusts his hands. Suddenly she runs to him and throws herself into his arms.*) Henry: help me. Find a way out of this for me; and I'll bless you as long as you live. Oh, how wretched I am! (*She sobs on his breast.*)

HE   And oh! How happy I am!

SHE   (*Whisking herself abruptly away*) Don't be selfish.

HE   (*Humbly*) Yes: I deserve that. I think if I were going to the stake with you, I should still be so happy with you that I should forget your danger as utterly as my own.

SHE (*Relenting and patting his hand fondly*) Oh, you are a dear darling boy, Henry; but (*Throwing his hand away fretfully*) you're no use. I want somebody to tell me what to do.

HE (*With quiet conviction*) Your heart will tell you at the right time. I have thought deeply over this; and I know what we two must do, sooner or later.

SHE No, Henry. I will do nothing improper, nothing dishonorable. (*She sits down plump on the stool and looks inflexible.*)

HE If you did, you would no longer be Aurora. Our course is perfectly simple, perfectly straightforward, perfectly stainless and true. We love one another. I am not ashamed of that: I am ready to go out and proclaim it to all London as simply as I will declare it to your husband when you see—as you soon will see—that this is the only way honorable enough for your feet to tread. Let us go out together to our own house, this evening, without concealment and without shame. Remember! We owe something to your husband. We are his guests here: he is an honorable man: he has been kind to us: he has perhaps loved you as well as his prosaic nature and his sordid commercial environment permitted. We owe it to him in all honor not to let him learn the truth from the lips of a scandalmonger. Let us go to him now quietly, hand in hand; bid him farewell; and walk out of the house without concealment or subterfuge, freely and honestly, in full honor and self-respect.

SHE (*Staring at him*) And where shall we go to?

HE We shall not depart by a hair's breadth from the ordinary natural current of our lives. We were going to the theater when the loss of the poems compelled us to take action at once. We shall go to the theater still; but we shall leave your diamonds here; for we cannot afford diamonds, and do not need them.

SHE (*Fretfully*) I have told you already that I hate diamonds; only Teddy insists on hanging me all over with them. You need not preach simplicity to me.

HE I never thought of doing so, dearest: I know that these trivialities are nothing to you. What was I saying?—oh yes. Instead of coming back here from the theater, you will come with me to my home—now and henceforth our home—and in due course of time, when you are divorced, we shall go through whatever idle legal ceremony you may desire. *I* attach no importance to the law; my love was not created in me by the law, nor can it be bound or loosed by it. That is simple enough, and sweet enough, is it not? (*He takes the flowers from the table.*) Here are flowers for you: I have the tickets: we will ask your husband to lend us the carriage to show that there is no malice, no grudge, between us. Come!

SHE   Do you mean to say that you propose that we should walk right bang up to Teddy and tell him we're going away together?

HE   Yes. What can be simpler?

SHE   And do you think for a moment he'd stand it? He'd just kill you.

HE   (*Coming to a sudden stop and speaking with considerable confidence*) You don't understand these things, my darling: how could you? I have followed the Greek ideal and not neglected the culture of my body. Like all poets I have a passion for pugilism. Your husband would make a tolerable second-rate heavyweight if he were in training and ten years younger. As it is, he could, if strung up to a great effort by a burst of passion, give a good account of himself for perhaps fifteen seconds. But I am active enough to keep out of his reach for fifteen seconds; and after that I should be simply all over him.

SHE   (*Rising and coming to him in consternation*) What do you mean by all over him?

HE   (*Gently*) Don't ask me, dearest. At all events, I swear to you that you need not be anxious about me.

SHE   And what about Teddy? Do you mean to tell me that you are going to beat Teddy before my face like a brutal prizefighter?

HE   All this alarm is needless, dearest. Believe me, nothing will happen. Your husband knows that I am capable of defending myself. Under such circumstances nothing ever does happen. And of course *I* shall do nothing. The man who once loved you is sacred to me.

SHE   (*Suspiciously*) Doesn't he love me still? Has he told you anything?

HE   No, no. (*He takes her tenderly in his arms.*) Dearest, dearest: how agitated you are! how unlike yourself! All these worries belong to the lower plane. Come up with me to the higher one. The heights, the solitudes, the soul world!

SHE   (*Avoiding his gaze*) No: stop: it's no use, Mr. Apjohn.

HE   (*Recoiling*) Mr. Apjohn!!!

SHE   Excuse me: I meant Henry, of course.

HE   How could you even think of me as Mr. Apjohn? I never think of you as Mrs. Bompas: it is always Aurora, Aurora, Auro—

SHE   Yes, yes: that's all very well, Mr. Apjohn (*He is about to interrupt again: but she won't have it.*) No: it's no use: I've suddenly begun to think of you as Mr. Apjohn; and it's ridiculous to go on calling you Henry. I thought you were only a boy, a child, a dreamer. I thought you would be much afraid to do anything.

And now you want to beat Teddy and to break up my home and disgrace me and make a horrible scandal in the papers. It's cruel, unmanly, cowardly.

HE   (*With grave wonder*)   Are you afraid?

SHE   Oh, of course I'm afraid. So would you be if you had any common sense. (*She goes to the hearth, turning her back to him, and puts one tapping foot on the fender.*)

HE   (*Watching her with great gravity*)   Perfect love casteth out fear. That is why I am not afraid. Mrs. Bompas: you do not love me.

SHE   (*Turning to him with a gasp of relief*)   Oh, thank you, thank you! You really can be very nice, Henry.

HE   Why do you thank me?

SHE   (*Coming prettily to him from the fireplace*)   For calling me Mrs. Bompas again. I feel now that you are going to be reasonable and behave like a gentleman. (*He drops on the stool; covers his face with his hands; and groans.*)   What's the matter?

HE   Once or twice in my life I have dreamed that I was exquisitely happy and blessed. But oh! the misgiving at the first stir of consciousness! the stab of reality! the prison walls of the bedroom! the bitter, bitter disappointment of waking! And this time! oh, this time I thought I was awake.

SHE   Listen to me, Henry: we really haven't time for all that sort of flapdoodle now. (*He starts to his feet as if she had pulled a trigger and straightened him by the release of a powerful spring, and goes past her with set teeth to the little table.*)   Oh, take care: you nearly hit me in the chin with the top of your head.

HE   (*With fierce politeness*)   I beg your pardon. What is it you want me to do? I am at your service. I am ready to behave like a gentleman if you will be kind enough to explain exactly how.

SHE   (*A little frightened*)   Thank you, Henry: I was sure you would. You're not angry with me, are you?

HE   Go on. Go on quickly. Give me something to think about, or I will —I will— (*He suddenly snatches up her fan and is about to break it in his clenched fist.*)

SHE   (*Running forward and catching at the fan, with loud lamentation*)   Don't break my fan—no, don't. (*He slowly relaxes his grip of it as she draws it anxiously out of his hands.*)   No, really, that's a stupid trick: I don't like that. You've no right to do that. (*She opens the fan, and finds that the sticks are disconnected.*)   Oh, how could you be so inconsiderate?

HE   I beg your pardon. I will buy you a new one.

SHE   (*Querulously*)   You will never be able to match it. And it was a particular favorite of mine.

HE   (*Shortly*)   Then you will have to do without it: that's all.

SHE   That's not a very nice thing to say after breaking my pet fan, I think.

HE   If you knew how near I was to breaking Teddy's pet wife and presenting him with the pieces, you would be thankful that you are alive instead of—of—of howling about five shillings-worth of ivory. Damn your fan!

SHE   Oh! Don't you dare swear in my presence. One would think you were my husband.

HE   (*Again collapsing on the stool*) This is some horrible dream. What has become of you? You are not my Aurora.

SHE   Oh, well, if you come to that, what has become of you? Do you think I would ever have encouraged you if I had known you were such a little devil?

HE   Don't drag me down—don't—don't. Help me to find the way back to the heights.

SHE   (*Kneeling beside him and pleading*) If you would only be reasonable, Henry. If you would only remember that I am on the brink of ruin, and not go on calmly saying it's all quite simple.

HE   It seems so to me.

SHE   (*Jumping up distractedly*) If you say that again I shall do something I'll be sorry for. Here we are, standing on the edge of a frightful precipice. No doubt it's quite simple to go over and have done with it. But can't you suggest anything more agreeable?

HE   I can suggest nothing now. A chill black darkness has fallen: I can see nothing but the ruins of our dream. (*He rises with a deep sigh.*)

SHE   Can't you? Well, I can. I can see Georgina rubbing those poems into Teddy. (*Facing him determinedly*) And I tell you, Henry Apjohn, that you got me into this mess; and you must get me out of it again.

HE   (*Polite and hopeless*) All I can say is that I am entirely at your service. What do you wish me to do?

SHE   Do you know anybody else named Aurora?

HE   No.

SHE   There's no use in saying No in that frozen pig-headed way. You must know some Aurora or other somewhere.

HE   You said you were the only Aurora in the world. And (*Lifting his clasped fists with a sudden return of his emotion*) oh God! You were the only Aurora in the world for me. (*He turns away from her, hiding his face.*)

SHE   (*Petting him*) Yes, yes, dear: of course. It's very nice of you; and I appreciate it: indeed I do; but it's not reasonable just at present. Now just listen to me. I suppose you know all those poems by heart.

HE   Yes, by heart. (*Raising his head and looking at her with a sudden suspicion*) Don't you?

SHE   Well, I never can remember verses; and besides, I've been so busy that I've not had time to read them all; though I intend to the very first moment I can get: I promise you that most faithfully, Henry. But now try and remember very particularly. Does the name of Bompas occur in any of the poems?

HE   (*Indignantly*) No.

SHE   You're quite sure?

HE   Of course I am quite sure. How could I use such a name in a poem?

SHE   Well, I don't see why not. It rhymes to rumpus, which seems appropriate enough at present, goodness knows! However, you're a poet, and you ought to know.

HE   What does it matter—now?

SHE   It matters a lot, I can tell you. If there's nothing about Bompas in the poems, we can say that they were written to some other Aurora, and that you showed them to me because my name was Aurora too. So you've got to invent another Aurora for the occasion.

HE   (*Very coldly*) Oh, if you wish me to tell a lie—

SHE   Surely, as a man of honor—as a gentleman, you wouldn't tell the truth: would you?

HE   Very well. You have broken my spirit and desecrated my dreams. I will lie and protest and stand on my honor: oh, I will play the gentleman, never fear.

SHE   Yes, put it all on me, of course. Don't be mean, Henry.

HE   (*Rousing himself with an effort*) You are quite right, Mrs. Bompas: I beg your pardon. You must excuse my temper. I am having growing pains, I think.

SHE   Growing pains!

HE   The process of growing from romantic boyhood into cynical maturity usually takes fifteen years. When it is compressed into fifteen minutes, the pace is too fast; and growing pains are the result.

SHE   Oh, is this a time for cleverness? It's settled, isn't it, that you're going to be nice and good, and that you'll brazen it out to Teddy that you have some other Aurora?

HE   Yes: I'm capable of anything now. I should not have told him the truth by halves; and now I will not lie by halves. I'll wallow in the honor of a gentleman.

SHE   Dearest boy, I knew you would. I—Sh! (*She rushes to the door, and holds it ajar, listening breathlessly.*)

HE   What is it?

SHE   (*White with apprehension*) It's Teddy: I hear him tapping the new barometer. He can't have anything serious on his mind or he wouldn't do that. Perhaps Georgina hasn't said anything. (*She steals back to the hearth.*) Try and look as if there was nothing the matter. Give me my gloves, quick. (*He hands them to her. She pulls on one hastily and begins buttoning it with ostentatious unconcern.*) Go further away from me, quick. (*He walks doggedly away from her until the piano prevents his going farther.*) If I button my glove, and you were to hum a tune, don't you think that—

HE   The tableau would be complete in its guiltiness. For Heaven's sake, Mrs. Bompas, let that glove alone: you look like a pickpocket.

Her husband comes in: a robust, thicknecked, well groomed city man, with a strong chin but a blithering eye and credulous mouth, He has a momentous air, but shows no sign of displeasure: rather the contrary.

HER HUSBAND   Hallo! I thought you two were at the theater.

SHE   I felt anxious about you, Teddy. Why didn't you come home to dinner?

HER HUSBAND   I got a message from Georgina. She wanted me to go to her.

SHE   Poor dear Georgina! I'm sorry I haven't been able to call on her this last week. I hope there's nothing the matter with her.

HER HUSBAND   Nothing, except anxiety for my welfare—and yours. (*She steals a terrified look at Henry.*) By the way, Apjohn, I should like a word with you this evening, if Aurora can spare you for a moment.

HE   (*Formally*) I am at your service.

HER HUSBAND   No hurry. After the theater will do.

HE   We have decided not to go.

HER HUSBAND   Indeed! Well, then, shall we adjourn to my snuggery?

SHE   You needn't move. I shall go and lock up my diamonds since I'm not going to the theater. Give me my things.

HER HUSBAND   (*As he hands her the cloud and the mirror*) Well, we shall have more room here.

HE   (*Looking about him and shaking his shoulders loose*) I think I should prefer plenty of room.

HER HUSBAND   So, if it's not disturbing you, Rory—?

SHE   Not at all. (*She goes out.*)

When the two men are alone together, Bompas deliberately takes the poems from his breast pocket; looks at them reflectively; then looks at Henry, mutely inviting his attention. Henry refuses to understand, doing his best to look unconcerned.

HER HUSBAND   Do these manuscripts seem at all familiar to you, may I ask?

HE   Manuscripts?

HER HUSBAND   Yes. Would you like to look at them a little closer? (*He proffers them under Henry's nose.*)

HE   (*As with a sudden illumination of glad surprise*)   Why, these are my poems!

HER HUSBAND   So I gather.

HE   What a shame! Mrs. Bompas has shown them to you! You must think me an utter ass. I wrote them years ago after reading Swinburne's *Songs Before Sunrise.* Nothing would do me then but I must reel off a set of Songs to the Sunrise. Aurora, you know: the rosy fingered Aurora. They're all about Aurora. When Mrs. Bompas told me her name was Aurora, I couldn't resist the temptation to lend them to her to read. But I didn't bargain for your unsympathetic eyes.

HER HUSBAND   (*Grinning*)   Apjohn: that's really very ready of you. You are cut out for literature; and the day will come when Rory and I will be proud to have you about the house. I have heard far thinner stories from much older men.

HE   (*With an air of great surprise*)   Do you mean to imply that you don't believe me?

HER HUSBAND   Do you expect me to believe you?

HE   Why not? I don't understand.

HER HUSBAND   Come! Don't underrate your own cleverness, Apjohn. I think you understand pretty well.

HE   I assure you I am quite at a loss. Can you not be a little more explicit?

HER HUSBAND   Don't overdo it, old chap. However, I will just be so far explicit as to say that if you think these poems read as if they were addressed, not to a live woman, but to a shivering cold time of day at which you were never out of bed in your life, you hardly do justice to your own literary powers—which I admire and appreciate, mind you, as much as any man. Come! Own up. You wrote those poems to my wife. (*An internal struggle prevents Henry from answering.*)   Of course you did. (*He throws the poems on the table; and goes to the hearthrug, where he plants himself solidly, chuckling a little and waiting for the next move.*)

HE   (*Formally and carefully*)   Mr. Bompas: I pledge you my word you are mistaken. I need not tell you that Mrs. Bompas is a lady of stainless honor, who has never cast an unworthy thought on me. The fact that she has shown you my poems—

HER HUSBAND   That's not a fact. I came by them without her knowledge. She didn't show them to me.

HE   Does not that prove their perfect innocence? She would have shown them to you at once if she had taken your quite unfounded view of them.

HER HUSBAND   (*Shaken*) Apjohn: play fair. Don't abuse your intellectual gifts. Do you really mean that I am making a fool of myself?

HE   (*Earnestly*) Believe me you are. I assure you, on my honor as a gentleman, that I have never had the slightest feeling for Mrs. Bompas beyond the ordinary esteem and regard of a pleasant acquaintance.

HER HUSBAND   (*Shortly, showing ill humor for the first time*) Oh! Indeed! (*He leaves his hearth and begins to approach Henry slowly, looking him up and down with growing resentment.*)

HE   (*Hastening to improve the impression made by his mendacity*) I should never have dreamt of writing poems to her. The thing is absurd.

HER HUSBAND   (*Reddening ominously*) Why is it absurd?

HE   (*Shrugging his shoulders*) Well, it happens that I do not admire Mrs. Bompas—in that way.

HER HUSBAND   (*Breaking out in Henry's face*) Let me tell you that Mrs. Bompas has been admired by better men than you, you soapy headed little puppy, you.

HE   (*Much taken aback*) There is no need to insult me like this. I assure you, on my honor as a—

HER HUSBAND   (*Too angry to tolerate a reply, and boring Henry more and more towards the piano*) You don't admire Mrs. Bompas! You would never dream of writing poems to Mrs. Bompas! My wife's not good enough for you, isn't she? (*Fiercely*) Who are you, pray, that you should be so jolly superior?

HE   Mr. Bompas: I can make allowances for your jealousy—

HER HUSBAND   Jealousy! Do you suppose I'm jealous of you? No, nor of ten like you. But if you think I'll stand here and let you insult my wife in her own house, you're mistaken.

HE   (*Very uncomfortable with his back against the piano and Teddy standing over him threateningly*) How can I convince you? Be reasonable. I tell you my relations with Mrs. Bompas are relations of perfect coldness—of indifference—

HER HUSBAND   (*Scornfully*) Say it again: say it again. You're proud of it, aren't you? Yah! You're not worth kicking.

Henry suddenly executes the feat known to pugilists as slipping, and changes sides with Teddy, who is now between Henry and the piano.

HE   Look here: I'm not going to stand this.

HER HUSBAND   Oh, you have some blood in your body after all! Good job!

HE   This is ridiculous. I assure you Mrs. Bompas is quite—

HER HUSBAND   What is Mrs. Bompas to you, I'd like to know. I'll tell you what Mrs. Bompas is. She's the smartest woman in the smartest set in South Kensington, and the handsomest, and the cleverest, and the most fetching to experienced men who know a good thing when they see it, whatever she may be to conceited penny-a-lining° puppies who think nothing good enough for them. It's admitted by the best people; and not to know it argues yourself unknown. Three of our first actor-managers have offered her a hundred a week if she'll go on the stage when they start a repertory theatre; and I think they know what they're about as well as you. The only member of the present Cabinet that you might call a handsome man has neglected the business of the country to dance with her, though he don't° belong to our set as a regular thing. One of the first professional poets in Bedford Park wrote a sonnet to her, worth all your amateur trash. At Ascot last season the eldest son of a duke excused himself from calling on me on the ground that his feelings for Mrs. Bompas were not consistent with his duty to me as host; and it did him honor and me too. But (*With gathering fury*) she isn't good enough for you, it seems. You regard her with coldness, with indifference; and you have the cool cheek° to tell me so to my face. For two pins I'd flatten your nose in to teach you manners. Introducing a fine woman to you is casting pearls before swine (*Yelling at him*) before SWINE! d'ye hear?

HE   (*With a deplorable lack of polish*) You call me a swine again and I'll land you one on the chin that'll make your head sing for a week.

HER HUSBAND   (*Exploding*) What!

He charges at Henry with bull-like fury. Henry places himself on guard in the manner of a well taught boxer, and gets away smartly, but unfortunately forgets the stool which is just behind him. He falls backwards over it, unintentionally pushing it against the shins of Bompas, who falls forward over it. Mrs. Bompas, with a

---

°*penny-a-lining:* penny-a-liners are second-rate writers; hacks
°*don't:* acceptable third-person singular at the time
°*cheek:* impudence

*scream, rushes into the room between the sprawling champions,
and sits down on the floor in order to get her right arm round her
husband's neck.*

SHE   You shan't, Teddy: you shan't. You will be killed: he is a prizefighter.

HER HUSBAND   (*Vengefully*) I'll prizefight him. (*He struggles vainly
to free himself from her embrace.*)

SHE   Henry: don't let him fight you. Promise me that you won't.

HE   (*Ruefully*) I have got a most frightful bump on the back of my
head. (*He tries to rise.*)

SHE   (*Reaching out her left hand to seize his coat tail, and pulling
him down again, whilst keeping fast hold of Teddy with the other
hand*) Not until you have promised: not until you both have
promised. (*Teddy tries to rise: she pulls him back
again.*) Teddy: you promise, don't you? Yes, yes. Be good; you
promise.

HER HUSBAND   I won't, unless he takes it back.

SHE   He will: he does. You take it back, Henry?—yes.

HE   (*Savagely*) Yes. I take it back. (*She lets go his coat. He gets
up. So does Teddy.*) I take it all back, all, without reserve.

SHE   (*On the carpet*) Is nobody going to help me up? (*They each
take a hand and pull her up.*)Now won't you shake hands and be
good?

HE   (*Recklessly*) I shall do nothing of the sort. I have steeped myself
in lies for your sake; and the only reward I get is a lump on the
back of my head the size of an apple. Now I will go back to the
straight path.

SHE   Henry: for Heaven's sake—

HE   It's no use. Your husband is a fool and a brute—

HER HUSBAND   What's that you say?

HE   I say you are a fool and a brute; and if you'll step outside with me
I'll say it again. (*Teddy begins to take off his coat for com-
bat.*) Those poems were written to your wife, every word of
them, and to nobody else. (*The scowl clears away from Bompas's countenance. Radiant, he replaces his coat.*) I wrote them
because I loved her. I thought her the most beautiful woman in
the world, and I told her so over and over again. I adored her: do
you hear? I told her that you were a sordid commercial chump,
utterly unworthy of her; and so you are.

HER HUSBAND   (*So gratified, he can hardly believe his ears*) You
don't mean it!

HE   Yes, I do mean it, and a lot more too. I asked Mrs. Bompas to
walk out of the house with me—to leave you—to get divorced

from you and marry me. I begged and implored her to do it this very night. It was her refusal that ended everything between us. (*Looking very disparagingly at him*) What she can see in you, goodness only knows!

HER HUSBAND   (*Beaming with remorse*) My dear chap, why didn't you say so before? I apologize. Come! don't bear malice: shake hands. Make him shake hands, Rory.

SHE   For my sake, Henry. After all, he's my husband. Forgive him. Take his hand. (*Henry, dazed, lets her take his hand and place it in Teddy's.*)

HER HUSBAND   (*Shaking it heartily*) You've got to own that none of your literary heroines can touch my Rory. (*He turns to her and clasps her with fond pride on the shoulders.*) Eh, Rory? They can't resist you: none of 'em. Never knew a man yet that could hold out three days.

SHE   Don't be foolish, Teddy. I hope you were not really hurt, Henry. (*She feels the back of his head. He flinches.*) Oh, poor boy, what a bump! I must get some vinegar and brown paper. (*She goes to the bell and rings.*)

HER HUSBAND   Will you do me a great favor, Apjohn. I hardly like to ask; but it would be a real kindness to us both.

HE   What can I do?

HER HUSBAND   (*Taking up the poems*) Well, may I get these printed? It shall be done in the best style. The finest paper, sumptuous binding, everything first class. They're beautiful poems. I should like to show them about a bit.

SHE   (*Running back from the bell, delighted with the idea, and coming between them*) Oh Henry, if you wouldn't mind?

HE   Oh, *I* don't mind. I am past minding anything.

HER HUSBAND   What shall we call the volume? To Aurora, or something like that, eh?

HE   I should call it How He Lied to Her Husband.

Questions

1. In *The Bear* Popova's highly romantic image of herself as the beautiful young inconsolable widow is exploded by the intrusion of the real world in the form of Smirnov. *How He Lied to Her Husband* offers the same theme in a slightly more complicated version. Who is the chief

cherisher of romantic images in this play? Who very speedily becomes the counterpart of Luka? Who is most like Smirnov? Don't jump to conclusions.

2. Much of the humor of the opening conversation depends on cross-purpose. What is Henry's mood, from his very first words onward? What is Aurora's, from *her* first words onward? What view of Aurora's feelings toward her husband enables Henry to be so unconcerned about Mr. Bompas's possible discovery of the poems? What view of those same feelings impels Aurora to be so concerned? What does she in fact now discover about her feelings toward Henry? Toward her husband? Toward the poems? What romantic image of herself has she evidently been half-cherishing or at least accepting? Why?

3. Though the play pokes fun at Henry for his illusions, and though he will be better off without them, the course of his disillusionment is as painful to him as it is comical to us. Trace the steps in his realization that he is not valued by Aurora in the ways he thought he was, and in his realization that she is not valuable in the ways he thought she was. In short, trace the stages in his growing up. What do you think Shaw means by saying in the preface to his play that Aurora is hopelessly his inferior in "spiritual distinction"? What evidence do we see of this in the play itself? Do you agree?

4. When the play is performed, audiences invariably laugh at Aurora's plea to Henry—"Surely, as a man of honor—as a gentleman, you wouldn't tell the truth: would you?"—because of the comic incongruity between being a man of honor (which usually goes with truth-telling) and telling lies. What comic incongruity is present in Mr. Bompas's reaction to Henry's statement that he never has been attracted to Aurora "in that way"? In his reaction to Henry's subsequent confession that he did indeed adore her? What further comic incongruity do we notice in the wife's two names—Aurora and Bompas? What larger comic incongruity of this kind underlies the whole play? What is a theater audience likely to expect when it sees a list of characters that consists of Her Lover, Her Husband, Herself? What, in Shaw's play, does it actually get?

5. How do the young man's actions and posturings (as Shaw describes them in the first long stage direction) communicate to the audience that the play is to be a farce? State in a brief directional note to yourself precisely how you would have the actor playing Henry go about communicating this idea, then carry out your instruction before an audience of some sort (your parents or some of your classmates) and see how they work. By the time you finish, your audience should be smiling, perhaps even chuckling, with anticipation.

T*he Bear* and *How He Lied to Her Husband* show that to live by the imagination can be dangerous if we fail to check it regularly—like a watch—against reality. We now come to a play which says "Reality? Forget it! Let me show you a world where imagination is king and reality a poor beggar. Once upon a time. . . ."

The Ugly Duckling

A. A. MILNE

Characters

THE KING
THE QUEEN
THE PRINCESS CAMILLA
THE CHANCELLOR
DULCIBELLA
PRINCE SIMON
CARLO

The SCENE *is the Throne Room of the Palace; a room of many doors, or, if preferred, curtain-openings: simply furnished with three thrones for Their Majesties and Her Royal Highness the Princess Camilla—in other words, with three handsome chairs. At each side is a long seat: reserved, as it might be, for His Majesty's Council (if any), but useful, as today, for other purposes. The King is asleep on his throne with a handkerchief over his face. He is a king of any country from any storybook, in whatever costume you please. But he should be wearing his crown.*

A VOICE   (*Announcing*)   His Excellency the Chancellor!   (*The Chancellor, an elderly man in horn-rimmed spectacles, enters, bowing. The King wakes up with a start and removes the handkerchief from his face.*)

KING   (*With simple dignity*)   I was thinking.

CHANCELLOR   (*Bowing*)   Never, Your Majesty, was greater need for thought than now.

KING   That's what I was thinking. (*He struggles into a more dignified position.*)   Well, what is it? More trouble?

CHANCELLOR   What we might call the old trouble, Your Majesty.

KING   It's what I was saying last night to the Queen. "Uneasy lies the head that wears a crown,"° was how I put it.

CHANCELLOR   A profound and original thought, which may well go down to posterity.

KING   You mean it may go down well with posterity. I hope so. Remind me to tell you some time of another little thing I said to Her Majesty: something about a fierce light beating on a throne.° Posterity would like that, too. Well, what is it?

CHANCELLOR   It is in the matter of Her Royal Highness's wedding.

KING   Oh . . . yes.

CHANCELLOR   As Your Majesty is aware, the young Prince Simon arrives today to seek Her Royal Highness's hand in marriage. He has been travelling in distant lands and, as I understand, has not—er —has not—

KING   You mean he hasn't heard anything.

CHANCELLOR   It is a little difficult to put this tactfully, Your Majesty.

KING   Do your best, and I will tell you afterwards how you got on.

CHANCELLOR   Let me put it this way. The Prince Simon will naturally assume that Her Royal Highness has the customary—so customary as to be, in my own poor opinion, slightly monotonous—has what one might call the inevitable—so inevitable as to be, in my opinion again, almost mechanical—will assume, that she has the, as *I* think of it, faultily faultless, icily regular, splendidly—

KING   What you are trying to say in the fewest words possible is that my daughter is not beautiful.

CHANCELLOR   Her beauty is certainly elusive, Your Majesty.

KING   It is. It has eluded you, it has eluded me, it has eluded everybody who has seen her. It even eluded the Court Painter. His last words were, "Well, I did my best." His successor is now painting the view across the water meadows from the West Turret. He says that his doctor has advised him to keep to landscape.

°From Shakespeare's *Henry IV, Part II*
°From Tennyson's *Idylls of the King*

CHANCELLOR   It is unfortunate, Your Majesty, but there it is. One just cannot understand how it can have occurred.

KING   You don't think she takes after *me*, at all? You don't detect a likeness?

CHANCELLOR   Most certainly not, Your Majesty.

KING   Good. . . . Your predecessor did.

CHANCELLOR   I have often wondered what happened to my predecessor.

KING   Well, now you know. (*There is a short silence.*)

CHANCELLOR   Looking at the bright side, although Her Royal Highness is not, strictly speaking, beautiful—

KING   Not, truthfully speaking, beautiful—

CHANCELLOR   Yet she has great beauty of character.

KING   My dear Chancellor, we are not considering Her Royal Highness's character, but her chances of getting married. You observe that there is a distinction.

CHANCELLOR   Yes, Your Majesty.

KING   Look at it from the suitor's point of view. If a girl is beautiful, it is easy to assume that she has, tucked away inside her, an equally beautiful character. But it is impossible to assume that an unattractive girl, however elevated in character, has, tucked away inside her, an equally beautiful face. That is, so to speak, not where you want it—tucked away.

CHANCELLOR   Quite so, Your Majesty.

KING   This doesn't, of course, alter the fact that the Princess Camilla is quite the nicest person in the Kingdom.

CHANCELLOR   (*Enthusiastically*) She is indeed, Your Majesty. (*Hurriedly*) With the exception, I need hardly say, of Your Majesty— and Her Majesty.

KING   Your exceptions are tolerated for their loyalty and condemned for their extreme fatuity.

CHANCELLOR   Thank you, Your Majesty.

KING   As an adjective for your King, the word "nice" is ill-chosen. As an adjective for Her Majesty, it is—ill-chosen.

(*At which moment Her Majesty comes in. The King rises. The Chancellor puts himself at right angles.*)

QUEEN   (*Briskly*) Ah. Talking about Camilla? (*She sits down.*)

KING   (*Returning to his throne*) As always, my dear, you are right.

QUEEN   (*To Chancellor*) This fellow, Simon—What's he like?

CHANCELLOR   Nobody has seen him, Your Majesty.

QUEEN   How old is he?

CHANCELLOR   Five-and-twenty, I understand.

QUEEN   In twenty-five years he must have been seen by somebody.

KING   (*To the Chancellor*)   Just a fleeting glimpse.

CHANCELLOR   I meant, Your Majesty, that no detailed report of him has reached this country, save that he has the usual personal advantages and qualities expected of a Prince, and has been traveling in distant and dangerous lands.

QUEEN   Ah! Nothing gone wrong with his eyes? Sunstroke or anything?

CHANCELLOR   Not that I am aware of, Your Majesty. At the same time, as I was venturing to say to His Majesty, Her Royal Highness's character and disposition are so outstandingly—

QUEEN   Stuff and nonsense. You remember what happened when we had the Tournament of Love last year.

CHANCELLOR   I was not myself present, Your Majesty. I had not then the honor of—I was abroad, and never heard the full story.

QUEEN   No; it was the other fool. They all rode up to Camilla to pay their homage—it was the first time they had seen her. The heralds blew their trumpets, and announced that she would marry whichever Prince was left master of the field when all but one had been unhorsed. The trumpets were blown again, they charged enthusiastically into the fight, and— (*The King looks nonchalantly at the ceiling and whistles a few bars.*)   —don't do that.

KING   I'm sorry, my dear.

QUEEN   (*To Chancellor*)   And what happened? They all simultaneously fell off their horses and assumed a posture of defeat.

KING   One of them was not quite so quick as the others. I was very quick. I proclaimed him the victor.

QUEEN   At the Feast of Betrothal held that night—

KING   We were all very quick.

QUEEN   The Chancellor announced that by the laws of the country the successful suitor had to pass a further test. He had to give the correct answer to a riddle.

CHANCELLOR   Such undoubtedly is the fact, Your Majesty.

KING   There are times for announcing facts, and times for looking at things in a broadminded way. Please remember that, Chancellor.

CHANCELLOR   Yes, Your Majesty.

QUEEN   I invented the riddle myself. Quite an easy one. What is it which has four legs and barks like a dog? The answer is, "A dog."

KING   (*To Chancellor*)   You see that?

CHANCELLOR   Yes, Your Majesty.

KING   It isn't difficult.

QUEEN   He, however, seemed to find it so. He said an eagle. Then he said a serpent; a very high mountain with slippery sides; two peacocks; a moonlight night; the day after tomorrow—

KING   Nobody could accuse him of not trying.

QUEEN   *I* did.

KING   I *should* have said that nobody could fail to recognize in his attitude an appearance of doggedness.

QUEEN   Finally he said "Death." I nudged the King—

KING   Accepting the word "nudge" for the moment, I rubbed my ankle with one hand, clapped him on the shoulder with the other, and congratulated him on the correct answer. He disappeared under the table, and, personally, I never saw him again.

QUEEN   His body was found in the moat next morning.

CHANCELLOR   But what was he doing in the moat, Your Majesty?

KING   Bobbing about. Try not to ask needless questions.

CHANCELLOR   It all seems so strange.

QUEEN   What does?

CHANCELLOR   That Her Royal Highness, alone of all the Princesses one has ever heard of, should lack that invariable attribute of Royalty, supreme beauty.

QUEEN   (*To the King*)   That was your Great-Aunt Malkin. She came to the christening. You know what she said.

KING   It was cryptic. Great-Aunt Malkin's besetting weakness. She came to *my* christening—she was one hundred and one then, and that was fifty-one years ago. (*To the Chancellor*)   How old would that make her?

CHANCELLOR   One hundred and fifty-two, Your Majesty.

KING   (*After thought*)   About that, yes. She promised me that when I grew up I should have all the happiness which my wife deserved. It struck me at the time—well, when I say "at the time," I was only a week old—but it did strike me as soon as anything could strike me—I mean of that nature—well, work it out for yourself, Chancellor. It opens up a most interesting field of speculation. Though naturally I have not liked to go into it at all deeply with Her Majesty.

QUEEN   I never heard anything less cryptic. She was wishing you extreme happiness.

KING   I don't think she was *wishing* me anything. However.

CHANCELLOR   (*To the Queen*)   But what, Your Majesty, did she wish Her Royal Highness?

QUEEN   Her other godmother—on my side—had promised her the dazzling beauty for which all the women in my family are famous— (*She pauses, and the King snaps his fingers surreptitiously in the direction of the Chancellor.*)

CHANCELLOR   (*Hurriedly*)   Indeed, yes, Your Majesty. (*The King relaxes.*)

QUEEN   And Great-Aunt Malkin said—   (*To the King*)   —what were
the words?

KING   I give you with this kiss
                                 A wedding-day surprise.
                                 Where ignorance is bliss
                                 'Tis folly to be wise.°

I thought the last two lines rather neat. But what it *meant*—

QUEEN   We can all see what it meant. She was given beauty—and
where is it? Great-Aunt Malkin took it away from her. The wedding-day surprise is that there will never be a wedding day.

KING   Young men being what they are, my dear, it would be much
more surprising if there *were* a wedding day. So how—   (*The
Princess comes in. She is young, happy, healthy, but not beautiful. Or let us say that by some trick of make-up or arrangement
of hair she seems plain to us: unlike the Princess of the story-
books.*)

PRINCESS   (*To the King*)   Hallo, darling!   (*Seeing the others*)   Oh, I
say! Affairs of state? Sorry.

KING   (*Holding out his hand*)   Don't go, Camilla.   (*She takes his
hand.*)

CHANCELLOR   Shall I withdraw, Your Majesty?

QUEEN   You are aware, Camilla, that Prince Simon arrives today!

PRINCESS   He has arrived. They're just letting down the drawbridge.

KING   (*Jumping up*)   Arrived! I must—

PRINCESS   Darling, you know what the drawbridge is like. It takes at
least half an hour to let it down.

KING   (*Sitting down*)   It wants oil.   (*To the Chancellor*)   Have *you*
been grudging it oil?

PRINCESS   It wants a new drawbridge, darling.

CHANCELLOR   Have I Your Majesty's permission—

KING   Yes, yes.   (*The Chancellor bows and goes out.*)

QUEEN   You've told him, of course? It's the only chance.

KING   Er—no. I was just going to, when—

QUEEN   Then I'd better.   (*She goes to the door.*)   You can explain to
the girl; I'll have her sent to you. You've told Camilla?

KING   Er—no. I was just going to, when—

QUEEN   Then you'd better tell her now.

KING   My dear, are you sure—

QUEEN   It's the only chance left.   (*Dramatically to heaven*)   My
daughter!   (*She goes out. There is a little silence when she is
gone.*)

°"*Where . . . wise*": From Thomas Gray's "Ode on a Distant Prospect of Eton Col-
lege."

KING   Camilla, I want to talk seriously to you about marriage.

PRINCESS   Yes, father.

KING   Now the great fact about marriage is that once you're married you live happy ever after. All our history books affirm this.

PRINCESS   And your own experience too, darling.

KING   (*With dignity*)   Let us confine ourselves to history for the moment.

PRINCESS   Yes, father.

KING   Of course, there *may* be an exception here and there, which, as it were, proves the rule; just as—oh, well, never mind.

PRINCESS   (*Smiling*)   Go on, darling. You were going to say that an exception here and there proves the rule that all princesses are beautiful.

KING   Well—leave that for the moment. The point is that it doesn't matter *how* you marry, or *who* you marry, as long as you *get* married. Because you'll be happy ever after in any case. Do you follow me so far?

PRINCESS   Yes, father.

KING   Well, your mother and I have a little plan—

PRINCESS   Was that it, going out of the door just now?

KING   Er—yes. It concerns your waiting-maid.

PRINCESS   Darling, I have several.

KING   Only one that leaps to the eye, so to speak. The one with the— well, with everything.

PRINCESS   Dulcibella?

KING   That's the one. It is our little plan that at the first meeting she should pass herself off as the Princess—a harmless ruse, of which you will find frequent record in the history books—and allure Prince Simon to his—that is to say, bring him up to the— In other words, the wedding will take place immediately afterwards, and as quietly as possible—well, naturally in view of the fact that your Aunt Malkin is one hundred and fifty-two; and since you will be wearing the family bridal veil—which is no doubt how the custom arose—the surprise after the ceremony will be his. Are you following me at all? Your attention seems to be wandering.

PRINCESS   I was wondering why you needed to tell me.

KING   Just a precautionary measure, in case you happened to meet the Prince or his attendant before the ceremony; in which case, of course, you would pass yourself off as the maid—

PRINCESS   A harmless ruse, of which, also, you will find frequent record in the history books.

KING   Exactly. But the occasion need not arise.

A VOICE   (*Announcing*)   The woman Dulcibella!

KING   Ah!   (*To the Princess*)   Now, Camilla, if you will just retire to your own apartments, I will come to you there when we are ready for the actual ceremony. (*He leads her out as he is talking; and as he returns calls out.*) Come in, my dear! (*Dulcibella comes in. She is beautiful, but dumb.*) Now don't be frightened, there is nothing to be frightened about. Has Her Majesty told you what you have to do?

DULCIBELLA   Y-yes, Your Majesty.

KING   Well now, let's see how well you can do it. You are sitting here, we will say. (*He leads her to a seat.*) Now imagine that I am Prince Simon. (*He curls his moustache and puts his stomach in. She giggles.*) You are the beautiful Princess Camilla whom he has never seen. (*She giggles again.*) This is a serious moment in your life, and you will find that a giggle will not be helpful. (*He goes to the door.*) I am announced: "His Royal Highness Prince Simon!" That's me being announced. Remember what I said about giggling. You should have a far-away look upon the face. (*She does her best.*) Farther away than that. (*She tries again.*) No, that's too far. You are sitting there, thinking beautiful thoughts—in maiden meditation, fancy-free,° as I remember saying to Her Majesty once . . . speaking of somebody else . . . fancy-free, but with the mouth definitely shut—that's better. I advance and fall upon one knee. (*He does so.*) You extend your hand graciously—*graciously;* you're not trying to push him in the face—that's better, and I raise it to my lips—so—and I kiss it— (*He kisses it warmly*) no, perhaps not so ardently as that, more like this (*He kisses it again*) and I say, "Your Royal Highness, this is the most—er— Your Royal Highness, I shall ever be—no— Your Royal Highness, it is the proudest—" Well, the point is that *he* will say it, and it will be something complimentary, and then he will take your hand in both of his, and press it to his heart. (*He does so.*) And then—what do *you* say?

DULCIBELLA   Coo!

KING   No, *not* Coo.

DULCIBELLA   Never had anyone do *that* to me before.

KING   That also strikes the wrong note. What you want to say is, "Oh, Prince Simon!" . . . Say it.

DULCIBELLA   (*Loudly*)   Oh, Prince Simon!

KING   No, no. You don't need to shout until he has said "What?" two or three times. Always consider the possibility that he *isn't* deaf. Softly, and giving the words a dying fall, letting them play around his head like a flight of doves.

DULCIBELLA   (*Still a little overloud*)   O-o-o-o-h, Prinsimon!

°*"maiden . . . free":* From Shakespeare's *A Midsummer Night's Dream*

KING Keep the idea in your mind of a flight of *doves* rather than a flight of panic-stricken elephants, and you will be all right. Now I'm going to get up, and you must, as it were, *waft* me into a seat by your side. (*She starts wafting.*) *Not* rescuing a drowning man, that's another idea altogether, useful at times, but at the moment inappropriate. Wafting. Prince Simon will put the necessary muscles into play—all you require to do is to indicate by a gracious movement of the hand the seat you require him to take. Now! (*He gets up, a little stiffly, and sits next to her.*) That was better. Well, here we are. Now, I think you give me a look: something, let us say, half-way between the breathless adoration of a nun and the voluptuous abandonment of a woman of the world; with an undertone of regal dignity, touched, as it were, with good comradeship. Now try that. (*She gives him a vacant look of bewilderment.*) Frankly, that didn't quite get it. There was just a little something missing. An absence, as it were, of all the qualities I asked for, and in their place an odd resemblance to an unsatisfied fish. Let us try to get at it another way. Dulcibella, have you a young man of your own?

DULCIBELLA (*Eagerly, seizing his hand*) Oo, yes, he's ever so smart, he's an archer, well not as you might say a real archer, he works in the armory, but old Bottlenose, *you* know who I mean, the Captain of the Guard, says the very next man they ever has to shoot, my Eg shall take his place, knowing Father and how it is with Eg and me, and me being maid to Her Royal Highness and can't marry me till he's a real soldier, but ever so loving, and funny like, the things he says, I said to him once, "Eg," I said—

KING (*Getting up*) I rather fancy, Dulcibella, that if you think of Eg all the time, *say* as little as possible, and, when thinking of Eg, see that the mouth is not more than partially open, you will do very well. I will show you where you are to sit and wait for His Royal Highness. (*He leads her out. On the way he is saying*) Now remember—*waft*—*waft*—not *hoick*. (*Prince Simon wanders in from the back unannounced. He is a very ordinary-looking young man in rather dusty clothes. He gives a deep sigh of relief as he sinks into the King's throne. . . . Camilla, a new and strangely beautiful Camilla, comes in.*)

PRINCESS (*Surprised*) Well!

PRINCE Oh, hallo!

PRINCESS Ought you?

PRINCE (*Getting up*) Do sit down, won't you?

PRINCESS Who are you, and how did you get here?

PRINCE Well, that's rather a long story. Couldn't we sit down? You could sit here if you liked, but it isn't very comfortable.

PRINCESS   That is the King's Throne.
PRINCE   Oh, is that what it is?
PRINCESS   Thrones are not meant to be comfortable.
PRINCE   Well, I don't know if they're meant to be, but they certainly aren't.
PRINCESS   Why are you sitting on the King's Throne, and who are you?
PRINCE   My name is Carlo.
PRINCESS   Mine is Dulcibella.
PRINCE   Good. And now couldn't we sit down?
PRINCESS   (*Sitting down on the long seat to the left of the throne and, as it were, wafting him to a place next to her*)   You may sit here, if you like. Why are you so tired?   (*He sits down.*)
PRINCE   I've been taking very strenuous exercise.
PRINCESS   Is that part of the long story?
PRINCE   It is.
PRINCESS   (*Settling herself*)   I love stories.
PRINCE   This isn't a story really. You see, I'm attendant on Prince Simon, who is visiting here.
PRINCESS   Oh? I'm attendant on Her Royal Highness.
PRINCE   Then you know what he's here for.
PRINCESS   Yes.
PRINCE   She's very beautiful, I hear.
PRINCESS   Did you hear that? Where have you been lately?
PRINCE   Traveling in distant lands—with Prince Simon.
PRINCESS   Ah! All the same, I don't understand. Is Prince Simon in the Palace now? The drawbridge *can't* be down yet!
PRINCE   I don't suppose it is. *And* what a noise it makes coming down!
PRINCESS   Isn't it terrible?
PRINCE   I couldn't stand it any more. I just had to get away. That's why I'm here.
PRINCESS   But how?
PRINCE   Well, there's only one way, isn't there? That beech tree, and then a swing and a grab for the battlements, and don't ask me to remember it all—   (*He shudders.*)
PRINCESS   You mean you came across the moat by that beech tree?
PRINCE   Yes. I got so tired of hanging about.
PRINCESS   But it's terribly dangerous!
PRINCE   That's why I'm so exhausted. Nervous shock.   (*He lies back and breathes loudly.*)
PRINCESS   Of course it's different for *me*.
PRINCE   (*Sitting up*)   Say that again. I must have got it wrong.

PRINCESS It's different for me, because I'm used to it. Besides, I'm so much lighter.

PRINCE You don't mean that *you*—

PRINCESS Oh yes, often.

PRINCE And I thought I was a brave man! At least, I did until five minutes ago, and now I don't again.

PRINCESS Oh, but you are! And I think it's wonderful to do it straight off the first time.

PRINCE Well, *you* did.

PRINCESS Oh no, not the first time. When I was a child.

PRINCE You mean that you crashed?

PRINCESS Well, you only fall into the moat.

PRINCE Only! Can you *swim?*

PRINCESS Of course.

PRINCE So you swam to the castle walls, and yelled for help, and they fished you out and walloped you. And next day you tried again. Well, if *that* isn't pluck—

PRINCESS Of course I didn't. I swam back, and did it at once; I mean I tried again at once. It wasn't until the third time that I actually did it. You see, I was afraid I might lose my nerve.

PRINCE Afraid she might lose her nerve!

PRINCESS There's a way of getting over from this side, too; a tree grows out from the wall and you jump into another tree—I don't think it's quite so easy.

PRINCE Not quite so easy. Good. You must show me.

PRINCESS Oh, I will.

PRINCE Perhaps it might be as well if you taught me how to swim first. I've often heard about swimming, but never—

PRINCESS You can't swim?

PRINCE No. Don't look so surprised. There are a lot of other things which I can't do. I'll tell you about them as soon as you have a couple of years to spare.

PRINCESS You can't swim and yet you crossed by the beech tree! And you're *ever* so much heavier than I am! Now who's brave?

PRINCE (*Getting up*) You keep talking about how light you are. I must see if there's anything in it. Stand up! (*She stands obediently and he picks her up.*) You're right, Dulcibella. I could hold you here forever (*Looking at her*) You're very lovely. Do you know how lovely you are?

PRINCESS Yes. (*She laughs suddenly and happily.*)

PRINCE Why do you laugh?

PRINCESS Aren't you tired of holding me?

PRINCE   Frankly, yes. I exaggerated when I said I could hold you forever. When you've been hanging by the arms for ten minutes over
a very deep moat, wondering if it's too late to learn how to swim
— (*He puts her down*) —what I meant was that I should *like*
to hold you forever. Why did you laugh?

PRINCESS   Oh, well, it was a little private joke of mine.

PRINCE   If it comes to that, I've got a private joke too. Let's exchange
them.

PRINCESS   Mine's very private. One other woman in the whole world
knows, and that's all.

PRINCE   Mine's just as private. One other man knows, and that's all.

PRINCESS   What fun. I love secrets. . . . Well, here's mine. When I
was born, one of my godmothers promised that I should be very
beautiful.

PRINCE   How right she was.

PRINCESS.   But the other one said this:

> I give you with this kiss
> A wedding-day surprise.
> Where ignorance is bliss
> 'Tis folly to be wise.

And nobody knew what it meant. And I grew up very plain. And
then, when I was about ten, I met my godmother in the forest one
day. It was my tenth birthday. Nobody knows this—except you.

PRINCE   Except us.

PRINCESS   Except us. And she told me what her gift meant. It meant
that I *was* beautiful—but everybody else was to go on being ignorant, and thinking me plain, until my wedding-day. Because, she
said, she didn't want me to grow up spoilt and wilful and vain, as
I should have done if everybody had always been saying how
beautiful I was; and the best thing in the world, she said, was to
be quite sure of yourself, but not to expect admiration from other
people. So ever since then my mirror has told me I'm beautiful,
and everybody else thinks me ugly, and I get a lot of fun out of it.

PRINCE   Well, seeing that Dulcibella is the result, I can only say that
your godmother was very, very wise.

PRINCESS   And now tell me *your* secret.

PRINCE   It isn't such a pretty one. You see, Prince Simon was going to
woo Princess Camilla, and he'd heard that she was beautiful and
haughty and imperious—all *you* would have been if your godmother hadn't been so wise. And being a very ordinary-looking
fellow himself, he was afraid she wouldn't think much of him, so
he suggested to one of his attendants, a man called Carlo, of ex-

tremely attractive appearance, that *he* should pretend to be the Prince, and win the Princess's hand; and then at the last moment they would change places—

PRINCESS   How would they do that?

PRINCE   The Prince was going to have been married in full armor—with his visor down.

PRINCESS   (*Laughing happily*)   Oh, what fun!

PRINCE   Neat, isn't it?

PRINCESS   (*Laughing*)   Oh, very . . . very . . . very.

PRINCE   Neat, but not so terribly *funny.* Why do you keep laughing?

PRINCESS   Well, that's another secret.

PRINCE   If it comes to that, *I've* got another one up my sleeve. Shall we exchange again?

PRINCESS   All right. You go first this time.

PRINCE   Very well. . . . I am not Carlo   (*Standing up and speaking dramatically*)   I am Simon!—*ow!*   (*He sits down and rubs his leg violently.*)

PRINCESS   (*Alarmed*)   What is it?

PRINCE   Cramp.   (*In a mild voice, still rubbing*)   I was saying that I was Prince Simon.

PRINCESS   Shall I rub it for you?   (*She rubs.*)

PRINCE   (*Still hopefully*)   I am Simon.

PRINCESS   Is that better?

PRINCE   (*Despairingly*)   I am Simon.

PRINCESS   I know.

PRINCE   How did you know?

PRINCESS   Well, you told me.

PRINCE   But oughtn't you to swoon or something?

PRINCESS   Why? History records many similar ruses.

PRINCE   (*Amazed*)   Is that so? I've never read history. I thought I was being profoundly original.

PRINCESS   Oh, no! Now I'll tell you *my* secret. For reasons very much like your own the Princess Camilla, who is held to be extremely plain, feared to meet Prince Simon. Is the drawbridge down yet?

PRINCE   Do your people give a faint, surprised cheer every time it gets down?

PRINCESS   Naturally.

PRINCE   Then it came down about three minutes ago.

PRINCESS   Ah! Then at this very moment your man Carlo is declaring his passionate love for my maid, Dulcibella. That, I think, is funny.   (*So does the Prince. He laughs heartily.*)   Dulcibella, by the way, is in love with a man she calls Eg, so I hope Carlo isn't getting carried away.

PRINCE   Carlo is married to a girl he calls "the little woman," so Eg has nothing to fear.

PRINCESS   By the way, I don't know if you heard, but I said, or as good as said, that I am the Princess Camilla.

PRINCE   I wasn't surprised. History, of which I read a great deal, records many similar ruses.

PRINCESS   (*Laughing*) Simon!

PRINCE   (*Laughing*) Camilla! (*He stands up.*) May I try holding you again? (*She nods. He takes her in his arms and kisses her.*) Sweetheart!

PRINCESS   You see, when you lifted me up before, you said, "You're very lovely," and my godmother said that the first person to whom I would seem lovely was the man I should marry; so I knew then that you were Simon and I should marry you.

PRINCE   I knew directly I saw you that I should marry you, even if you were Dulcibella. By the way, which of you *am* I marrying?

PRINCESS   When she lifts her veil, it will be Camilla. (*Voices are heard outside.*) Until then it will be Dulcibella.

PRINCE   (*In a whisper*) Then good-bye, Camilla, until you lift your veil.

PRINCESS   Goodbye, Simon, until you raise your visor.

(*The King and Queen come in arm-in-arm, followed by Carlo and Dulcibella, also arm-in-arm. The chancellor precedes them, walking backwards, at a loyal angle.*)

PRINCE   (*Supporting the Chancellor as an accident seems inevitable*) Careful! (*The Chancellor turns indignantly round.*)

KING   Who and what is this? More accurately who and what are all these?

CARLO   My attendant, Carlo, Your Majesty. He will, with Your Majesty's permission, prepare me for the ceremony.

(*The Prince bows.*)

KING   Of course, of course!

QUEEN   (*To Dulcibella*) Your maid, Dulcibella, is it not, my love? (*Dulcibella nods violently*) I thought so. (*To Carlo*) She will prepare Her Royal Highness.

(*The Princess curtsies.*)

KING   Ah, yes. Yes. *Most* important.

PRINCESS   (*Curtsying*) I beg pardon, Your Majesty, if I've done wrong, but I found the gentleman wandering—

KING   (*Crossing to her*) Quite right, my dear, quite right. (*He *pinches her cheek, and takes advantage of this kingly gesture to say in a loud whisper*) We've pulled it off! (*They sit down; the King and Queen on their thrones, Dulcibella on the Princess's throne, Carlo stands behind Dulcibella, the Chancellor on the right of the Queen, and the Prince and Princess behind the long seat on the left.*)

CHANCELLOR (*Consulting documents*) H'r'm! Have I Your Majesty's authority to put the final test to His Royal Highness?

QUEEN (*Whispering to King*) Is this safe?

KING (*Whispering*) Perfectly, my dear. I told him the answer a minute ago. (*Over his shoulder to Carlo*) Don't forget. Dog. (*Aloud*) Proceed, Your Excellency. It is my desire that the affairs of my country should ever be conducted in a strictly constitutional manner.

CHANCELLOR (*Oratorically*) By the constitution of the country, a suitor to Her Royal Highness's hand cannot be deemed successful until he has given the correct answer to a riddle. (*Conversationally*) The last suitor answered incorrectly, and thus failed to win his bride.

KING By a coincidence he fell into the moat.

CHANCELLOR (*To Carlo*) I have now to ask Your Royal Highness if you are prepared for the ordeal?

CARLO (*Cheerfully*) Absolutely.

CHANCELLOR I may mention, as a matter, possibly, of some slight historical interest to our visitor, that by the constitution of the country the same riddle is not allowed to be asked on two successive occasions.

KING (*Startled*) What's that?

CHANCELLOR This one, it is interesting to recall, was propounded exactly a century ago, and we must take it as a fortunate omen that it was well and truly solved.

KING (*To Queen*) I may want my sword directly.

CHANCELLOR The riddle is this. What is it which has four legs and mews like a cat?

CARLO (*Promptly*) A dog.

KING (*Still more promptly*) Bravo, bravo! (*He claps loudly and nudges the Queen, who claps too.*)

CHANCELLOR (*Peering at his documents*) According to the records of the occasion to which I referred, the correct answer would seem to be—

PRINCESS (*To Prince*) Say something, quick!

CHANCELLOR —not dog, but—

PRINCE Your Majesty, have I permission to speak? Naturally His

Royal Highness could not think of justifying himself on such an occasion, but I think that with Your Majesty's gracious permission, I could—

KING   Certainly, certainly.

PRINCE   In our country, we have an animal to which we have given the name "dog," or, in the local dialect of the more mountainous districts, "doggie." It sits by the fireside and purrs.

CARLO   That's right. It purrs like anything.

PRINCE   When it needs milk, which is its staple food, it mews.

CARLO   (*Enthusiastically*)   Mews like nobody's business.

PRINCE   It also has four legs.

CARLO   One at each corner.

PRINCE   In some countries, I understand, this animal *is* called a "cat." In one distant country to which His Royal Highness and I penetrated it was called by the very curious name of "hippopotamus."

CARLO   That's right. (*To the Prince*)   Do you remember that ginger-colored hippopotamus which used to climb onto my shoulder and lick my ear?

PRINCE   I shall never forget it, sir. (*To the King*)   So you see, Your Majesty—

KING   Thank you. I think that makes it perfectly clear. (*Firmly to the Chancellor*)   You are about to agree?

CHANCELLOR   Undoubtedly, Your Majesty. May I be the first to congratulate His Royal Highness on solving the riddle so accurately?

KING   You may be the first to see that all is in order for an immediate wedding.

CHANCELLOR   Thank you, Your Majesty. (*He bows and withdraws. The King rises, as do the Queen and Dulcibella.*)

KING   (*To Carlo*)   Doubtless, Prince Simon, you will wish to retire and prepare yourself for the ceremony.

CARLO   Thank you, sir.

PRINCE   Have I Your Majesty's permission to attend His Royal Highness? It is the custom of his country for Princes of the royal blood to be married in full armor, a matter which requires a certain adjustment—

KING   Of course, of course. (*Carlo bows to the King and Queen and goes out. As the Prince is about to follow, the King stops him.*)   Young man, you have a quality of quickness which I admire. It is my pleasure to reward it in any way which commends itself to you.

PRINCE   Your Majesty is ever gracious. May I ask for my reward *after* the ceremony? (*He catches the eye of the Princess, and they give each other a secret smile.*)

KING   Certainly. (*The Prince bows and goes out. To Dulcibella*)   Now, young woman, make yourself scarce. You've done your work excellently, and we will see that you and your—what was his name?

DULCIBELLA   Eg, Your Majesty.

KING   —that you and your Eg are not forgotten.

DULCIBELLA   Coo! (*She curtsies and goes out.*)

PRINCESS   (*Calling*)   Wait for me, Dulcibella!

KING   (*To Queen*)   Well, my dear, we may congratulate ourselves. As I remember saying to somebody once, "You have not lost a daughter, you have gained a son." How does he strike you?

QUEEN   Stupid.

KING   They made a very handsome pair, I thought, he and Dulcibella.

QUEEN   Both stupid.

KING   I said nothing about stupidity. What I *said* was that they were both extremely handsome. That is the important thing. (*Struck by a sudden idea*)   Or isn't it?

QUEEN   What do you think of Prince Simon, Camilla?

PRINCESS   I adore him. We shall be so happy together.

KING   Well, of course you will. I told you so. Happy ever after.

QUEEN   Run along now and get ready.

PRINCESS   Yes, mother. (*She throws a kiss to them and goes out.*)

KING   (*Anxiously*)   My dear, have we been wrong about Camilla all this time? It seemed to me that she wasn't looking *quite* so plain as usual just now. Did *you* notice anything?

QUEEN   (*Carelessly*)   Just the excitement of the marriage.

KING   (*Relieved*)   Ah, yes, that would account for it.

Curtain

Questions

1. What clues are given us immediately that this is a storybook world without serious problems? On what kind of "problem" does the Chancellor come to consult the King? What makes their interview funny? How long has the Chancellor been Chancellor? What happened to his predecessor? Why is that, too, funny?

2. The play's title, *The Ugly Duckling*, alludes to a story by Hans Christian Andersen in which a duckling, laughed at by all the other ducklings for its face and figure, turns out to be the most beautiful of all for

it grows up to be a swan. How far is that same situation present in this play? When is Princess Camilla to be revealed as truly a swan? How do the King and the Queen intend to make her appear one? How do you account for Prince Simon's knowing immediately that she is one? Does his unerring instinct have anything to do with this being a world where the imagination is supreme?

3. The "joker one-upped" is an ancient comic formula: Someone intends to play a little private joke on someone else but then the joke turns out to be really on him. To what extent is the formula visible in Milne's play? How many "little private jokes" are there before the play ends? Sometimes intended jokes inflict pain. What prevents the jokes in this play from doing so?

4. Much of the comedy in the play's dialogue is also based on having one's little private joke, especially in the King's speeches. What little private joke is the King enjoying when he says to his Chancellor: "It's what I was saying last night to the Queen. 'Uneasy lies the head that wears the crown,' was how I put it"? When he says to his Queen: "As always, my dear, you are right"? When he says to Dulcibella: "Always consider the possibility that he isn't deaf"? Pick three other comments of the King's that strike you as funny and explain their humor.

5. What audiences often find most delightful of all in this play is the collection of fairy-tale conventions to which the playwright has given a fresh and original turn. Show how Milne has given a new twist to: (a) the convention of the beautiful princess; (b) the convention that to win her all suitors must pass a test involving great risk of their lives and, if they fail, must be put to death; (c) the convention that the princess is in some sort of sleep or other enchanted condition that can only be broken when the right prince kisses her; (d) the convention that the hero is a man of supreme physical prowess; (e) the convention that a princess's waiting-maids are women of courtly refinement and delicate tastes. Can you think of any other fairy-tale conventions that are played with here? Could it be said that through his handling of these conventions, Milne has brought our old friend Reality in by the back door? Explain.

6. Suppose a person were not aware of the fairy-tale conventions Milne is fooling with here, would the play still be good fun and funny? What kind of people would find it silly or soupy—and what would that response tell about them?

7. Choose a friend and play over the conversation between the King and Dulcibella as he instructs her in the art of behaving like a princess. Begin by miming without speech, one of you imitating the movements of the King, the other those of Dulcibella. When you have mastered those sufficiently so that the scene is funny without words, add the words and perform it before the class.

One of the oldest games people play is minding other people's business for them. After all, how can other people get along without our superior insight? And one of the neatest turns in that game comes when the busybodies get one-upped, either by design or just dumb luck. In this play, a Jamaican couple get their not-so-strictly-matrimonial lives straightened out in a way that busybodies hadn't planned on.

Strictly Matrimony

ERROL HILL

Characters

MANNY BONAPARTE, a strapping laborer
BELLA, his common-law° wife
SLICK, Bella's half-brother, who lives by his wits
LADY POLLY LOVE-MUGGINS, a socialite
THE REVEREND TIMOTHY SHRIMP, a clergyman

SCENE: *Manny's house in the Jamaican countryside.*

Scene 1

(*The house in which Manny Bonaparte and his common-law wife, Bella, live is a one-room cottage in the Jamaican countryside. This single room serves as living, dining, and sleeping quarters,*

°*common-law:* a common-law marriage is one in which a man and woman live together as husband and wife without having gone through a religious or civil ceremony.

109

*and although the furniture is necessarily crowded in, the room
presents an appearance of cozy tidiness. One section, cut off by a
folding screen, is used as a bedroom and holds a four-poster bed
whose canopy spreads a starched white sheet across that part of
the board ceiling. A curtain stretched between the screen and the
wall covers the entrance to the bedroom. Over the top of the
screen are thrown certain items of a workingman's attire: dirty
shirt, trousers, and vest.*

*The furniture in the visible part of the room is strong and
roughly made. Down close to the audience are two straightback
chairs, a rocker, and a center table with a vase of flowers. On the
wall are a mirror and some passe-partout° pictures of the family
and friends. This serves as the sitting room. Immediately above
this is a dining table and two chairs, a wire safe, a washstand
and, on the back wall, a shelf from which hang cups, pots, and
pans. This is the dining area. The table is laid for one.*

*Sunday morning. The village church bell clangs noisily. Bella
is on the back doorstep bending over a coal pot preparing breakfast. She is an honest, hard-working type, endowed with an am-
plitude of feminine virtues which she happily surrenders to her
man. At the moment, she is busily fanning the coals and singing a
hymn. Her lucid notes wrestle with the nerve-racking clangor of
the church bells. And, as if these were not enough to disturb the
peace of Sunday morning, the duet is joined by the heavy snoring
of Manny who is asleep behind the screen.*

*Bella sets out breakfast on table. It consists of a large flour
bake, run-down mackerel, and a mug of cocoa. She goes to the
curtained opening and calls into the bedroom.*)

BELLA   Manny! Wake up, wake up, boy. Day break long.
MANNY   (*Off*) Eh . . . oh . . . what time it is there?
BELLA   Time to get up. Nine gone.
MANNY   (*Off*) Gone! Why you didn't call me before?

(*Manny appears around the curtain. He is not quite awake and
speaks drowsily.*)

MANNY   But how come the clock didn't alarm this morning? You
mean I going late for work again!
BELLA   Late for work! What wrong with you, boy, you stale drunk? Is
Sunday morning.

°*passe-partout:* inexpensively framed with gummed paper around the edges

MANNY   Sunday! Yes, in truth. Well, what the hell you disturb my sleep for? I tired tell you when Sunday come . . .

BELLA   Tea ready. I don't want it get cold. (*She gets a duster, begins to wipe off the furniture, singing meanwhile.*)

MANNY   I going back and catch my second nap. You could hot over the tea later. (*He retires. Bella sings more loudly.*) Bella, what for you keeping so much noise in my head? (*She persists. Manny reenters the room.*) You gone crazy or what? I ask you again: What you shouting so for?

BELLA   Big Sunday morning you want to sleep till sun-high.

MANNY   When else I going sleep then. "Six days thou shall labor and rest the seventh." I breaking my back Monday till Saturday from sun up to nightfall. When I going sleep late if not Sunday.

BELLA   Your tea getting cold. You better eat it. I don't have no time to warm it over.

MANNY   No time to warm it over? But what wrong with you this morning, Bella? First thing, you stir before cockcrow. Big Sunday, you don't even stay abed to pass a little time with me. Next thing, you make the tea before sleep well leave my eye and you start harassing me to eat it. And third to begin with, you singing in my ears as if judgment come and St. Peter ask you to wake the dead. What wrong with you?

(*While he speaks, Bella pours water into the washbasin, gets a towel from the bedroom and puts it on his arm, then continues dusting. Manny shrugs his shoulders and goes to wash up. He keeps glancing at Bella, who is vigorously tidying the room.*)

MANNY   You feed the fowls?

BELLA   Yes. One of Rosa chickens dead.

MANNY   You milk the goat?

BELLA   Yes. I think is time you fix the piece of fencing.

MANNY   But why she so brisk-brisk today? (*He draws on his trousers. Bella pulls out a chair at the dining table for him. He sits.*) You eat already?

BELLA   No. I had a cup of coffee.

MANNY   Where your plate then?

BELLA   I will eat what you leave.

MANNY   None of that. When Sunday come I like my wife to sit down beside me at table. If we poor self we could still behave like decent people. Sunday is the one day of the week we have together.

BELLA   Hmph! (*She sits. Manny fetches a plate, cup, and spoon for her. They begin to eat.*)

MANNY   I like Sunday breakfast. No hustlement. And I like how you does prepare my meal good.

BELLA   I glad.

MANNY   You's a good woman, Bella. If is no lie you have your little contrariness. A man couldn't ask for nothing better. (*He slaps her fondly on her buttocks.*)

BELLA   So you say.

MANNY   I mean it. You know, work ain't sweet and when I out there on the wharf lifting old load and that foulmouth foreman bawling out his liver string after me, I does feel sometimes to throw up the whole caboodle and go away to England or someplace. Then I remember you. I remember how on a Sunday we does sit down peaceful-like and talk together and eat good food and thing. And I decide to stick my grind. It worth it.

BELLA   That's good.

MANNY   Eat some more, nuh? You finish already?

BELLA   Yes. What about you?

MANNY   I done too. My stomach feel a little upside-down after last night.

BELLA   (*Begins to clear table*)   Well, take a bath and tidy yourself while I wash up the things.

MANNY   (*Sits on rocker*)   Come over here, nuh.

BELLA   What you want?

MANNY   Draw nearer. I ain't going bite you.

BELLA   (*Up to him*)   Yes? (*Manny makes a sudden lunge and pulls her down on his lap, laughing. He begins to fondle and kiss her as she struggles.*)   Oh shucks, man, you going ramfle up my hair and my clothes!

MANNY   What I care about clothes. You shouldn't have on none. Come, give me a little love-up, girl.

BELLA   Take time, take time with me, I say. I busy bad this morning.

MANNY   You too busy to kiss me? What is this at all? (*He kisses her flush on the lips.*)   After all, we is man and wife.

BELLA   I not your wife.

MANNY   Eh?

BELLA   I say I is not your wife.

MANNY   Well who wife you is, then? Gombo Li-Li?

BELLA   I is your concubine.°

MANNY   My how much?

BELLA   Your concubine. Look it up in the Bible what you always quoting. It write down there in black and white. You like to talk decency but you ain't talk the right thing yet.

°*concubine:* mistress

MANNY   What you telling me at all?

BELLA   I saying that I not your lawful wife.

MANNY   (*Pushes her off and gets up*)   And what you bringing that up for now, sudden-like?

BELLA   Yes, you don't want to hear the truth, because you know you wrong.

MANNY   Know I wrong? Woman, what fool-fool thing you talking?

BELLA   I talking plain as day. If you don't like the song, is up to you to change the tune.

MANNY   Talk straight, girl. Come out from behind the pretty-pretty word and talk straight.

BELLA   You don't want to hear the word mention, but I will mention it: Matrimony.

MANNY   Look, Bella, is Sunday morning. The Lord give us this day to rest and relax. Don't disturb it with no marriage talk. Is years we living together . . .

BELLA   Living in sin.

MANNY   All right—in sin. We born in sin. So the Book say. We in it already and we might as well stay there so longst we happy.

BELLA   My eyes was close. Now they open.

MANNY   Okay, open them. Only don't see no marriage contract write up on the wall. You know what I think about that already.

BELLA   Time going. I have to clear the table.

MANNY   Pass me a cigarette there and ask Jamesy if he finish with the newspaper.

BELLA   And I think you hadst better tidy yourself before you loll off. In case anybody come.

MANNY   (*Gets cigarette himself and settles down in rocker*)   Anybody like who? You expecting company?

BELLA   You never know who to drop in after church.   (*She brings him bath towel and soap.*)

MANNY   (*Laughing*)   All right, missis, I know you have some sort of surprise cook up for me. But tell me who you expecting, nuh? I hope is not your half-brother, Slick. The last time he come here all the silvers vanish like smoke.

BELLA   Slick never thief nothing.   (*She takes the garments off the screen and folds them up.*)

MANNY   I didn't say he thief, nuh? But I think the knives and forks get up off the table and walk down the road after him. Slick must be had magnet in his pocket.

BELLA   He borrow them for an "At Home" and somebody misplace them. He promise to pay us back when he working.

MANNY   That is when cock have teeth.

BELLA   Well, he working now.

MANNY   How you know that? Slick come by here since last time? (*A silence*)   Answer me, Bella.

BELLA   Give the boy a break, nuh? Because he get in a little scrape once you always charging him.

MANNY   What he come here for?

BELLA   Slick get a work in the district. He come to tell me.

MANNY   You check all the things. I miss a gray pants three days now.

BELLA   Is I send it to the laundry. Give the boy a break! He get a respectable work with the white people and he coming to make a visit this morning after church with important company. So I begging you please to behave yourself and don't disgrace me.

MANNY   Well, Slick take up religion now. When the devil start going to church, zip up your pocket quick-sharp.

BELLA   Come off the boy back, nuh!

MANNY   All right. I ain't going pass on him till he try. But so help me, this time he better walk good. As he slip, he slide with me.

BELLA   Go on and bathe. Church nearly over.

(*Manny goes out through the back door. Bella resumes her tidying. A face shows at the window. It is Slick.*)

SLICK   Pss . . . pss . . . Bella!

BELLA   Hey! Is you Slick?

SLICK   Eh-heh. Where Manny?

BELLA   Bathing.

SLICK   Is all right to come in?

BELLA   Yes, man. But watch your step with him.

(*Slick enters through the front door. He is handsomely decked out in a neat-fitting parson-gray suit and a gray felt hat. He holds a briefcase under his arm.*)

BELLA   Church over already? Where the white lady?

SLICK   She coming later with the parson-feller. I couldn't take no more of that sermon. The man is a mamapoule.° He ain't long come out from England. If you hear the stupidness pop out his mouth. He must be think because people black they ignorant, nuh? All you take tea yet?

BELLA   Just finish. You want some?

SLICK   Tumble a sandwich on me. And something to wash it down with.

BELLA   I make bake this morning.

SLICK   All going the same place. (*Bella prepares a tray for Slick. He*

°*mamapoule:* lit. female chicken; a wishy-washy person

picks a flower from the vase and places it in his button-hole.) This work I doing well hard, you know. No rest, not even on Sunday. Look me, dress up to kill, like I going to Grace Kelly wedding, nine o'clock in the hot morning sun when I should be coasting an old sleep.

BELLA   Anyhow you looking well sharp.

SLICK   Is Lady Love-Muggins give me this outfit. How you like it? The tie is my own. I think she catch a fall for the old style, you know. Me with my sweet talk and nice ways and the old Alan Ladd smile.

BELLA   You ain't playing you like yourself, nuh, Slick! (*She hands him the tray.*)

SLICK   That look good. I had was to hustle off to church this morning before I finish eat good. And I was damn near late too. The parson-man talk out all the food in my belly. (*He begins to eat.*)

BELLA   Before Manny come back inside, you getter prime me up what to say.

SLICK   You tell him anything yet?

BELLA   I drop a few spratt,° but he ain't biting. His face set against this marriage business like is jail self.

SLICK   Don't fret. Polly going fix him up good-good.

BELLA   Who Polly that?

SLICK   Lady Love-Muggins. Between you, me and the bedpost, I does call her Polly sometimes—in private. She have a likeness for spades.°

BELLA   Boy, you too rude. (*They smile together understandingly.*) Tell me again how you does convince people to do this thing, nuh?

SLICK   Charm, Bella, just charm. And after I hypnotize them I hit them couple few smart words, you know, like how the cost of living going up and withouten you married, nobody don't respect you; you is a conks . . . a conks . . .

BELLA   Concubine.

SLICK   Yes, something so. But mostly, is charm.

(*Manny comes in, half-dressed. He pauses at the back door and looks steadily at Slick who returns his look with uneasiness. Manny bursts out laughing and comes forward.*)

MANNY   Hey, Slick boy, you look as if is the last supper you eating. What happen, friend?

°*spratt:* tiny fish, used for bait
°*spades:* Blacks (used approvingly)

SLICK   (*Much relieved*) How you do, Manny.

MANNY   I there, man. Sit down and finish eat. I hear you working now. You bring the money for the silvers and them what you thief . . . I mean, lost? (*He puts on a shirt and tie during the scene. Bella removes the tray and goes behind the screen to change her dress.*)

SLICK   I land this job only last week. But I promise you as soon . . .

MANNY   Slick, your promise same like Moses and the promised land: It never reach. Where you working?

SLICK   (*Begins to feel more at home. He pulls out a cigar and lights up.*) I employ with the S.P.P.W.R.

MANNY   Tonnerre!!° What it mean in English?

SLICK   The full name is the Society for the Protection and Preservation of Women's Rights.

MANNY   God almighty!

BELLA   (*Off*) It spread all over the world. Slick belong to a branch here that run by a social lady name Lady Polly Love-Muggins.

MANNY   You really climbing high this time. Take care you fall, boy.

SLICK   Easy-cai,° man. Don't frighten for Slick. Look, nuh, is after ten. All you ain't ready yet? (*He goes to window and looks out.*)

MANNY   Ready for what?

SLICK   Bella didn't tell you?

BELLA   (*Coming out*) Slick invite the new parson and Lady Love-Muggins to come and meet us after prayers.

MANNY   Oh-ho! And you bound to make so much fuss about that?

SLICK   See them coming down the road now! I best hadst give all you a few ideas how to behave in social company.

BELLA   Listen good, Manny. We don't want to shame weself in front the white people and them.

MANNY   Nobody ain't ask them to come here. What you exciting-up yourself for?

SLICK   All right now. When her ladyship reach, everybody must stand up and you must say: "Honored to meet you, my lady." Don't stick out your hand until she put out hers; and, if you want, Bella, to make a good impression, you could drop a little curtsy, like this. (*He demonstrates awkwardly, Bella following him.*) And you, Manny, you should . . .

MANNY   Look, saga-boy,° maybe this house ain't no palace, but I is king in it. If Lady Love-bird don't like it here, she could fly back where she come from.

°*Tonnerre:* lit. thunder (Fr.); expression of mystification, roughly equivalent to "Wait a minute!"
°*Easy-cai:* no problem; nothing to worry about
°*saga-boy:* equivalent to "hot shot"; someone who lives by his wits

BELLA   Behave yourself, nuh, boy!

(*Lady Polly's voice is heard off. She speaks rapidly and unceasingly, in a high-pitched, near-falsetto and penetrating voice, punctuating her flow of language with occasional burbles of laughter. She is a tall, well proportioned woman with striking blond hair framing a handsome, if masculine, face. Her manner is authoritative and slightly condescending, with a trace of vulgarity. She is talking now to the Reverend Timothy Shrimp as they come through the Bonapartes' front gate.*)

LADY POLLY   (*Off*) And so, my dear Reverend, I would strongly advise you to consider giving up this outmoded theological jargon and come straight to the point. Who wants to be a soldier of the Lord? What does it mean? There's too much war in the world altogether. Talk about everyday problems, if you see what I mean . . . (*Slick opens the front door and stands there like a commissionaire. Bella and Manny rise. Lady Polly sweeps in.*) Oh, how do you do? I'm so pleased to meet you both. (*She takes their hands.*) Mr. Bonaparte, isn't it, and Miss er . . . Miss er . . . Of course, we understand, don't we? (*She emits a ripple of laughter.*) Bonaparte, such a lovely name, so romantic, so vigorous, so full of history. I always think, don't you, what a pity he was so diminutive. I mean Napoleon, of course. I like tall, well-built men. You, Mr. Bonaparte, you couldn't be more admirably suited to the name. What a splendid torso you have, if you don't mind my mentioning it. Robust and er . . . virile, no doubt. Well, let's be seated, shall we? You sit there, Mrs. Bona . . . I mean, Miss . . . well, my dear, what shall we call you?
MANNY   She name Bella.
BELLA   But in the village I goes by the name of Miss Bonaparte.
LADY POLLY   Yes, well we'll call you Bella—for the present. It's much simpler. You sit over there, Mr. Bonaparte can sit here beside me. Crawford, you'd better sit on my other side. Now we're all set. Oh, Mr. Shrimp!

(*Shrimp has been hovering half-in and half-out of the front door. He is a little man, middle-aged, quite out of his depth in this environment, terrified of Lady Polly, and longing for the seclusion of his rural English parsonage.*)

LADY POLLY   Come along in and find a seat, Mr. Shrimp. I suppose it's necessary to have a representative of the church here? Now we're all set. Ah, by the way, I imagine you know Mr. Shrimp? He's the new minister. Mr. Shrimp, Mr. and Mrs. er . . . I mean, Mr.

Bonaparte and his er . . . Well now, I daresay that Mr. Crawford told you I represent the S.P.P.W.R., a worldwide organization whose sacred duty it is to protect and preserve the rights of women everywhere. I'm president of the local branch and I'm sure our Mr. Crawford prepared you for . . .

MANNY   (*Lugubriously cutting in to assert his headship*) Excuse me, missis, I not too sure what all this is about, but my mind tell me . . .

LADY POLLY   What your mind tells you, Mr. Bonaparte, is really of no interest to us here, I think? Yours is a passive role in this affair. You must listen and when the appropriate time comes, act. (*She pats his hand affectionately and adds*) You big, strong man. (*A burble of laughter*) As I was saying, the purpose of our visit is to enlighten you on the moral, social, and economic dangers of the sort of relationship you have both condoned for some years now, I believe? (*The question, requiring no confirmation, is directed at Slick. He nods assent.*) This relationship, I regret to say, though very prevalent in this country, is indefensible on social, ethical, or legal grounds, and can lead only to untold complications and unhappiness. That is why the S.P.P.W.R. is doing all it can to remove this blemish on the good name of Jamaican women. And remove it we shall in this village, and throughout the island, with the aid of people like Mr. Crawford here and Mr. Shrimp . . . Mr. Shrimp! (*Shrimp is dozing away in a corner. He starts up guiltily.*) Really, Mr. Shrimp, didn't you sleep well last night or were you otherwise engaged—at your age too. Hmph! Well, as I was saying, socially, Mr. Bonaparte, your mate is an outcast unless she can carry your full name.

MANNY   I don't stop her using it.

LADY POLLY   That's not the point. She has no legal right to it. We hardly know how to address her. It's embarrassing, to say the least. You can't be invited out together; she is, in a way, deprived of playing her full role as a leader in the social life of the village. This is bound to make her dissatisfied and unhappy.

MANNY   Bella and me been living together happy for six years and we never had no trouble till all you come and put this marriage talk in her head. That ain't true, Bella?

LADY POLLY   Ah, but think what you've been missing all these years, both of you. Now we turn to the legal side of the matter. Mr. Crawford, will you . . . ?

SLICK   (*Takes out a notebook from his briefcase and makes a show of consulting it*) Well, yes, as I was saying, the legal side. For instance, to begin with, living in conks . . . conks . . .

LADY POLLY   . . . Living in concubinage means that the woman is not entitled by law to anything that her husband possesses and, in case of death, she has no claim to his estate. She has no security, her so-called husband can walk out on her at any time, and where there are children, the responsibility is entirely hers. For though the law can compel a man to contribute toward the upkeep of his offspring, it is incumbent on the mother to prove who the father is; and that's not easy nowadays. (*A tinkle of laughter*) All this is very complicated, of course, and I don't expect you, Mr. Bonaparte, to understand the intricacies of the law. I merely cite a few instances to show you how much you stand to lose by persisting in this sham liaison.

MANNY   Nothing sham about it. If Bella and me like it so, I don't see why all you have to interfere.

LADY POLLY   But we don't live unto ourselves. There are others to consider. And now, here is where Mr. Shrimp comes in. He will explain the attitude of the church in this matter.

SHRIMP   (*His big moment has come. He rises, clears his throat, and prepares to deliver his sermon*) It is written: "He that covereth his sins shall not prosper." Though we're all of us sinners, in the sight of God, it behooves each and every one of us to search our hearts . . .

LADY POLLY   Yes . . . I really think, Mr. Shrimp, we can defer this heart-searching to another occasion? Sometime, perhaps, when you can conveniently probe with Mr. Bonaparte and his er . . . wife? In camera?° Good. Now we have one or two small details to settle and then you can sign the documents. First of all, in case you're worried about the finances. Let me reassure you that all expenses of the wedding will be borne by my Society. The ring will come from America, the shoes from Italy, the hat from Paris. The wives of twelve different countries will be contributing to your wedding. The bride's dress, of course, will have to be made here, but we have received the most exquisite silk from China only last week. I'd better have your measurements right away. (*She produces a measuring tape from her handbag and hands it to Slick. He passes it on to Shrimp and signals to him that he must take Bella's measurements.*) Isn't it exciting to think of all those wonderful people all over the world who are in-

°*In camera:* privately

terested in your welfare, Mr. Bonaparte? I'm afraid we have no provision for the husbands, but if you need it, I'm sure I could rustle up something suitable for you to wear. (*She glances over his figure admiringly.*) Really, it's most exciting. We shall have the usual VIP's in attendance and lay on a chicken mayonnaise dinner . . .

(*The company is now divided in two groups, Lady Polly and Manny seated on one side. She continues to talk interminably and he tries hard to keep his temper. On the other side are Bella, being measured by Shrimp, and Slick, who is writing down the measurements. Shrimp is obviously embarrassed by Bella's nearness and circles round her trying to avoid coming in too close contact.*)

SLICK   Length?

SHRIMP   Forty-seven.

LADY POLLY   You realize, of course, that you two will be the first couple in the village to benefit from our current S.P.P.W.R. campaign. We hope that with your precedent, scores of others in similar unfortunate circumstances will come forward to declare for upright and decent living. I want to surpass our record in Bogles where· twenty-seven couples were married together—a mass wedding and a great day for the sanctity of Jamaican womanhood. I remember the address given by the Custos of the Parish when he said: "You will feel the difference tomorrow morning"—he was speaking to the new brides—"you will feel the difference when instead of saying, 'Anyone see Mass Joe?,' you will stick out your chest and ask, 'Where is my husband?' " (*She burbles a laugh.*)

SLICK   Waist?

SHRIMP   Thirty-eight.

LADY POLLY   Now I must have your full names for this form. You will be er . . . "Bella Crawford," I suppose, and er . . . yours, Mr. . . . ?

BELLA   My title is Carrington, not Crawford. You see, Slick and me is half-brother and sister. Same mother but not same father.

LADY POLLY   I see. Perhaps one day soon we can look into that situation too. And Mr. Bonaparte?

BELLA   My husband name "Manny." "Manny Bonaparte."

LADY POLLY   (*Writing*) Manny Bonaparte.

SLICK   Hips?

SHRIMP   Forty-two.

LADY POLLY   Well, those are very pretty names, but I really don't think the abbreviations improve them. I should like to have your full names.

BELLA But Bella is my right name, my lady.

LADY POLLY Dear child, surely you weren't christened "Bella"—and if you were, that was an oversight. Now let me see: "Annabel Carrington" and er . . . er . . . "Emanuel Bonaparte." That's much better. They would sound so much more impressive in the newspaper report—I always write one myself—something like this: "After long years of faithful and devoted er . . . companionship"—we have to choose our words carefully—"wedding bells have at last pealed for Annabel Carrington and Emanuel Bonaparte of Havendale. Preceded by flowergirls and bridesmaids, the bride, in radiant attire provided by the wives of twelve nations, entered the church to the strains of the Bridal Chorus from Wagner's *Lohengrin*"—we'll get the Police Band to play for us. "This was the first of what is expected to be a cavalcade of nuptial ceremonies in the village, sponsored by the S.P.P.W.R. of which Lady Polly Love-Muggins is president." I always include my name at the end to make sure the report is printed on the social page.

SLICK Bust? (A brief silence.) Bust? (*Shrimp is struggling futilely to encircle Bella. Manny's anger, which has been slowly mounting, now erupts.*)

MANNY No, by God! No! No! NO!!

BELLA No what?

MANNY There ain't going be no wedding. You hear what I say? I not having no pappyshow wedding. Who you think I is? Dressing up in a monkey suit and parading myself and my woman like a couple of blasted chimpanzees! I say no! We not in no circus.

SHRIMP Mr. Bonaparte! Please moderate your language. In front of Lady Love-Muggins, too!

MANNY You shut your mamapoule mouth! Mad Benjy by the street corner got more sense than you. This is my house and if I want to damn and blast I going damn and blast in front of Missis Queen self!

BELLA But Manny, how you could get on so? Where your breeding?

MANNY You going taste breeding when I down hand in your skin. You is the ringleader in this plot to deceive me, you and that lousing half-brother you have there. (*Slick melts into his chair.*) But I warning all of you. I's a peaceful, pacific, law-abiding man and I don't want no trouble. Don't make the blood fly up in my head or, bejeez, is the grave for all you and the gallows for me.

LADY POLLY But, Mr. Bonaparte, nobody wants to harm you. We're here to help you really, you and Annabel.

MANNY I didn't ask for no help. With all due respects, Lady, if you would mind your business and I mind mine, we wouldn't cross each other path. You don't know the ways of woman as I know them. You don't have no experience of how our people does get on. Me and Bella living nice together, we love one another, and we content to stay as we is. She free to walk through one door, and I free to walk through the other. That is how we accustom living and I don't see why all you should come with your high-and-mighty ideas and interfere in what don't concern you.

BELLA   But, Manny, we not living right!

MANNY   Look, I done say my piece. I not having no wedding. No bells ringing and no band playing. If you want Yankee ring, buy one in the store. If you want chicken dinner, I have fowls in the yard. I not letting no woman tie me up like a crab because next day they break off your gundy and drop you in hot water. And another thing, your name is Bella where I concern. Now I going down the road by George to fire one, and I want my house nice and quiet and peaceful—like how it was before these marriage-mongers come—by the time I reach back. Is Sunday morning. (*He stomps out angrily.*)

SLICK   Well, Lady Polly, you can't say I didn't warn you. The man is a mad bull when his temper raise.

SHRIMP   I did what I could to calm him down.

BELLA   (*Crying*) I know Manny would've blow up. I know all the time he would never agree to this thing. What we going do now?

LADY POLLY   Do? Why nothing, of course. Just carry on with our plans as if nothing happened to disrupt them. I've come across this kind of behavior more than once. In fact, I should've been surprised if Mr. Bonaparte, who is every inch the caveman, didn't act like one. I expected much more violence. Never mind, my dear, I have ways and means of getting round him. Don't worry, you'll have your wedding bells sooner than you think, and a full military band too. The S.P.P.W.R. is not easily balked; we won't let you down. I assure you. (*She rises.*) Well good-bye Annabel. You'll hear from us. Get these papers signed, Mr. Crawford, and have them processed in the usual way. You've got all the measurements?

SLICK   Bust? (*Shrimp snatches up the tape measure and leaps back to the task.*)

The curtain falls
followed immediately during the blackout by wedding
bells and the strains of the "Wedding March."

Scene 2

A Mime

It is another Sunday morning, a month later. The room is the same, but simple rusticity has given way to the new and gaudy. The furniture is now of the Morris style, heavy and vulgar, crowding the room even more than before, with cushions covered in a loud flowered print material. The wall pictures display screen stars, the curtains and drapes are also brightly colored. The atmosphere has changed from modest cosiness to cheap gaudiness.

The room is empty. Manny enters from the backyard. He holds a sick chicken in one hand and a paper bag of chick feed in the other. He finds a small cardboard box, deposits the chicken in it and places the box on the table, then pours in some feed. He looks at the coal pot at the door on which he is trying to prepare breakfast. The fire is dying out. He bends down and blows into the arch to fan the coals but succeeds only in covering his face with ash and smoke. He coughs and splutters, crosses to the washstand, but there is no water in the basin or pitcher. He glares at the bedroom and yells: "Bella! Bella!" There is no reply.

Manny wipes his face in a towel and proceeds to lay out dishes for breakfast. He picks up the teapot from the fire and burns his fingers. He drops it back and plunges his fingers in the flower bowl to cool them in the water. A rose thorn sticks him. He seizes the roses and throws them on the floor. He sits down to eat. An insistent bleating comes from the yard. He stops and listens. The bleating continues. He yells again: "Bella!" No response. The goat appears in the doorway. Manny takes it out to feed it.

Bella enters from the bedroom, drawing on her housecoat. She has changed. She is legal mistress in her own house and has acquired the airs befitting a mistress. She is in silk pajamas, a Chinese kimono, and gay slippers. She stretches lazily, looks around for a hairbrush which Manny has left on the table. She fetches this and stands before a wall mirror, brushing and putting her hair in paper bows.

Manny returns and sits at table eating and glowering at Bella. She ignores him, begins to hum a calypso tune: "Mama, Look a Boo-Boo." Once or twice he thinks of having it out with her, but changes his mind and restrains himself. Each time he makes to rise, Bella senses his intention and begins to hum louder, thereby asserting her authority. Manny pushes away his plate in disgust, gets up, crosses to washbasin, takes up empty pitcher, and goes outside to fetch water.

Bella puts away the hairbrush, pins, etc., gets towel and soap, and waits for Manny to return. He comes in with filled pitcher which she promptly takes from him and begins to wash her hands and face. Manny crosses to window, picking up roses from the floor. He throws them through the window. Bella moves to dining table, pours a cup of cocoa, brings cup and saucer down to rocker, sits, puts cup on center table, takes up a bottle of nail varnish and begins to touch up her nails, still la-la-ing a calypso tune. Manny turns sharply on her, attempts to speak, changes his mind again, sits in a chair facing Bella. He lights a cigarette. Bella continues to polish, sip her cocoa, and hum. A pause.

A knock at the front door. Manny looks at Bella, she looks at him. She puts down the nail polish, smoothes her housecoat and waits. A visitor, perhaps, after church. The knock is repeated. Manny goes to answer it. It is only the newspaper boy. Manny turns back into the room with the paper. As he crosses Bella she holds out her hand for the paper. He hesitates a moment, then hands it over. Without once looking up at him, she extracts the comic section, puts it on her lap, and hands him the rest of the paper. He stands there fuming.

Bella drains her cup of cocoa, holds out the empty cup and saucer for Manny to put away. This is the last straw. With a mighty sweep he knocks the dishes away. Bella rises majestically —there is an echo of Lady Polly in her movement—looks him up and down, and marches into the bedroom with her comic sheets. Manny is a monument of controlled rage. He begins, very slowly and deliberately, to rip the newspaper into pieces and drop them on the floor.

Curtain
followed immediately by a gay
passage from the "Wedding March."

Scene 3

(The room as in Scene 2. Sunday morning, a week later. Manny is packing his things. A battered suitcase is open on the table and two carton boxes are on the chairs. He folds and puts away a few garments, takes up a pair of heavy workingman's boots and pauses, wondering where to put them. Slick appears at the window.)

SLICK   Hey Manny, you get my message? (*Manny ignores him.*) I ask Jamesy to tell you I want to see you—important-like. (*Manny dumps the boots in the suitcase and continues packing.*) I could come inside? I have a piece of news to your benefit. (*He leaves the window and enters by the front door. He is dressed in a gay sports shirt and colored gabardine trousers. He approaches Manny tentatively.*) You packing?

MANNY   No. I playing dolly-house.

SLICK   Where Bella?

MANNY   What you want with her?

SLICK   Nothing, nothing. But she ain't here?

MANNY   She gone traipsing off to one of them Women's Rally. What you have to tell me?

SLICK   You leaving Bella?

MANNY   Mind your damn business.

SLICK   I have a piece of news give you.

MANNY   Well, spill it then and stop dancing me around.

SLICK   I want to know how matters stand first.

MANNY   Look, Slick, you done capsize my life already. Is only because I was mook enough to agree to it that I ain't beat out your brains yet. But don't try your luck too far. If you don't have nothing to say, hoist yourself out my house quick-sharp.

SLICK   Man, I come here in your interest and you getting on like a Russian! Like you don't trust me.

MANNY   You dead right.

SLICK   Okay, if is so you want it . . . (*He moves to the door and stops.*) You don't want to hear the ballad.

MANNY   How come you not at the Rally this morning, Slick?

SLICK   I don't have to go every time, man.

MANNY   (*Approaches Slick menacingly*) Come clean, Slick. I could see the lie forming up behind your eyes. Where your monkey clothes?

SLICK   The truth is, Manny, I let go the work.

MANNY   You mean they fire you?

SLICK   Fire who? Is I walk out. It was getting kind of dull—you know how—so much woman all about, however you turn you bounce up with one. And when you talk about talk! My ears didn't stop buzzing two weeks solid! Look, I going tell you something, eh. When nighttime come, instead of coasting a nice limn with a brownskin as mate, I beating a bottle hard with the boys behind Joe bar. And why? Because I sick-sick hearing woman-talk. I too young for that, boy.

MANNY   You working now?

SLICK   I taking a rest after all the hustlement.

MANNY   That is why you hanging round here. You come to see what you could pick up? (*He collars Slick.*) You expect soon I will walk out my house in disgust the way Bella getting on, and you will take over. You louse!

SLICK   No, Manny, no! You charging me wrong!

MANNY   What for you come here this morning!! Talk sharp, my patience running out!

SLICK   Is a lawyer friend I have. He say he could get your marriage annul if you want.

MANNY   Annul? What you mean?

SLICK   Break up, squash, like how you was before.

MANNY   How he could do that?

SLICK   Some legal mixup in the business. I ain't too well understand the ins and outs. But he's a good lawyer. You could trust him.

MANNY   How soon he could fix me up?

SLICK   He say in a week or two.

MANNY   What he name?

SLICK   He tell me don't mention his name to nobody—you know how it is—being as the business not strictly aboveboard.

MANNY   I suppose he want a pound and a crown for that?

SLICK   He's a good lawyer, you know, and seeing that he taking a big risk, you will have to compensate him good.

MANNY   How much?

SLICK   I tell him how you's my family and all that, so he willing to cut down the price for you.

MANNY   Jeeze-and-ages! How much? You don't understand English?

SLICK   Fifty pounds.

MANNY   Fifty what? Where in France I going get that kind of money.

SLICK   That is what he charge at first, but I beat him down to thirty. And too beside, you could pay him off by degrees. He tell me bring anything you have as a bind.

MANNY   (*Collaring Slick again*) You ain't lying? You ain't trying to bamboozle me again? Because if you do, so help me . . .

SLICK   No, Manny, no! I could really fix you up!

MANNY   You could?

SLICK   I mean the lawyer-feller. Jeezu-web,° man, and we is family? I wouldn't fool you.

MANNY   Slick, if you could do this thing for me you's a real friend. I don't want to leave Bella, but I can't go on no longer in this tanglement. From the time she get married, Bella change. Like the ring take away all her born sense. Every striking day is some-

---

°*Jeezu-web:* from "Jesus wept"; used as a mild expletive

thing new. First thing, she make me buy up a whole new set of furniture and put me in debt. Me who never owe the chinee shop for a pound of rice, I owing the joinershop, the shoemaker, and the store. Next thing, she can't do no more housework; she don't want the neighbors see her milking the goat or cleaning out the fowl coop; if Emily get a kimono, she want one too; Doris wearing sack, she want one too, and all day and night the woman flying out the house like she mad going to rally and social and soiree. And on top of that, if I call her Bella, she ignore me. Is Annabel or Emanuel, otherwise nothing doing. You think any God-fearing man would stomach that stupidness?

SLICK Is a hard life.

MANNY Not she alone what turn, you know. The whole village gone crazy with this society living. George throw out Agnes last week. Harry and Emily in noise every living day. Is you I blame for the whole commess.° You and that nosy white woman.

SLICK Manny, boy, I agree is my fault and I trying my best to equalize matters. Leave it to papa. Me and my lawyer friend going straighten you out. How much you have on you?

MANNY (*Takes a cloth bag from his grip*) I have eleven, no twelve pounds save up here. I could give you five as an advance.

SLICK You better make it eight. We don't want the lawyer man to turn down the case.

MANNY All right. Here. (*He hands over the money.*) Tell him don't waste no time. The sooner the better.

SLICK Eh-heh. You smart. (*He moves to the door.*) Well, I better peel off now. I have to make my rounds.

MANNY Stay and take a drink, nuh, man? I feel better already.

SLICK Next time. We going pick up. (*He opens the door, makes to leave but jumps back inside and closes the door again.*) Is Lady Polly. She coming in here.

MANNY What the hell she want now?

SLICK I going out the back way. I don't want her see me.

MANNY (*Suspicious now, he forcibly restrains Slick*) No, stay here. We going see what she want.

(*Slick drifts disconsolately into a corner as Lady Polly knocks at the door and enters peremptorily without waiting to be admitted.*)

LADY POLLY Good morning, Mr. Bonaparte, I . . . (*She sees Slick and pauses melodramatically, then decides it is better to ignore*

°*commess:* total confusion; complete mess

him completely.)   I'm sorry to have to visit you unceremoniously like this, but it's rather urgent and I'm pressed for time. The point is—and I very much regret to say this—there has been a slight miscarriage in the arrangements made for your wedding some weeks ago. I've only now discovered that it was not conducted strictly er . . . shall we say, according to the book. It happens that certain important documents were mislaid and not registered . . .   *(She glares at Slick.)*   . . . and other legal requirements were overlooked at the time. It's all our fault, of course; the S.P.P.W.R. assumes full responsibility, but it does mean we shall have to repeat the ceremony—merely a formality. Of course, on this occasion we shall do it quietly. No sense in making a fuss about it a second time. Now if you will just sign these documents . . . ?

MANNY   You mean to say—I not really married to Bella?

(Slick tries to edge his way toward the door. Manny, realizing he has been tricked, attempts to forestall him. During the following scene with Lady Polly, they play a private game of cat-and-mouse.)

LADY POLLY   Well you are and you aren't. In the eyes of the church, you most certainly are. But legally . . .

MANNY   Legally?

LADY POLLY   I'm afraid not. I know this must upset you terribly . . .

MANNY   Oh, yes, mum. It upset me a lot!

LADY POLLY   And I don't mind telling you, Mr. Bonaparte, because I know you will understand and be discreet about it, a certain member of our staff, who is also, I regret to say, a member of your family, misled us dreadfully, deceived us in fact, that he had got the signatures and complied with all the regulations. It was with horror that I discovered otherwise and it has caused the S.P.P.W.R. a great deal of embarrassment in the village and in official circles. Needless to say, disciplinary action has been taken against that member and he is no longer in our employ. However, that is past history now. We are trying to repair the damage at the earliest possible moment, so if you would just sign . . . ?

MANNY   Just leave the papers there, mum. I'll be happy to sign them for you. Just leave them there.

LADY POLLY   Very well. And get Annabel to sign too. I've filled them up myself. I will have the forms picked up tomorrow and taken to the record office. Now if you'll excuse me, I have several other calls to make. Good morning!   *(She leaves.)*

MANNY   *(Pounces on Slick who cowers behind a piece of furni-*

ture) You damn worthless scamp! So you know a lawyer who could fix things, eh? Give me my money back, you bloody thief!

SLICK   (*Returning the money*) Look the raise, Manny. I was only joking you. Don't take it serious, I beg you.

MANNY   Boy, I should blade your skin with my poui.° But I let you off this time. But look my trouble, nuh? (*He laughs uproariously.*) So you fire the job because you fed up. Ho-ho-ho! How come you forget to take in the marriage papers?

SLICK   I was running a booze that weekend and as the liquor fly in my head the work fly out. I can't tell what the France happen to the forms and them.

MANNY   Thank your stars, boy, thank your stars and sing hallelujah! I could tell you now. I had every intention when all this finish to bathe you with licks. Because you was at the back of everything. Anyhow, let that pass. Reach a grog there and come fire one.

SLICK   Let me hear that tune again. Is my favorite.

MANNY   (*Chanting*)

Fire one, I say, fire one,
Take a shot before life done,
Warm up the wet and cool down the sun,
So fire one.

SLICK   (*Gets a bottle of rum and glasses. He pours the drinks*) I didn't tell you what really cause the old mass between me and Polly. Pardner, after the first novelty wear off, I didn't have no more uses for her. She run kind of stale, you understand. Them kind of people ain't have no zip. Anyhow, one morning she get a great idea in her head. Whaddap! She come out with how it ain't look decent to have me in the setup as a single man, so much women all around, and how is high time I get married, and she think some old fowl name Josephine would make me a good wife. Well I never hear that in forty-four years! Me, Slick, who ain't even cut my eyeteeth good—look, my mother's features still on me, the woman want to come blight my future with wedding ring. And come see the Josephine! She been down here since the days of Methuselah! (*He makes a grimace.*) I sure is spite Polly want to spite me. Boy, is then the old man decide to bail out fast. Never me in woman affair again, boy.

MANNY   But you know the woman well bold-face. She have the brass to come back here, after what I done pass through, and talk about . . . (*Mimicking Lady Polly*) . . . "I know this must upset you terrible, but we trying to repair the damage . . ."

°*poui:* stick from the hardwood tree by that name

SLICK   (*Joining in the fun*)   And "if you will just sign here, Mr. Bonaparte, and get Annabel to sign too . . ."

MANNY   Annabel! Annabel my eye. Now we going see who is man.

SLICK   What you going do?

MANNY   Just watch me. (*Very deliberately he sets about disarrang-
ing the room. He throws pieces of clothing over the screen and on
the chairs, spills food on the table, scatters a newspaper about the
floor. Slick helps himself to another rum and recites.*)

SLICK   I am monarch of all I survey,
        My right there is none to dispute,
        From the center all round to the sea,
        I am lord of the fowl and the brute.°
I remember that poetry from third standard. Hey, Manny, I just
think up a master plan. Listen. How about me and you starting
up a society too. We could charge shilling-a-week subscription
and we could call it S.S.S.P.P.W.R.

MANNY   What the devil name is that?

SLICK   The Society for the Suppression of the Society for the Preservation and Protection of Women's Rights. What you saying? Every
man-jack would join up. Is a good idea.

MANNY   Eh-heh. Is a good idea.

(*Slick laughs uproariously and pours more drinks. Manny rises
quickly and takes up his poui-stick.*)

MANNY   Ss . . . hh! She coming.

(*Bella enters. She is outrageously overdressed with gloves and
hat. She closes the door and hesitates, looking from Manny to
Slick and back to Manny. Finally, she approaches him slowly.*)

BELLA   Emanuel, I hear . . .

MANNY   Manny!

BELLA   Manny, I hear that . . .

MANNY   Good. Say it again. Say my name again let me hear.

BELLA   Manny.

MANNY   And you. What your name is again?   (*A pause.*)   Tell me, I
forget it. What your name is?

BELLA   Bella.

MANNY   Good. Now, Bella, take off them society gloves and don't let
me see you wearing them again. Hands make for work, not for
show. (*She removes her hat and gloves.*)   And I find the house
looking kind of dirty. You ain't find so? Clean it up give me
please, and wipe off the table, and wash out the basin. When you

---

°"*I am . . . brute*": from William Cowper's "The Solitude of Alexander Selkirk"

finish, go outside and feed the fowls and the goat. And I think I would like my food ready by one o'clock sharp. If you don't mind?

(*Bella turns away, a pitiful figure of submission. She fetches an apron, puts it on, gets the broom and duster and begins to clean up. Manny sits brooding. Slick pours another drink and tries to cheer him up.*)

SLICK   That's the way, Manny, that's the way. "I am monarch of all I survey. . . ."

MANNY   You get to hell out of here. Out off, I say!   (*He hurls Slick out by the scruff of his neck.*)   A no-good louse! I don't want to see him round here again. I done with him—for good.

(*Manny watches Bella as she moves about her chores sadly. He relents. He collects the scattered newspaper, puts away the rum and glasses, begins to unpack his clothes from the suitcase. Bella stops and looks at him. He looks at her. They reach for each other.*)

Final Curtain

Questions

1. The first problem with this play is how to handle the language of Manny, Bella, and Slick. In the West Indies there are a number of creole languages, meaning languages that are a mixture of two languages, with one dominating, in this case English. Mr. Hill, who is from Trinidad, says that the speech here carries elements of several creoles he is familiar with and that he has not tried to reproduce Jamaican Talk, the creole language of native Jamaicans. Speak the lines aloud often enough to make them flow easily, and you'll find yourself enjoying the unusual word order and word choice and the pleasurable lilt of the phrasing. Take turns reading aloud a page or so of the dialogue. (Do what you will with Lady Love-Muggins and The Rev. Timothy Shrimp; they're ripe for hamming up.)

2. Show that Manny, Bella, and Slick come across as real flesh and blood people. Describe what you think they look like, using suggestions found in the text, and then compare your descriptions with those of others in the class. How much general agreement do you find? In contrast, show that Lady Love-Muggins and the Rev. Shrimp are clearly caricatures, exaggerations of typical attitudes, not real people at all.

3. Why is Lady Love-Muggins prying into the lives of people like Manny and Bella? What grounds does she have for doing so, if any? Why does Bella like the idea? Why does she give in so easily when Slick's foul-up is discovered? In what sense has Lady Love-Muggins really done her a favor? What did Lady Love-Muggins want to do for Manny? What does she actually do for him?

4. If the situation of the play were removed from its dramatic context and discussed as if it were a problem posed for a "Dear Abby" type of commentary, what would be your attitude toward it (a common-law marriage, a completely dominant male, a seemingly chaotic household)? What makes the situation as actually experienced in the play very different?

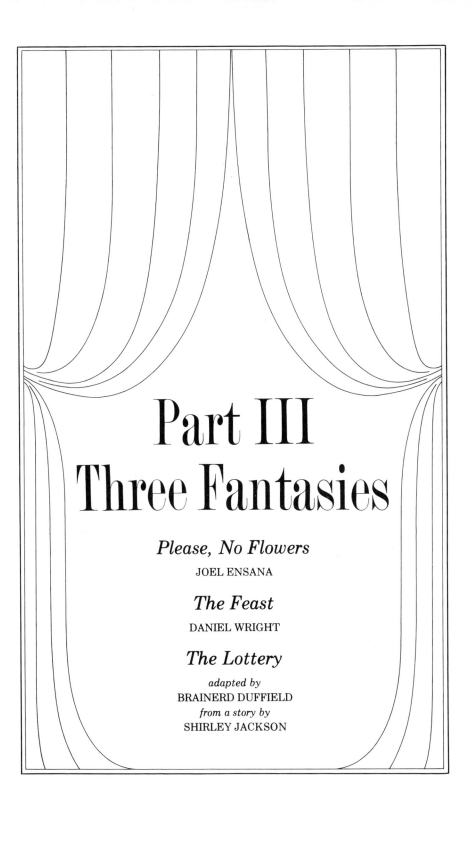

Part III
Three Fantasies

Please, No Flowers

JOEL ENSANA

The Feast

DANIEL WRIGHT

The Lottery

adapted by
BRAINERD DUFFIELD
from a story by
SHIRLEY JACKSON

E sther and Lena, laid out in their coffins in a funeral parlor, find they can communicate with each other (though not with anyone still living) and proceed to recount, between visits from mourners, a capsule history of the harsh and unpitied lives that have made them willing, even eager, to give life up. The first mourners who come, with their self-satisfied indifference and lack of understanding, tend to confirm the two dead women in their view that life held nothing worth clinging to, at least for them; but the second set of mourners introduce a new and complicating factor into the situation. And then, as the dead women begin to sense their mistake. . . .

Please, No Flowers

JOEL ENSANA

Characters

CARETAKER
LENA GROSSMAN
ESTHER RUBEL
MRS. HIRSHMAN
MR. HIRSHMAN
MRS. BLEEKER
MRS. LEHR
THE YOUNG MAN
SANDY

SCENE: *A funeral parlor in San Francisco, California.*

Although the time is the present, the ornate room seems to date back to the twenties. There are faded red velvet drapes fringed with gold tassels, Spanish style paneling and arched entrances, wrought-iron standing candelabra, four gilded folding chairs and, most conspicuously, two caskets, one somewhat more elaborate than the other. Adjacent to the main entrance to the room, there is a baroque table which holds a large "Visitors' Register."

The setting may be realistic or impressionistic—perhaps using biers for the caskets—but whatever the style of design, the feeling should be ethereal.

The elderly Caretaker enters, silently lights the candles, then slowly crosses around one of the caskets and with his sleeve polishes a brass handle. This completed, he starts toward the door, stops, removes a handkerchief from his pocket and diligently dusts a bronze statue of a cherub and a faun. As he does so, he shakes his head and sighs, as if to say: "The help these days!" He then leaves the room. A moment later, a tapping sound is heard from within one of the caskets.

LENA   (*In a low-pitched voice*) Yoo-hoo!   Anybody   there—? Hello . . .

ESTHER   (*From the other casket; hesitantly*)   Wait . . . yes, yes, I'm here. Hello, it's me! I can hear you.

LENA   Your voice sounds familiar. What's your name?

ESTHER   Esther. Esther Rubel.

LENA   That sounds familiar, too. Mine's Lena Grossman. Tell me, did you belong to the B'nai B'rith?°

ESTHER   No, I never belonged to any organizations. I wasn't a joiner.

(*The door slowly opens and the Caretaker returns*)

LENA   Sh! Someone's coming . . .

(*There is silence as the Caretaker lifts the lids of the caskets, revealing in one, Esther Rubel, a plainly dressed and homely woman of thirty-five; in the other, Lena Grossman, a woman in her late sixties. A second or two passes, then Esther suddenly bursts into song in order to test the Caretaker's reaction*)

ESTHER   (*Singing*) "Somewhere over the rainbow . . ."

(*Silence again. The Caretaker does not react. Esther, then, kicks her legs up in the air. Still, no response*)

ESTHER   (*Looking over at Lena; shrugging her shoulders*)   Well, I guess we're ghosts.

°*B'nai B'rith:* a Jewish fraternity founded in New York City in 1843; now worldwide; the name means, in Hebrew, "the Sons of the covenant"

(*The Caretaker slowly crosses to the baroque table, opens the "Visitors' Register," checks the inkstand and, as he consults his vest-pocket watch, leaves the room*)

LENA What a relief! Phew, it's so restful . . . (*She sits up in the casket and makes herself quite comfortable. Then, with a surprised glance at Esther*) My goodness, you're a young woman! So, tell me, what happened? Childbirth, maybe—?

ESTHER (*Leaning over the edge of the casket*) Suicide. I was number three-hundred-and-fifty off the Golden Gate Bridge.

LENA Listen, life like it was—who can blame you? You know, you *look* familiar. Maybe you were a customer of mine? For twenty years, after my husband died, I ran a delicatessen . . .

ESTHER (*Now sitting on the edge of the casket, her legs dangling*) I didn't indulge very much in delicatessen, only the packaged meats. But, sometimes, I would splurge, like on my birthdays— I'd buy onion rolls and prune Danish at the Ukrainian bakery. You see, I was too busy trying to keep up with Pacific Gas and Electric and the landlord and . . .

LENA Me, I just let go. I could hear them talking—my niece, the doctors and nurses—"If she's got the will she'll make it, just a little of the old fight." Just like on a TV soap opera. Fight? I was tired of fighting. A whole lifetime of fighting . . .

ESTHER You are so right.

LENA So, I let go of my niece's hand. I let go and I let my hands fall limply. I remember thinking—*fight?* Why? What for? Maybe three years, ten years—it wasn't worth it. I was tired of "Who's going to run for president?" and "What's happened to the new generation?" and . . .

ESTHER Yes, how true . . .

LENA So, just like Marilyn Monroe said, "So long, fame, I've had you," me, I said, "So long, life, I've had enough of you!" Yes, believe me, I felt you, life, tightly with love, frightened, in passion, and besides, my niece, Sandy, she's young, let her enjoy my money. Let her use it. And, believe me, it was such a relief when I took that last breath . . .

ESTHER (*Leaping off the casket*) Look, no flowers, no mourners! I'm glad there's no one to cry for me—because I'm—I'm so happy. It's wonderful being free! Free of loneliness and worries, no more fears of what was going to be—it's here, the to-be, and it's all over. You know, when I jumped from the bridge, I turned and yelled through the fog, "Goodbye PG&E, you bastards, you . . . !"

LENA Yes, Yes, goodbye, PG&E and also, all those hungry doctors with their big bills. Come, come and look at the label in my coffin! It says the *Hollywood Model*, and feel, just feel the silk and soft foam. All my life I've slept in a Murphy bed° between sheets bought at "white sales" at Penney's—now, now it's silk for an eternity!

ESTHER   Yes, it's wonderful, oh, so wonderful! But it's such a funny feeling. It's like . . . an epilogue, this being nowhere . . . just in between, like I finished a book and I'm going to start a new one— and now, this is like an epilogue . . .

LENA   I'm not so sure I like that thing—an epilogue. I always like to know what's coming next.

ESTHER   (*Leaning against Lena's casket*)   I wonder what the next book will be like? A tropical paradise, a burning furnace or maybe, just nothing—years and years of nothing—just lying there —like lying in bed on Sunday, not moving or anything—just so glad to be there. But, at least seven o'clock Monday morning will never come again! . . . Yes, I'm glad I did it, so glad. I'm sure it would have gotten worse as I got older . . .

LENA   I just hope someone takes care of my birds and my dog, that's all. You know, animals, they're so much nicer than people. They never hate.

ESTHER   Yes, animals are great, really great . . . (*A tiny pause*)   But I wonder what *people* are saying? Not that I care! (*Then, reflectively*)   The people at the office . . . the girls I would sit next to at the Ali Baba ballroom next Saturday night, that little old bachelor who'd always ask me to dance . . . Imagine, ten years of going regularly to the Ali Baba! . . . . And Mr. Hirshman. His payroll won't get out on time and the union representative will chew him out but good! (*In a change of tone*)   But just think, they're all reading about me. Yes, Esther Rubel, who received little attention before, now in the newspapers! I can just hear them saying, proudly, "Why, I knew this girl! Look, look, I used to . . ." (*Turning to Lena*)   Do you think I made the headlines, Mrs. Grossman?

LENA   Sure, you made the headlines. Those papers we had in San Francisco—and you being number three-hundred-fifty. You set a record.

ESTHER   But who's to miss me, *really* miss me? No, no one will ever say, "What happened to Baby Esther?" (*Sadly, she begins to sing to the tune of "I Wonder What's Become of Sally"*)   "I wonder what's become of Esther . . ."

°*Murphy bed:* a bed that can be folded into a wall to save space

LENA   Me, I'd like to see my relatives' faces when they hear I left everything to my niece. I remember how after my mother's funeral, the arguing. "You take the silver, I'll take the linen and china . . ." Me, they left me the wind-up phonograph and a few cracked records . . .

ESTHER   (*Impulsively*) You know, Mrs. Grossman, I feel like a new person! Just suppose those people were right about reincarnation. I might go back a raving beauty!

LENA   Or a mouse. Who knows? Maybe worse yet, an ant . . .

ESTHER   Even *that* might be better! Ants stick together. They share. Anything's better than being alone, not sharing. I had a studio apartment, furnished in the brightest colors, but to me, it was dark and empty because there was no one there to share it, to love. I mean, that's really important, having someone to love. A woman like me needed love. At least, a mother, a father—even a cousin who maybe'd write once a year, but there was no one. A person needs roots, the warmth from someone close. I had nothing but headaches, it was one thing after another, and every day seemed to become colder, darker. If it had been just a little balanced. You know, a little love, then a little trouble . . .

LENA   So, where did you get the nerve? Imagine such a big bridge! I would look down and get dizzy.

ESTHER   After a whole week-end of sitting around, depressed and lonely—and as age creeps up on you, the depression and loneliness become more frightening—I took inventory of my, let's say, stock. The warehouse was empty. On top of that, I had a fierce sinus headache, a plugged-up toilet, a pile of bills and, well, I just pretended I was diving into the pool at the Jewish Community Center . . .

LENA   Imagine, such *chutzpa* . . .

ESTHER   At least, you had a husband, some loving, someone needing you. I can see—you must have been a beautiful woman.

LENA   Who? Me? Never. Still, I was lucky for a while. (*Reflectively*) Yes, he was a fine husband. Then, one night he got up to go to the bathroom. I heard him, then went back to sleep. Suddenly, I didn't feel him. I would always snuggle up close, such a warm person. "Irving, Irving," I called. I got up and there he was, on the bathroom floor. A heart attack. . . . I was never the same after that. Maybe we were too close. After they . . . (*She indicates the lid of the casket; then*) Do you think I might see my Irving?

ESTHER   I don't know. But then, who am I to say? I always thought we just came to an abrupt end. We died and that was all, but look, here we are and it hasn't ended.

LENA   (*Calling out in a small voice*) Irving . . .

ESTHER   Sure, sure, Lena, you'll see your Irving! Why not? After this, *anything* is possible.

LENA   I—I think I'll get up for a while. Walk around a bit—you know, for old times' sake . . .

ESTHER   (*Assisting Lena as she climbs out of the casket*) Here, let me help you.

LENA   Just for a little while . . .

ESTHER   It might be a helluva long time before we can do this again.

LENA   Tell me, you said you *never* had love? A nice young woman like you?

ESTHER   Nice? Me? With this absurd face and figure? (*A second*) Maybe if I'd had money . . . (*Another second*) Yes, I loved a young man, not the best looking or the smartest—very poor taste, always dandruff on his shoulders, but still, I loved him. Yet, I never really knew if . . . (*With a sad little laugh*) There I am, still wondering, hoping! I thought all that would end when I left my camera and purse on the bridge . . .

LENA   A camera? You were going to take pictures?

ESTHER   No, but the guards don't pay any special attention to you that way. You look like just another tourist. (*Then, after a moment*) . . . Oh, we had a few dates, but I'm sure he didn't love me or he would have said so . . .

LENA   Esther, did *you* say so?

(*They are interrupted by the muffled sound of voices from the foyer. A second later, Mr. Hirshman, an older, extremely well-dressed man, enters, followed by Mrs. Hirshman, a stout woman. She, too, is splendidly turned out. They quietly go to the table and sign the register. The only sound in the room, for the moment, is the loud scratching of the worn penpoint. Then*)

ESTHER   (*Startled*) Lena! It's my boss! Mr. Hirshman and his wife.

(*Mr. and Mrs. Hirshman solemnly cross the room and stand before Esther's casket*)

MRS. HIRSHMAN   (*Putting on her glasses and staring intently into the casket*) They did a good job, but still, she has that crazy look on her face. Like the characters you see in the Haight Ashbury.° Those hippies . . .

MR. HIRSHMAN   Funny, how you work with a person so many years and

°*Haight Ashbury:* section of San Francisco once known as "hippie" territory

you really don't know them. I mean, jumping off a bridge . . . (*With a little sigh*) But then, somehow she always did seem a little odd—a bit *meshuga*°—living alone, always complaining . . .

ESTHER (*Now standing beside the Hirshmans*) Complaining! (*Turning to Lena*) Who wouldn't complain? He paid me practically nothing! Such a little man, such a little person! Could you believe it, he even kept track of how long a typewriter ribbon lasted! Can you imagine, Lena? To him, I was nothing *but* a typewriter!

LENA That's why I had my own business. I did as I pleased.

ESTHER Every time I'd say, "Mr. Hirshman, may I speak to you?", he'd yell, "If it's about a raise, forget it. Look, I can get another girl, it's an easy job. Besides, business is bad and what with taxes like they are . . ." Oh, the lousy capitalist! A few dollars, just a few dollars more . . .

MR. HIRSHMAN But her work was good—yes, it wasn't bad, and always on time. (*Another sigh*) I don't think I'll ever be able to find another girl to replace her. As a matter of fact, I was just thinking about giving her a promotion and a little raise . . .

ESTHER (*Angrily, clenching her fist*) Hypocrite! Lousy hypocrite!!

MRS. HIRSHMAN (*Glancing at her wristwatch*) Please, Max, let's go. The dinner starts at seven and I don't want to miss the fruit cup.

MR. HIRSHMAN What could I have done to . . . ?

MRS. HIRSHMAN You did enough for her! What more? You took care of all her unpaid bills—including that damned one from PG&E— imagine, being three months behind! And now, you've paid your respects. So, come, come on, Max, it gives me the shudders. The girl surely must've been sick. Who in their right mind . . . ?

ESTHER Go on, get the hell out of here! (*She gives Mrs. Hirshman a swift kick, as they slowly start to depart, arm in arm*) It's people like *you* who are sick, it's *me* who's smart. I'm through with your lousy world! Yes, through! (*The Hirshmans disappear*) And . . . and I feel wonderful, truly wonderful! Like a fat girl who's suddenly lost a hundred pounds, yes, a hundred pounds of living!

(*Mrs. Bleeker and Mrs. Lehr, nicely groomed women in their early sixties or thereabouts, enter and sign the register*)

MRS. BLEEKER (*As she signs in*) The page's blank. We're the first and only visitors for poor Lena . . .

MRS. LEHR The way she behaved, what did you expect? A royal turn-

°*meshuga:* crazy

out? She lived like a hermit and died like a hermit.

MRS. BLEEKER   (*Turning over the pen to Mrs. Lehr*) Work, work,
always in that store or else talking to those stupid birds and that
flea-bitten old dog . . .

MRS. LEHR   What kind of existence is that, can you tell me?

(*Lena stands, alert, now brushing back a few wisps of gray hair.
Mrs. Bleeker and Mrs. Lehr approach Lena's casket. They walk
softly and carefully, in an experienced manner from having at-
tended so many of these rites*)

LENA   Esther! Friends of mine from the B'nai B'rith. I—I haven't seen
them in ages! Their husbands made a lot of money during the war
and—suddenly—they were too good for the neighborhood . . .
and *me* . . .

(*Mrs. Bleeker and Mrs. Lehr stand staring into Lena's casket,
both shaking their heads while their lips almost move in unison,
silently mumbling prayers*)

MRS. BLEEKER   She looks better than ever.

MRS. LEHR   See what a little make-up does for a person?

MRS. BLEEKER   Look, look how restful. Before her husband died, she
was a handsome woman.

MRS. LEHR   I wonder who bought the dress? Always, she wore that
faded smock in the store, remember?

MRS. BLEEKER   I've got to sit down for a few minutes. Funeral parlors
always make me a little unsteady on my feet.

MRS. LEHR   (*As she and Mrs. Bleeker leave the side of the casket and
sit in the folding chairs*) She was a changed woman after her
husband went.

LENA   (*Turning to Esther*) Naturally, Esther, I had to work from
morning to night, lugging orange crates, going to the vegetable
market at four, before dawn. Do you think anyone would offer to
help?

MRS. BLEEKER   So many times, believe me, I planned to call her, ask
her over for dinner . . .

MRS. LEHR   I was going to bake a special cake for her, for the holidays.
Deliver it personally. I was sure she wasn't eating right, being
busy in that store and, after all, when you're alone who feels like
baking?

MRS. BLEEKER   . . . But there was always something . . .

MRS. LEHR   You're right, something always interferes with good inten-
tions.

MRS. BLEEKER   Besides, I didn't know how she'd react, not having seen her in so many years. And, especially, after the stories I heard . . .

MRS. LEHR   That's the way it goes, that's life . . .

(*They both sigh, deeply and simultaneously*)

LENA   How many times I wished *someone* would call. I would've given —I don't know how much!—if someone had just called, Esther, not to talk or gossip for hours or go on about themselves. Just a "So, how are you—are you still alive, Lena?"

ESTHER   (*Compassionately*) I know, Lena. (*A second*) It was that crazy world. Everyone for themselves.

MRS. BLEEKER   It's getting late. We'd better be going. This neighborhood—it's changed since we moved. It isn't safe after dark anymore.

MRS. LEHR   The whole city has changed. . . .

(*Mrs. Bleeker and Mrs. Lehr rise and once again approach Lena's casket for a final look. Suddenly, Mrs. Bleeker's gaze is diverted toward Esther's casket*)

MRS. BLEEKER   So young! When a person dies so young it's a real tragedy. (*She moves a bit closer to Esther's casket*) That face looks awfully familiar.

MRS. LEHR   (*Standing beside Mrs. Bleeker*) Why, it's the one in the paper! I remember, I even remarked to my Morris, "Look, honey, a Jewish girl is number three-hundred-and-fifty off the bridge!"

MRS. BLEEKER   Unbelievable, so young . . .

MRS. LEHR   Anyway, she made the headlines. Even my Morris said, some people will do anything for a little publicity.

ESTHER   Publicity? Who needed publicity! *Attention, perhaps!* . . . I was a typist, eighty words a minute. A typist, not a movie star!

MRS. BLEEKER   (*To Mrs. Lehr*) Come . . .

(*As Mrs. Bleeker and Mrs. Lehr silently return to Lena's casket, The Young Man enters. He is wearing a shapeless tweed suit and carrying a bouquet of mixed flowers. Noticing the other two visitors, he hesitates, then steps back into the shadows of the room*)

MRS. BLEEKER   (*Taking Mrs. Lehr's arm*) There's nothing more we can do.

MRS. LEHR   Crying won't bring her back.

(*As they leave, Lena shouts after them*)

LENA   So, why didn't you call? Friends! Who needs friends like you! (*Turning back to Esther*) I would've starved if I waited for their dinner or "special holiday cake" . . .

(*As Mrs. Bleeker and Mrs. Lehr disappear, The Young Man, visibly upset, comes forward and approaches Esther's casket*)

ESTHER   (*Surprised*) Lena! It's *him!* The young man I told you about . . . Oh, I feel funny! (*Nervously and excitedly, she hastily brushes back her hair, straightens her dress*) I mean, I wonder what he thought when he heard about it? And, oh, I must look awful, all that water, being dragged in a net like a fish . . .

LENA   Don't worry, Esther, you look terrific.

(*The Young Man stands before Esther's casket and begins to sob*)

ESTHER   He's crying! Look, Lena, for me, he's crying!

LENA   It must be nice to have someone crying for you.

ESTHER   Oh, God, I can't believe it!

LENA   It must give you a good feeling.

ESTHER   (*Incredulously*) *I'm missed!* Imagine, *me*, being missed!

THE YOUNG MAN   (*Quietly sobbing*) Oh, Esther, why—why did you do it? Why couldn't you have waited just a little while longer? Just until I finished my night course in traffic management—was a little more secure . . .

ESTHER   Security? What's security! You and me, that's security . . . (*Turns to Lena*) Funny, listen to me, still talking in the present tense.

THE YOUNG MAN   God, please, let her rest in peace. If I'd only realized that she was so close to giving up. I must've been blind! (*A second; then*) Security—hell—a person—so much more important . . . I loved you, Esther!

ESTHER   (*Screams*) *Oh, my God!* My God!! He loved me. You heard that, Lena, he loved me.

THE YOUNG MAN   I was blind and stupid! I needed you, Esther, my darling—oh, how I needed you . . .

(*The Young Man collapses into a chair, grief-stricken. Esther rushes to his side, her hands gently tracing his face, his body— never touching him—as though trying to capture his features to treasure for an eternity. She now is kissing his hair, his hands, then suddenly, she turns about in anguish, in realization*)

ESTHER   (*Miserably*) Why *now?* Why not yesterday? Why did he wait, Lena? *Why?* If he'd only told me, explained . . . (*She turns back to The Young Man*) I'd have loved you, no matter what—even if you didn't have a cent. I'd have taken pride in laundering your shirts, shining your shoes, even trimming your hair so's to save on the barber's fee. But now, now it's too late . . .

LENA (*Hastening to Esther's side*) Don't, please, don't upset yourself. Besides, you'll wake up tomorrow and who knows? We'll be
in a better place, you'll see. Things, so they say, usually happen
for the best.

ESTHER (*Desperately; clasping Lena's hands*) Lena, maybe it's all a
dream? Maybe I ate too much before going to bed last night? Yes,
yes, I distinctly remember having a piece of cheese on seeded rye,
with plenty of mustard. I'll wake up in the morning and I'll—I'll
call him the very first thing! He needs me, Lena. You heard,
you're a witness—*he needs me* . . .

LENA Please, don't—don't do this to yourself . . .

(*Sandy, an attractive young lady, enters and goes to Lena's casket. As she begins to weep, The Young Man quickly wipes his own
tear-stained face with a pocket handkerchief*)

LENA Sandy! My lovely niece . . . (*To Esther*) You know, it does
feel good having someone to cry for you. Suddenly, I feel important, like maybe it wasn't all for nothing after all.

(*The Young Man rises and approaches Sandy*)

THE YOUNG MAN Is there something I can do?

SANDY No. Thank you. My aunt, she—she was such a wonderful person. Never an ugly word about anyone. Never envious or bitter,
like so many old people.

THE YOUNG MAN Well, she's resting now. She looks very peaceful.

SANDY Yes, she's at peace, all right, but if she only knew . . . She
struggled, worked hard all her life and for what? A pack of greedy
relatives who've already begun to battle over her money . . .

LENA I left a will. What's to fight?

SANDY (*Turns to The Young Man*) They're saying she was *incompetent*. Imagine! Just because a person stays to herself, she's judged
incompetent and incapable of making proper decisions. Perhaps
she *was* a little out of tune with the times, but that was one of the
nice things about her. She was a complete individual and I—I
always found it refreshing to spend a couple of hours with her.

THE YOUNG MAN We all have our strange little ways . . .

SANDY I wish she had never left anything to me! You ought to hear
them, especially my uncles—what they've called me, the accusa-
tions . . . (*A moment; then*) Just before I came over here, they
phoned—said they were going to contest the will because *I had
influenced her! That's why I had visited her whenever I could*
. . . They've already engaged a lawyer. Imagine, she's not even
buried yet—God rest her soul!—and they've already begun the
battle.

THE YOUNG MAN   That's the way it usually is whenever there's some money involved. People turn into vultures. Never give, just get.

LENA   Esther, did you hear? That's the last thing I wanted, to cause her trouble. *Incompetent!* My own brothers calling me that? What kind of family . . . ? (*A pause*) If only I had given her everything while I was still alive . . .

SANDY   (*To The Young Man; indicating Esther's casket*) Was she your—wife?

THE YOUNG MAN   No, but I—I was about to . . . (*Again overtaken with emotion*) Yes, I was . . .

ESTHER   Imagine, Esther Rubel, a *wife*, someone's partner . . .

(*She leans against the foot of her casket and weeps; except for her sobbing, there is silence as the others remain deep in thought*)

LENA   (*Breaking the silence*) *Incompetent!* So, I kept a lot of birds and an old dog and I went no place. So, I lived in the back of my store and denied myself little luxuries. *It was my privilege!* It's a free country—no? My work, my pets, my independence were everything. I never asked for anything from anybody!

(*The Caretaker comes in and quietly walks over to Sandy and The Young Man*)

CARETAKER   We close at eight. Sorry . . .

SANDY   Eight o'clock, already?

THE YOUNG MAN   Even here, where you face eternity, there's a time limit.

(*The Caretaker leaves. Sandy and The Young Man silently take their places, respectively, before Lena and Esther's caskets for one final look, one last prayer, an eternal goodbye*)

THE YOUNG MAN   Goodbye, Esther. I really loved you and I'm—I'm going to miss you.

(*Esther clutches his legs, sobbing*)

THE YOUNG MAN   True, we weren't together a lot, yet we were . . .

SANDY   Goodbye, dear Tante Lena. God—please be good to her, let her finally find peace . . .

LENA   *Peace?* Will I *ever* find peace—?

(*The Young Man turns to Sandy and they start to leave together. Esther, desperately, follows The Young Man to the door, attempting to touch him, kiss him, but never quite able to reach him*)

THE YOUNG MAN   *(To Sandy)* I hope you get a good lawyer. Your aunt's wishes should be followed to the letter . . .

SANDY   I'm not sure whether I *want* to fight it. Right now, I—I couldn't even think about it . . .

(As Sandy and The Young Man disappear)

ESTHER   *(Crying out)* No, please, please . . . !

LENA   *(Calling after them; anxiously)* Sandy, get Mr. Shapiro for a lawyer! He has proof, papers. He knew me all my life. Knew I *wasn't* incompetent, just a little strange, maybe, the neighborhood character, but he has proof, Sandy! Oh, why did I let go? Look, she didn't even hear me. Maybe if I think hard enough . . . *(Closing her eyes tightly)* . . . They say thoughts can carry sometimes—like a breeze . . .

(Esther wearily returns to the side of Lena's casket. There is a moment of silence)

ESTHER   Lena, isn't it all like a joke? As if someone said, "You thought it was all over—you were so happy, well, I've got news for you."

LENA   *(Nods)* Maybe I went too peaceful, Esther, so someone is giving the screw another twist to make up for it, someone is saying, "Ah-ha, let's play a little joke on her." *(She stops, listening)* Wait . . .

ESTHER   What is it?

LENA   I heard someone laughing.

(The sound of laughter suddenly fills the stage. It is the laughter of the Fat Woman, the mechanical woman who stands in front of the Fun House at Playland and just laughs and laughs)

ESTHER   *(Gazing up at the ceiling)* It came from up there . . .

LENA   No, it sounded like it came from someplace down there . . .

ESTHER   What's funny? Some joke, eh?

LENA   The biggest joke of all, Esther, was that crazy life, that crazy world. First, it's "hate" the Germans and the Japs—then, it's "like" the Germans and the Japs—then, it's fight for peace, then, you want peace, suddenly you're a Communist . . .

ESTHER   Yes, how true . . .

LENA   And the cruelest joke of all is you've just learned about life, how to enjoy it, embrace it, and then, all of a sudden you become tired and old. *(A moment)* Believe me, Esther, it was a crazy world and you're not missing anything. So, please, no regrets!

ESTHER   You're right, no regrets . . . *(The sound of laughter increases)* I just wish they would let us in on their joke! I never had much laughter . . . (*She picks up the bouquet of flowers, holds them tenderly*)

LENA   I'm glad someone's happy. Look, don't pay any attention. (*The laughter subsides, as she returns to her casket*) My feet, they're starting to hurt, just like they used to. I guess nothing has really changed . . . (*Then, after a moment*) Esther, please, would you let me smell one of the flowers? That one—the yellow . . .

(*Esther selects a yellow rose from the bouquet and gives it to Lena*)

LENA   Funny, I'm not able to smell it—still, I can remember and so, I can smell. (*As though she were inhaling the fragrance of the rose*) How fresh and nice and sweet . . .

ESTHER   (*Impulsively*) Lena! I've changed my mind. I want to go back to that crazy world!

LENA   (*Staring intently at the rose*) Yes . . . me, too, but let's be honest—it's too late for both of us. (*Then, in a change of tone*) Listen, I would advise you to return to your—your— how I hate to use that word—! (*Instead, she points to Esther's casket*) . . . And keep thinking of all the bad things. It'll make you feel that what you did wasn't such a big mistake after all— and just think you missed the cruelest joke of all . . .

ESTHER   You mean, *I* actually missed out on something?

LENA   Yes, believe me, getting old. You're lucky . . .

ESTHER   Tell me, Lena, keep telling me all the *bad* things I missed. Maybe it will make me feel better about . . .

LENA   Aches and cramps, watching young people do things you can't do anymore, being left out like you were some horrible disease or a dress out of style, living in a country where they worship youth, losing people you loved or were close to—each year, another person and then having to say, "Oh, no, so when did this happen?" —another building torn down, one with special memories, now maybe a parking lot—yes, always finding yourself apologizing, "But in the good old days, we would . . ."

ESTHER   But being older, you had something I didn't have . . .

LENA   What? More gray hairs?

ESTHER   No. More memories . . .

LENA   (*A second*) But somehow, Esther, it's the *bad* memories that stay with you. I know from experience. I think back, like hunting for an old letter in a bureau drawer and it's always, strangely, the unhappy memories that seem the clearest. Just think—in a box for an eternity—me and all those memories!

ESTHER   Imagine, though, if they should ever open it, it would be like a Pandora's box—all those memories, the good packed along with the bad—still, memories—spreading over the earth . . . (*She shudders*) Funny, I wasn't afraid on that bridge. But now—now, I feel cold. Like when the first puffs of wet fog suddenly catch up with you . . . (*Then, with a sudden little cry*) Tell me, Lena, will time just drag on and on and on?

LENA Esther! The bad memories, remember . . .

ESTHER (*As she returns to her casket, tightly clutching the bouquet of flowers*) I'll try, I'll try real hard, but forever is such a long time —I mean, just that word! If only he hadn't brought these damn flowers, maybe it wouldn't have been so hard . . .

LENA (*Urgently*) Listen, hurry! I hear the old man locking the front door . . .

ESTHER (*Quickly shoving the bouquet under her pillow and beginning to recall the more unpleasant memories*) Let's see—working for Mr. Hirshman, that crowded bus, getting nowhere, TV commercials, cold mashed potatoes, people who shove, people who whistle, people . . .

(*The Caretaker returns and starts to shut the lid of Lena's casket as the speeches of both women overlap*)

LENA (*Speaking bitterly at first*) . . . People, Nazis, gas chambers, bread lines, assassinations—(*She begins to sob*) . . . You're right, Esther, no flowers, please. No flowers! (*Then, resuming in a warm, emotional tone*) . . . Walking with my dog, fresh onion rolls, big fat clouds, children running—playing as if there was no tomorrow—my birds, my wonderful beautiful little birds, eating fresh celery leaves, newly laundered bedclothes . . .

(*The lid on Lena's casket now is closed. The Caretaker proceeds to Esther's casket*)

ESTHER (*Desperately*) Lena! Mrs. Grossman!! (*Then, lowering her voice*) . . . Chocolate ice cream in sugar cones, riding the cable car on a spring evening, hot dogs and player pianos, foghorns drifting in from the Bay, Bette Davis movies, flowers, Wonton Soup, parades, seagulls, after-Christmas sales, Halloween and the pumpkins in the windows . . .

(*The Caretaker has shut the lid on Esther's casket. Then, he laboriously crosses to the baroque table, closes the "Visitors' Register," puts out the candles and, as the stage is darkened, the sound of laughter resumes, now building to a crescendo*)

Curtain

Questions

1. What problems and experiences in Esther's life led her to suicide? What in Lena's led her to "just let go" in the hospital (after, presumably, a heart attack)? In answering, consider all that is revealed in the play as a whole, not just the causes that the two women explicitly mention.

2. What do you make of the laughter that is heard during the play's last minutes? Do you think the author wants us to imagine it as Fate, or Life, or the Universe laughing at the cruel joke it has played on the two women? Or as a symbol of the mindless stupidity of the world they have put behind them? Or do you see some other interpretation? Discuss fully whatever evidence you think the play provides on this point.

3. *Please, No Flowers* indulges in fantasy—that is to say, in imagining an action that could not possibly take place in the real world in order to say something about the real world. As you see it, what does the play say about the real world? What recurrent regrets do you notice in the reflections made during their visits by (a) Mr. Hirshman (b) Mrs. Bleeker and Mrs. Lehr (c) the young man? In the same vein, what do you take to be the implication of the sudden shift in Lena's last list of earthly experiences? What is the implication of Esther's last list? How would you relate the play's title to what the play seems to be saying?

4. A problem that every playwright faces is how to capture the interest and curiosity of the audience immediately. How does the setting chosen by Ensana—what we first see when the curtain lifts—work for him in this respect? What is the point of the first entrance of the Caretaker? Observe carefully what he does and try to grasp the playwright's reasons for each action assigned him: (a) lighting the candles, (b) polishing and dusting, (c) shaking his head and sighing. If instead of sighing, he gave a great groan, or alternatively, a visible shudder, would his action be better or worse suited to the mood of this play? Why or why not? What is the point of his second entrance? (Again observe what he does.) Is he in some sense the stage manager of the play as well as the Caretaker of the funeral parlor? What are his actions at the play's end? Observe, too, what he does *not* do when Esther bursts into song. By this means what does the playwright tell us?

5. How should Lena be played? With what clothing? Hair? Face? Voice? And Esther? The Young Man? Sandy? (Be sure to note all the explicit clues on these matters offered by the play before you consult your own imagination.) Make a sketch of the two coffins indicating how you would differentiate them. List the other properties needed for the play.

6. Write a short dialogue, several lines for each speaker, in any (or all) of the following situations: You are walking your dog just before dusk in a

big city, and as you wait at a street corner for the light to change, you are approached by (a) a small child, (b) a pretty girl, (c) a handsome young man, (d) a policeman, (e) a woman who eyes you nervously, (f) a man who eyes you with hostility. Try to make your dialogue reflect some imagined inner state in the other person and in yourself.

A n old man, a factory worker, on his lunch hour, starts up a con-versation with a young man, also a factory worker, also about to eat his lunch, and slowly, against considerable resistance on the young man's part, draws him away from the drab reality of the lunch-pail and paper-sack to an imagined great feast. The odd thing is that real glasses with real champagne in them actually appear, along with a real cellist to play an obbligato, to which the old factory worker reads a real ode he has written to Bacchus, the god of wine. There must be some-thing crazy here—but what?

The Feast

DANIEL WRIGHT

Characters

BLUE JEANS
OLD MAN
ANGRY YOUNG MAN
ELF WITH CHAMPAGNE   (*Blue Jeans disguised*)
DROWSY CELLIST   (*Likewise*)

The curtains open . . . and . . . it must be some kind of mistake. The stage crew is still putting up sets. But no one seems to be much bothered by the fact. It might be a nice touch, though, to have a director, troubled species, to look up and notice. He might shout some muffled expletive off stage about who was the fool who opened the curtains etc., when they weren't ready. But in any case, the stage work-lights remain on, the stage work con-

*tinues, somebody's complaining about a costume that doesn't fit,
and damnitall if the curtains don't stay open. Now some character in blue jeans and spotted shirt comes out along the front of the
stage. He is carrying an easel over his shoulder, a large piece of
cardboard in his hand, and a pot of paint. For the sake of somebody's reputation, he might smile an apology to the audience. At
any rate, when he gets to the opposite end of the stage, he sets up
his easel, places the cardboard upon it facing the audience, and
paints—rather scrawls, "THE FEAST." He puts his pot of paint
aside and sits down on the stage next to his easel. He looks out at
the audience and, twirling his glasses in his hand, begins:*

BLUE JEANS   Well, now . . . no one said it was going to be an extraordinary sort of play . . . I mean, as a matter of fact, it's quite an
ordinary sort of . . . Believe me, it doesn't deserve much of . . .
You know, come to think of it, it's such an ordinary . . . I mean,
I, for one, wouldn't feel so bad about dispensing with . . . uh . . .
that is, I don't want to bother them for the sake of the feast. After
all, you start stomping around on the grounds of every whim and
. . . well, people get mad. So, we'll just let them go on working
. . . go on, go right on and . . . then we can maybe sneak in this
bit . . . (*He saunters back among the stagemen and, in a pantomime, wangles two tin buckets, which he brings forward, arranging them about five feet apart.*) . . . I've got friends . . . or,
sometimes I seem to . . . CHARLIE (*Calls over audience*) hey
. . . HEY CHARLIE . . . (*A spot comes on, and Blue Jeans
waves it over to where he is standing between the buckets. The
stage work-lights remain on. B.J. places a can on top of one of the
buckets.*) I've got characters too, or sometimes I seem . . . they
are supposed to arrive . . . (*Factory whistle. Blue Jeans holds
up his hand to the audience, nods his head.*) . . . a whistle, if
you hadn't guessed, and it signals the start of this play. It makes
a suitable sound to start a play? . . . right? It blows, and people
change . . . you know, it toots, and people are possessed by it.It
beckons in the harbor, and people look up expectant. Maybe it
calls from the factory stacks . . . feet move, sometimes a smile
. . . and you know it's our own creation, but we pray in our exer-
tion . . . A CHERUB OUT THERE perhaps. He looks down
and chuckles at our business, but he takes up his horn and sounds
pause, "take pause" . . . (*The whistle blows again. B.J. is
about ready to climb down in the orchestra—but one final
word.*) . . . and so on, so forth. (*He makes himself comfortable
in the first row. Old Man is heard humming outside.*)

OLD MAN   (*Enters through the audience down the center aisle. He is wearing spotted, baggy work pants supported from the shoulders of a red plaid wool shirt by suspenders. He is characterized by an ambling, joyful gait, and when he speaks, it is with the friendly, booming quality of a man who has found a sense of self-assurance and contentment. Go ahead and ham him up . . . no danger. You might as well. He walks all the way down the center aisle, swinging a lunch pail at his side, singing. He sings to the tune of "Freight train, freight train. . . ."*) Lunch hour, lunch hour, goin' so faaaast . . . Lunch hour, lunch hour, goin' so faaast . . . Dum de dum, de dum de donn . . . so they won't know where I've gone . . . (*Climbs stage, eventually sees the tin can on the one bucket*) . . . AH HA! Miserable tin can of a man that I am . . . counting the minutes till your lunch hour comes . . . (*Kicks the can off the bucket*) TAKE THAT! . . . (*Old Man gazes after the can and chuckles contentedly.*)

(*Several of the stage crew members are still working on the sets, but they are making less noise now. One of the crew calls "Lights!" off stage, and the stage work-lights go off. The red and white border lights remain on, along with the spot centered on the Old Man and on the two buckets . . . Old Man puts his lunch pail in front of him, and as he opens it, Angry Young Man enters from the side. He is wearing old pants and a denim jacket—on his head a battered tweed golf cap. He sits down on the second bucket and . . . facing the audience like the Old Man, explores the contents of his paper bag. During the conversation that follows, Old Man eats his lunch out of his lunch pail, Young Man, out of his paper sack. Old Man chews his lunch in delight. Young Man rips at his lunch in anger. They are about finished with lunch by the time the "feast" begins. Young Man is characterized by brooding, suspicious expressions of a rebelliousness which, I guess, he considers attractive. Certainly he holds no distinct notions of revolt, because you see, indications are that Young Man isn't all that bright. But anyway, Old Man hums; Young Man broods, and neither seems conscious of the other until Old Man glances over at Young Man and says offhandedly*)

Ah, you are here too . . . So you have come to join in the Great, Green Lunch Hour—that moment of rapture and dizzy joy, that . . . uh, moment of freedom! and . . . (*No response from Angry Young Man*) . . . so you have come too?

YOUNG MAN   (*Glances around, realizes that Old Man has spoken to him*) Yeah, sure, I mean, what do you mean? . . . of course I am here . . . I mean I DON'T EVEN KNOW YOU, OLD MAN!

OLD MAN   As you wish . . . was just trying to make conversation.

YOUNG MAN   Humph. (*Lights begin to fade.*)

OLD MAN   There's this little game, see, that I know . . . makes new acquaintances come much easier . . .

YOUNG MAN   Humph. (*Spot remains on.*)

OLD MAN   It starts out, you see, by me asking a question . . . I ask you, "What did you have for breakfast this morning, stranger?"

YOUNG MAN   Yeah?

OLD MAN   Well, what did you have for breakfast this morning, stranger?

YOUNG MAN   (*Suspiciously*) Well, let me see now . . . I had a big bowl of Sugar Crisp—yes, and a cup of coffee from the machine.

OLD MAN   Now I tell you what I had for breakfast. I had this magnificent combination of Wheat Chex . . . I really like Wheat Chex . . . and orange juice, sausage, eggs—poached with pepper—and toast with plenty of kumquat jam . . .

YOUNG MAN   Look here, what kind of a game is this?

OLD MAN   Why . . . it's called the comparative breakfasts game.

YOUNG MAN   (*Throwing his hat to the floor*) LOOK HERE, OLD MAN . . . WHAT DIFFERENCE DOES IT MAKE WHAT I HAD FOR BREAKFAST ANYWAY . . . I mean, A MAN'S BREAKFAST IS HIS OWN BUSINESS . . . (*Y.M. sputters, dusts off his hat and goes back to his lunch bag.*)

OLD MAN   Exactly . . . you see, disclosing one's breakfast, a very intimate matter indeed, presumes acquaintance and avoids all sorts of embarrassment. Now if I were to tell you what I'm having for lunch . . . for instance, I say, "Well, lemme see, I've got a boiled egg and a thermos of vegetable beef soup and . . . a salomy 'n' lettuce on rye . . . (*Gleefully exhibits the contents of his lunch pail*)

YOUNG MAN   LOOK HERE . . . I don't happen to be interested in your breakfast, or your lunch, or even you fridgin'° dinner, for that matter . . .

(*Long pause*)

OLD MAN   It's such a pleasant day out. I just thought maybe . . .

YOUNG MAN   Hey, Dad . . . So happens I think it's a lousy rotten day, and so happens I don't like eating lunch out here in this lousy, rotten storage lot . . . out of a lousy, rotten paper bag. So happens it's a grubby, lousy city in a grubby, rotten world filled up with a lotta grubby, lousy, rotten people . . . try that out for size on the old wazoo.

°*fridgin'*: meaningless swear word, equivalent to "damned"

(*Old Man takes a crunchy bite from an apple.*)

OLD MAN   Why, I'd say you are bitter . . . you are bitter, aren't you?

YOUNG MAN   Yeah . . . I am . . . I'm real bitter (*Throws hat on floor again*) WHAT'YA MEAN BITTER, ANYWAY? . . . WHAT KIND OF QUESTION'S THAT? AND WHAT IF I AM . . . (*Turns his back on O.M., who shrugs his shoulder. They go back to their lunch.*)

OLD MAN   Well . . . I was just interested, you know . . . I mean bitter people don't usually . . . don't come here, that is . . .

YOUNG MAN   (*Challenged*) What do you mean?

OLD MAN   But . . . come to the feast, of course.

YOUNG MAN   The WHAT?

OLD MAN   . . . the feast . . .

YOUNG MAN   Oh, "the feast" . . . look, if that's some underhanded way of telling me you don't like my company, it don't wash, see Dad . . . I've got as much right to this crummy can as the next Joe . . . and so maybe you don't like me, well that's just tough potatoes.

OLD MAN   Oh, you can do what you like . . . the feast is quite open, you know . . . I don't mean to say you weren't invited, in fact this very moment I ask you to be my special guest.

YOUNG MAN   Guest?

OLD MAN   Yes, at the feast.

YOUNG MAN   Yeah, sure, what feast?

OLD MAN   Right now . . . here.

YOUNG MAN   What the fat kind of a feast you expect to have out in this crummy lot . . . I know about feasts, you think I'm dumb or something? . . . You think I'm dumb? My old lady used to tell me about feasts. She used to work at the Regis, and she used to bring junk back to the place and tell me about all the food and the people getting potted and dancing and smoking big cigars.

OLD MAN   Well, you see, this feast is a little different. I mean, your mother . . .

YOUNG MAN   You can leave her out of this. What gives you the right to sit there and . . .

OLD MAN   Really, I'm sure your mother is a very fine woman. I just want to explain . . .

YOUNG MAN   Well, for your information, so happens the old lady can take it in the ear for all I'm concerned.

(*Long pause*)

OLD MAN   Let me explain about the feast.

YOUNG MAN OK, OK, I'm willing to go along with a gag . . . the feast . . . shoot.

OLD MAN Well take, for example, that little fellow over there on the corner playing the flute.

YOUNG MAN Where . . . you mean that corner?

OLD MAN Yes, over there . . . the little fellow with the flute.

YOUNG MAN Oh, yeah. You mean the traffic cop—sure, I see the traffic cop.

OLD MAN NO! NO! Not the traffic cop . . . "traffic cop" . . . the little fellow on the corner with a red bandana on his head playing the *flute!*

YOUNG MAN The newsboy . . . maybe?

OLD MAN NO! Not the newsboy . . . you mean to say you don't see a little man wearing a green coat and a red bandana, dancing around the bus stop sign, playing a flute? (*He makes a motion as if playing a flute.*)

YOUNG MAN LOOK! I don't see any little guy in a green coat and a red bandana dancing around any bus stop sign, playing any fridgin' flute on THAT CORNER!

OLD MAN Well, I suppose that's understandable.

YOUNG MAN OK. What's the catch?

OLD MAN My fine young man, any fool, if he uses his eyes, can plainly see that there is no little man with a flute and a bandana . . . quite obviously, he is not there.

YOUNG MAN (*Pause, nods his head, barely restraining his impulse to throw his hat on the floor*) Yes, I . . . I see . . . yes, that . . . come to think of it . . . that's surely the reason why I couldn't see the guy with the flute.

OLD MAN Now, the feast is about the same as the little man with the flute, you know.

YOUNG MAN Yeah, I get it, you mean I'm not going to be able to see the feast either . . . well, you didn't have to tell me that!

OLD MAN NO, NO . . . not in the least . . . you see the feast is like the little man because it is not . . . for the most part, essentially and in *factum* . . . there.

YOUNG MAN Yeah, sure . . . but, uh . . . how we going to have the feast if it is not there? . . . or here?

OLD MAN Oh . . . no more time to explain . . . the feast is about to begin. But there's one small matter to settle first.

YOUNG MAN And what's that?

OLD MAN Why, the sort of feast that you prefer, of course.

YOUNG MAN Now, don't tell me we have a choice even . . . of feasts, that is.

OLD MAN   Absolutely! You have the broadest choice of all the choices, so you just say which it is that you prefer, and we will see what we can do.

YOUNG MAN   Yes, well . . . I'm not exactly up on this feast jazz. What sort of choices do I have?

OLD MAN   GREAT SCOTT! Let's see . . . you have wedding feasts, birthday feasts, feasts for coronation celebrations, vengeance feasts . . . whether you win or love, you always have a feast . . . and you have feasts for kings, feasts for thieves, demagogues, churchmen, salesmen, boatmen, law men, small men . . . let's see, there are New Year feasts, Easter feasts, Christmas, Halloween, Arbor Day, Ground Hog's Day . . .

YOUNG MAN   Yes, but there's really no fridgin' reason to have a feast, come right down to it.

OLD MAN   I was hoping you'd say that, because you see, that's the best sort of feast to have.

YOUNG MAN   Sure . . . what's that?

OLD MAN   Why, the feast for no fridgin'. . . er, Phrygian° reason, as you put it.

YOUNG MAN   Yeah, sure . . . that's bound to be the best . . . uh, feast.

OLD MAN   Certainly the best . . . no red tape of emotion to tangle up the revelry, no sticky cause, you see . . . no cloud of duty hanging overhead . . . yes, the feast for feast's sake is, without a doubt, the best.

YOUNG MAN   Anything you say, Dad . . . it's your show, but seriously, how're you going to have any kind of a feast when all you've got left is half a salomy 'n' lettuce, and me . . . (*Holding up his sandwich fragment*) . . .

OLD MAN   Come, lad . . . the feast is not essentially a matter for eating. Food is but a key to the door where most any key will fit, you see . . . It is that moment when the appetite is satisfied, when hunger is bubbled away   (*Slaps his stomach*)   and the door opens on the magical landscape of the FEAST! (*Old Man strikes a dramatic pose and slowly lifts his hands to the ceiling. Young Man sits awed at the Old Man's invocation. The spotlight is by now the only light on the stage.*)   OH, BACCHUS!° SPIRIT OF MIRTH! SPIRIT OF SONG! LOOK DOWN WITH FAVOR UPON US . . . SMILE THE SMILE OF MERRIMENT, for why have we come but for the sake of merriment? Do we come to

---

°*Phrygian:* the Old Man, to avoid using the Young Man's swear word, sees in his own mind the same sounds spelled as a reference to a people of ancient Phrygia in Asia Minor

°*Bacchus:* god of wine in classical mythology

honor the living or the dead? Do we come to goad ourselves to victory or to cheer the victory already won? NO! Do we come in the guise of charity and pity? Or do we come in the guise of business and serious matters? NO! NONE OF THESE! WE HAVE COME TO THIS GRAND FEAST FOR NO FRIDGING . . . er, PHRYGIAN REASON AT ALL! . . . so to speak—but for the sake of merriment. Let us, oh Bacchus, celebrate this moment!

YOUNG MAN   (*Whispering to Old Man*) Hey, cut it out! You want somebody to see us and think we're nuts? You want to be shipped off to the booby hatch or something?

OLD MAN   . . . I look upon the vaulted hall, the ranks of bountiful tables smiling in their candlelight. I see kindred faces, expectant faces . . . How best to celebrate this occasion which is, of course, no occasion, we ask. I present to you our special guest (*Old Man waves an arm in Young Man's direction. Young Man shrinks back.*) Here is a mind of vigor and youth. He represents a promise for our age . . .

YOUNG MAN   (*Whispering*) Look here, Old Man, I don't know what you're up to, but I sure as fat don't like it. I didn't ask to get into this. I . . . I was sucked into this flaming feast, you know damn well I was . . . come on now.

OLD MAN   Ladies and gentlemen, I present to you a young man with depth of spirit, breadth of heart, and fullness of imagination . . .

YOUNG MAN   (*Still whispering*) This is no fair, you tricked me . . . you trapped me . . . you . . . (*Shouts in Old Man's ear*) . . . FRUITCAKE! (*Old Man not fazed. Young Man hastily stoops to pick up his bag and lunch papers, puts on his cap in preparation for flight.*)

OLD MAN   . . . in short, I present to you the Angry Young Man. (*Old Man catches Young Man by the sleeve and leads him into the spotlight.*)

YOUNG MAN   Look here, this gag of yours has gone far enough . . . go right ahead and spout off if you want, just leave me out of it . . . uh, just feast it by yourself, why don't you?

OLD MAN   (*Whispering*) Don't spoil it all . . . this is part of the bit. There always has to be some sort of a keynote speech at every feast.

YOUNG MAN   But really, Dad. This is ridiculous . . . I mean, really.

OLD MAN   I don't know what you're so worried about. All you have to do is to say a few words to them . . .

YOUNG MAN   To WHO?

OLD MAN   To them . . . (*Indicates the audience*) It's just part of the bit, you know.

YOUNG MAN   OK, OK. Nobody's going to say I'm not a good sport, a good Joe, an allright guy . . . just so long as you agree that if someone happens to come by, it's all a joke, see . . . Let's make this short . . . what am I supposed to say?

OLD MAN   Well, let me see . . . you ought to say something about the reason for the feast which, of course, will be a hard part . . . you just say what you like. Yes, and add something about how distinguished the audience is . . . appeal to the emotions, their pity, amuse them, flatter them, agree with them . . .

YOUNG MAN   OK, anything you say. Remember, I'm just going along with the gag. (*Takes off his hat and faces the audience with an embarrassed smile, then turns towards the Old Man again*)   Aw, come on. This is crazy.

OLD MAN   (*Whispering*)   Go on, go on . . .

YOUNG MAN   (*Turns to the audience, smiling again*)   Ladies and gentlemen . . . I'm not much on speeches really . . . (*Turns*)   How's that?

OLD MAN   Fine, fine. Their sympathy is already with you.

YOUNG MAN   (*Facing the audience again*) . . . and believe me, it's like a great honor to be here at this moment before you. Now let me tell you about a funny thing that happened to me during my lunch hour. I was sitting there, see, and this old geezer invites me to this feast, just for a gag (*Glances at Old Man*) and so . . . uh, here I am. And the introduction that the Old Man gave me was way out . . . I mean it was too much. But, consider the reason why we are all here . . . What is the reason we're all here, after all? . . . Damned if I know. Man, the whole thing is really . . . uh, crazy. (*Glances at Old Man*)   Well, there doesn't seem to be any reason for being here—how about all the reasons for not being here? Just put that in your pipe and smoke it. Just think of all the things you might be doing instead of wasting your time at this, uh . . . feast. You could be putting the garbage out. You could be running over rabbits in your car (*Whispers "Pity" to Old Man, who nods his head in approval*) . . . you could be shoplifting in a super-market or thinking up nasty comments to make to your mother-in-law. Just THINK of all the temptations you might be yielding to if you weren't wasting your time here, feasting it up . . . It's great to have you here and . . . So go right ahead and feast it up because it's great to be here (*Glances at Old Man for approval*) and besides that, you are all really great people, and I really agree with you about everything . . . thank you. (*Turns to Old Man*)   How was that?

OLD MAN   That was great, just great . . . but wait, you may be called on to make a few toasts.

YOUNG MAN   (*Brow-beaten and confused*)   Just give the word, Dad

. . . I can't make any more a fool of myself. (*He sits down, shaking his head.*)

OLD MAN   We thank the Angry Young Man for his remarks, always apt, well-chosen, short, and to the point. But the time for invocation has passed; the moment of preparation is accomplished . . . Therefore, GIVE US WINE! Let us lift up our glasses and so lift up our hearts. (*Old Man looks down at the front row seat where Blue Jeans is sitting.*) PSSSST! That's your cue . . . the wine . . . (*Blue Jeans gets up from his seat, goes back up the ladder, and is to be seen at one end of the stage, putting on a short green coat and wrapping a red bandana around his head, both of which were handed out to him from the wings.*)

YOUNG MAN   Wine?

OLD MAN   Of course. How can you drink a toast without wine?

YOUNG MAN   Yeah, sure. This I gotta see. (*Follows Blue Jeans off stage in amazement*)

OLD MAN   . . . Bring flushes to our cheeks and so flush the general spirit with unencumbered mirth. (*A cart is pushed out onto the stage, and Blue Jeans trundles it out towards the spotlight. The cart holds a bucket of ice with a bottle of champagne and several glasses.*) Sniff gently the wine's bouquet and rejoice in its sweet vapor. Smile, laugh . . . feel warmth. (*Elf with champagne, i.e., Blue Jeans, rolls the cart into the spotlight. Young Man stares at him wide-eyed. Blue Jeans answers the stare with an embarrassed shrug. B.J. pours out two glasses and hands one to Old Man, one to Young Man.*) I PROPOSE A TOAST . . . (*Lifts up his glass*) . . . TO THE FEAST . . . THE FEAST FOR NO FRIDG-IN' . . . PHRYGIAN REASON, so the expression goes. (*Drinks, motioning to Young Man to do the same*)

YOUNG MAN   (*After lowering his glass*) This is ridiculous . . .

OLD MAN   TO THE RIDICULOUS, THEN! (*They drink.*)

YOUNG MAN   This is UNREAL!

OLD MAN   TO THE UNREAL, IF YOU LIKE! (*They drink again.*)

YOUNG MAN   But I mean . . . really . . .

OLD MAN   DRINK! (*Drinks again. As Blue Jeans refills the glasses, Old Man whispers to Young Man.*) Now it's your turn to make the toast . . . (*Young Man hesitates.*) Go on, go on.

YOUNG MAN   Well, OK . . . I propose a toast to, uh . . .

OLD MAN   WHY NOT?!

YOUNG MAN   (*Slumping down on the bucket*) This is too much . . . (*Blue Jeans has been sneaking a few drinks himself.*)

OLD MAN   All right, all right. So much for the toasts. (*Smacks his lips*) Let's on to the reading of the ode.

YOUNG MAN   Yeah, sure, "The Ode"!

OLD MAN   Any kind of feast that's worth its salt has a reading of a commemorative ode . . . (*Takes a piece of paper from his shirt pocket and unfolds it*) . . . You don't want to read the ode, do you? Some people say the special guest should always read the ode.

YOUNG MAN   Oh, no . . . uh, you just go right ahead, and I'll just sort of sit here and listen.

OLD MAN   As you prefer. (*During this time, Blue Jeans has taken off his green coat and bandana, handing them off stage. He runs to the other side of the stage and slips into a tail coat and buttons on a white tie. He carries a cello and a small stool out to the edge of the spotlight, sits down and prepares to play. He yawns and stretches, waiting for Old Man to begin the reading of the ode.*) I present to you the ODE, forever commemorating this feast . . . our feast without reason or occasion.

(*Old Man motions for the Cellist to begin his background music, waits a moment, then sighing, begins. As the ode progresses, Cellist falls almost asleep, bowing of cello is spasmodic, but recorded music plays on.*)

Old Man's Ode

Oh Bacchus, look this way!
See the anger mapping lines upon our brow, trace the print of
trouble's foot around our eyes—
Dismal creatures we must seem, cowering behind the days's affairs,
Grasping tight to tin toy soldiers of our objective lives, staring, as
imagination dies;
See our mental siege and send down laughing legions to set us
free.

Thus did we call out to Baccus, and he raised a drunken eyebrow
to our plea.
He sent to us, not legions, but a Cherub from his troop,
One small, fat, sodden Cherub (*Looks at Blue Jeans*)   from his
troop.

Oh Cherub, harken to our woe!
Listen, minor spirit of the feast, fledgling sent by Bacchus giving
answer to our plea,
Thou, who now would far rather be thronged among thy master's
ranks,

Voicing his choral praise, or tipping the Olympian cup upon your
lip to drain his liquid revelry,
Listen to our labor's chant, and grant, at least, a momentary
feast!
Thus, did we call out to the Cherub Bacchus sent, still pouting
from his journey,
He blinked his eyes, and then his pudgy mouth gaped open in a
yawn,
But he gave us music, and he gave us wine before our time was
up.

(*Factory whistle blows. All characters look up. The lights begin to
fade on again. Blue Jeans takes his cello and stool off stage, along
with his costume. He comes back out and grabs the glasses away
from Young Man who resists, and from Old Man, who is resigned.
Blue Jeans trundles the champagne cart off stage. The lights
come up quickly now. The stage work-lights are flipped on. The
stage crew members begin to return to their task of putting up
sets.*)

YOUNG MAN   (*Looking around him, bewildered*) The wine . . . the
  guy with the . . . uh, violin? Where have they gone? The feast
  . . . what happened?
OLD MAN   Time was up, that's all.
YOUNG MAN   What do you mean, the time was up . . . I mean they
  were all here . . . and your ode? Where's your ode?
OLD MAN   (*Checking through his pockets*) I guess I lost it . . . (*He
  had set it down on the cart.*) . . . anyway, you heard the whistle, didn't you . . . back to work, you know. (*Cheerful*)
YOUNG MAN   I guess so . . . (*Old Man climbs down the ladder after
  gathering up his things. Young Man puts his lunch papers in the
  paper bag and crumples it up. He gazes up the aisle as Old Man
  leaves.*)
OLD MAN   (*Turns somewhere up the aisle*) So long, Young Man . . .
YOUNG MAN   So long, Old Man . . . (*Turns and walks slowly off
  stage pondering something. As he goes, Blue Jeans bustles out
  from the wings, gathers up his easel and cardboard and ladder. In
  his rush he bumps into Young Man, says, "Excuse me . . ."
  Young Man barely notices.*)

(*Blue Jeans bustles off the other side of the stage; someone
among the stage crew looks up, and noticing that some damn fool
has opened the curtain when they weren't ready, shouts some
expletive off stage. The curtains close hurriedly.*)

Questions

1. "Beauty," it is sometimes said, "lies in the eye of the beholder," or "What we are determines what we see." What inner attitude determines what the old man sees on his lunch hour? What inner attitude determines what the young man usually sees on *his* lunch hour? What significance is there in the fact that the old man eats his lunch with delight, opens the conversation, tells what he had for breakfast, shows what he's having for lunch? Explain. Clearly the old man, since he's still working in a factory in his old age, has not been "successful" in the usual material sense. How then can he be so much less bitter than the young man, who still has his life ahead of him?

2. The young man obviously has great difficulty in "joining" the old man in the feast. What stands in his way? How does a little man wearing a red bandana and playing a flute help him "see" more clearly. How does Blue Jeans help him further? When the young man says, still dragging his feet, "I propose a toast to, uh. . . ." and the old man replies loudly, "WHY NOT?!," what do you gather the toast would have been to? What is he referring to when he says, "This is too much. . . ."?

3. So far we have ignored the fact that the conversation of the old man and the young man actually takes place on a stage in a theater: They are actors and Blue Jeans is a stage manager or director. Plainly, at the beginning we are asked to see the stage as a stage, stagehands apparently getting ready for some other play, one of them suddenly coming forward with a title on a placard and an aside to us that he will try to "sneak in this bit" while the rest go on working. Later, when the old man and the young man are eating their lunch, we are asked to imagine that the stage is a park or a vacant lot or anywhere near a factory that workers might take their lunch. When is this "imagined reality" broken into again by the reminder that this is a stage and these are actors? Why does the playwright ask us to move back and forth between these two worlds of "reality" and "imagined reality"? Do these worlds have any kind of parallel inside the play, with the vision of the old man and the vision of the young man? How could it be said that the old man's role within the play is somewhat like that of a playwright and the young man's like that of a theater audience? Might it even be said that what the old man does within this play for his young companion parallels what its author aims to do for us—persuading us to make-believe in order to learn something about ourselves? What does the young man within the play learn? (Consider his two speeches just after the factory whistle blows.)

4. What do you think this play is saying about the proper attitude toward "reality" and "imagined reality"?

5. A great deal is communicated to us at the beginning of the play by the entirely different attitudes and feelings that the old man and the young man express in their ways of eating. Try first of all imitating the young man's way: Imagine you have a sandwich in your hand and express resentment, anger, frustration simply by the way you eat. Then try the old man's way: Let your eating convey a feeling of pure delight and happy wonder that the world could be so good to you. Finally, see how many of the following moods, situations, or characteristics you can express so that they are recognizable to a classmate simply by the way you eat an imaginary sandwich or piece of fruit: (a) boredom, (b) hunger, (c) distress, (d) femininity or masculinity, (e) elegance, (f) a gradually developing stomach ache.

Some very ordinary people—just like most of us—gather together in the village square of a small New England farming community for a time-honored jearly ritual. They exchange pleasantries and memories and reveal in the most matter-of-fact way that they are friendly, easy-going, and neighborly. Then these very ordinary people do a very extraordinary thing.

The Lottery

adapted by
BRAINERD DUFFIELD
from a story by
SHIRLEY JACKSON

The scene is a bare stage with a few stones lying here and there. It represents a village square on the twenty-seventh of June of the present year. The stage is in darkness. Gradually a pool of amber light comes up at stage center. Two boys, Tommy and Dickie, enter, looking about on the ground. From time to time, one of them picks up a stone and puts it in his pocket. The search should continue for about a minute before either of them speaks.

TOMMY I'm keepin' the best ones right in my pocket.
DICKIE Me, too.
TOMMY (*Indicating right stage*) We oughta make an extra pile over here. Then we could take turns guardin'.
DICKIE Sure. Then if some other kids tried to swipe any, we'll be ready for 'em. (*He and Tommy begin to build a stockpile of stones at right.*)

(A Girl somewhat younger enters and crosses to watch them, but the boys ignore her. During this leisurely pantomime, a steeple bell has begun to chime, and the amber light widens, gradually illuminating the full stage.)

DICKIE   *(Muttering)*   Girls always got to be hangin' around.

(The little girl has attempted to assist Dickie and Tommy by adding a stone or two to the pile, but they turn their backs on her and, feeling hurt, Girl goes out.)

(During the preceding, two men, Martin and Delacroix, enter and cross to center, conversing quietly.)

MARTIN   *(Glancing over)*   Children are always the first to gather.

DELACROIX   Sure—but everybody'll be comin' now, soon as they hear the bell.

MARTIN   *(Scanning sky)*   Beautiful day for it.

DELACROIX   Yes, fine. I don't care if it *is* my home town, we got the purtiest village green of any in the state.

(Another man, Hutchison, has entered, leading his small son, Davy, by the hand. They cross to join the others.)

DELACROIX   *(To Hutchison)*   How are you, Bill?

HUTCHISON   Fred . . . Horace . . .   *(Shakes hands with both men)*   Good to see you. You both know Davy?

MARTIN   *(Patting Davy on head)*   Well, I should hope so. How are you, Davy?   *(To Hutchison)*   This is his first year, ain't it?

HUTCHISON   That's right. Never seen a Lottery before, have you, Dave?

(Davy nods.)

MARTIN   Gonna grow up and be a good farmer like your dad?   *(Davy nods.)*   That's the boy.

DELACROIX   *(Amiably)*   My son, Chester, wants to go off to the Agricultural School and learn a lot of book rubbish. I tell him he'd do better to stay home and learn of his father, same as I did of mine.

MARTIN   That's right, too. Pitch in and help pay the taxes.

DELACROIX   I told him a farmer don't need to develop his mind, long as he builds up his muscles.

HUTCHINSON   A strong back, that' what you need when you take up farmin'.

DELACROIX   Where's the wife, Bill?

HUTCHISON   *(Slight pause)*   Oh, she'll be along.   *(Frowns and looks about anxiously)*

(*Mrs. Dunbar and Mrs. Watson enter and cross toward the children. The men continue to talk in pantomime.*)

MRS. DUNBAR   (*As they cross*)   How does the weather suit you, Stella?

MRS. WATSON   Couldn't be better.

MRS. DUNBAR   We always seem to get good weather for the twenty-seventh. Never knew it to fail.

MRS. WATSON   Been right cold and wet for June.

(*Miss Bessom enters and starts toward the other women.*)

MRS. DUNBAR   Oh, that rain done us lots of harm. (*Shakes her head*)   Too *much* rain!

MRS. WATSON   Guess the Lottery ought to change our luck.

MRS. DUNBAR   That's how the sayin' goes. (*Sees Miss Bessom*)   Look who's here. Howdy, Miss Bessom. Why, you ain't changed a particle!

MISS BESSOM   (*Slightly piqued*)   Who ever said I had?

MRS. DUNBAR   (*Scrutinizing her*)   They told me you were gettin' real fleshy, and it ain't so.

MRS. WATSON   Course it ain't. Hear you had a weddin' in the family.

MISS BESSOM   Yes, my sister Nina's girl got married to young Sam Gilliatt over to Rigby township.

MRS. WATSON   I s'pose that means she'll be drawin' over there from now on?

MISS BESSOM   Oh, sure! She's got to draw with *his* family now. (*To Mrs. Dunbar*)   I declare, Janey, it's been a month of Sundays since I seen you. Don't you *never* come into town?

MRS. DUNBAR   Not if I can help it. Ain't been further than m'own chicken yard—not since Decoration Day, and that's a fact.

MRS. WATSON   One thing about the Lottery, it does bring everyone out, like it or not.

MISS BESSOM   Well, Janey's got Clyde to wait on, too. How's he makin' out?

MRS. DUNBAR   Oh, he'll be fine! Except he's terrible mad to have to stay home and miss the excitement.

MISS BESSOM   I'll bet. (*She and Mrs. Watson cluck sympathetically, and the women continue to converse silently.*)

(*Dickie and Tommy have drifted away by now to continue their search for stones off stage. Other Villagers now drift in. They chat ad lib, building to a general murmur.*)

MARTIN   (*On spoken cue, "I'll bet"*)   Now I got that tractor, I was figurin' I might make the switch from grass to hay silage.

HUTCHISON   Costs about the same to harvest an acre, don't it?

MARTIN   Just about. Cattle don't seem to mind what they're eatin', and I thought I could get away from the risk of bad weather—

DELACROIX   (*Slight chuckle*) Don't you fret about the weather, Horace. "Lottery in June, corn be heavy soon."

HUTCHISON   (*Nodding, with a faint smile*) That's what they always told us, ain't it, Fred?

(*Delacroix nods.*)

MISS BESSOM   (*Glancing about*) Don't see Tessie Hutchison any-place, do you?

MRS. WATSON   No, I don't. Bill's standin' right there, though, and little Davy, too.

MISS BESSOM   Got a recipe I borrowed and want to give back to her. It's for the watermelon pickles she won a prize with at the social.

(*Jack Wilkins enters and nods to the ladies.*)

JACK   'Scuse me, ladies. Hi, Miz Dunbar. How's Clyde doin'?

MRS. DUNBAR   Fine, thanks, Jack. Doctor's goin' to take the cast off next week.

JACK   How's he goin' to get the news today?

MRS. DUNBAR   I promised to send Tommy runnin', soon as the drawin's over.

JACK   (*Grinning*) That's good. (*Goes to join other men*)

(*Women beam at one another.*)

MISS BESSOM   *Such* a nice boy—Jack Wilkins.

MRS. WATSON   He's got his mother's looks and that's a blessin'.

MRS. DUNBAR   So many of the young ones seem to drift away. This place's gettin' smaller every year.

MISS BESSOM   I know it. Joe Summers told me there's less'n two hundred names on the registration this time.

MRS. DUNBAR   You don't mean it?

MRS. WATSON   Isn't that awful?

(*Old Man Warner has made a slow entrance, crossing to center. Villagers have a greeting for him as he passes.*)

DELACROIX   Well, here's Old Man Warner, lookin' spry as ever!

HUTCHISON   How're you feelin', Mr. Warner?

WARNER   Not so bad. (*Winks*) Rheumatism comes and goes.

MARTIN   How's it seem to be the oldest citizen?

WARNER   You don't hear *me* complainin'.

HUTCHISON   (*Chuckling*) How many Lotteries does this make?

WARNER   I'm eighty-one last November. Seen my first at the age of five. You figure it out.

DELACROIX   Never missed one in all those years!

JACK   He hears very good, too, don't he?

DELACROIX   Oh, he's a marvel!

WARNER   And I'll be comin' back for a few more!

JACK   (*Grinning*)   You tell 'em, old-timer!

MARTIN   (*Calling across to women*)   Hear that? Old Man Warner says he's good for a few more!   (*General murmur of approval from others on stage*)

MRS. WATSON   He's seen seventy-six of them.

MRS. DUNBAR   Imagine!

WARNER   Oh, you fellers ought to been here in the old days. Not like now. Lottery meant somethin' when I was a boy.

(*Belva Summers has entered, and stops at one side of the stage, opposite the other women. She wears black, and carries some knitting with her, at which she works during the following action. She remains by herself, content to speak to no one.*)

MISS BESSOM   Almost time to get started.

MRS. WATSON   (*Looking off*)   Guess we're goin' to, Miss Bessom. There's Joe Summers now, on the post-office steps.

MRS. DUNBAR   He's bringin' out the box.

MISS BESSOM   Where's his sister? She here?

MRS. DUNBAR   (*Nodding toward Belva*)   Beats me how he can stay so cheerful with that one to put up with.

MRS. WATSON   I'd hate to have her in *my* house.

(*The murmur of the Villagers swells. Dickie and Tommy have entered again. They see a stone and both grab simultaneously for it. They tussle with each other to gain possession of the stone.*)

TOMMY   You didn't, neither! I seen it first!

DICKIE   You give that back!

TOMMY   The heck I will!   (*Shoves him.*)

DICKIE   Cut it out, will you? Watch who you're shovin'—

(*There is a tussle again. Mrs. Dunbar comes forward and grasps Tommy by the wrist.*)

MRS. DUNBAR   You stop that!

TOMMY   Leggo, Ma! I seen it first, honest!

MRS. DUNBAR   Never you mind. You got stones aplenty!

(*Mrs. Watson attempts to collar Dickie, but he escapes.*)

MRS. WATSON   You come here to me. Wait till I get you home.

MARTIN   (*Sharply, to Dickie*)   Obey your mother. Mind what I say.

DICKIE   (*Dutifully*)   Yes, Uncle Horace. (*Crosses to Mrs. Watson, unwillingly.*)

JACK   (*Pointing off with gesture of thumb*)   Joe Summers is comin'. It won't be long now.

DELACROIX   (*Good-humoredly*)   We'd better line up by families and wait for the bad news.

(*Villagers begin to shift and reassemble according to family groups.*)

HUTCHISON   (*To Davy*)   Now, Davy, stick close to me. There's nothin' to be a-scared of.

(*Joe Summers enters, crosses to center. He is carrying a large black wooden box and a wooden paddle. A Townsman follows with a high stool, on which Joe places the black box in a dignified and solemn manner.*)

JOE   Thank you, Norbert.

(*During Joe's entrance, there has been a growing murmur from Villagers.*)

VILLAGERS   (*Ad libbing upon Joe's entrance*)   Here he comes. Howdy, Mr. Summers. There's the head man comin'. He's got the old black box. Howdy, Joe. Let's get goin'.

(*Joe takes a sheaf of papers from his hip pocket and places them on box. He pauses now to mop his forehead with a handkerchief. Most of the Villagers are in small groups covering right half of stage. The remainder of the left side of stage is clear, except for Belva.*)

JOE   (*Brightly*)   Little late today, folks. (*Waves to Jack*)   Here, you! The Wilkins boy. Give me a hand and stir these names up. Stir 'em good and hard. (*Jack stirs box with paddle, which Joe hands him. Then Joe turns to Townsman.*)   Norbert, you hold it steady for him. Better use both hands. (*Townsman, using both hands to steady box, helps Jack with stirring business. Joe notices Belva, and moves toward her, passing others en route.*)   How are you, folks?

VILLAGERS   Mr. Summers! Howdy, Joe. How are you? (*Belva, occupied with her knitting, awaits him with an enigmatic smile. During scene which follows between Joe and Belva, Villagers converse in pantomime.*)

BELVA   (*Drily*)   Almost ready, are you, Joe? Hope you haven't forgotten, and left my name out.

JOE   No, Belva. You're down there. I just been checkin' the list.

BELVA   (*Looking over his shoulder*)   Oh, you got a long ways to go yet. A terrible responsibility. Everybody says so. (*Shakes head with mock sympathy.*)   Poor Joe Summers. Doin' his duty. And with that naggin' sister, too.

JOE   (*Grimly*)   Well, if everybody says so, Belva, there must be somethin' to it.

BELVA   (*Knitting as she talks*)   I must say *I* enjoy myself. Watchin' an important man at work. Joe Summers—up there runnin' things—devotin' all his time and energy to civic activities. And how you love it!

JOE   (*glancing over at Villagers*)   You'd oblige me, Belva, by lowerin' your voice a little.

BELVA   (*Smiling*)   Why should I? Nobody asked you to come over and speak to me.

JOE   You might give a thought to the neighbors.

BELVA   (*Contemptuously*)   The neighbors! If everybody wasn't so scared of their neighbors, maybe we'd give up some heathen customs that don't make sense any more. Half the young folks growin' up don't have the faintest notion what a Lottery stands for.

JOE   (*Turning away*)   Oh, what's the use of talkin' to you!

BELVA   There's no tellin' these days where the wisdom stops and superstition begins.

JOE   (*Turning back to her*)   The Lottery has got to be taken serious. People get set in a way of doin' things and you can't change 'em. It's human nature.

BELVA   (*Stops knitting, speaking softly, but with intensity*)   I don't like this town nor anybody in it. But you're the worst of 'em, Joe Summers. You drove him away. Our own brother and you drove him away.

JOE   It was more your doin' than mine. You're the one brought him up to be a weaklin' and a coward. You started him goin' out on the street and preachin' against tradition.

BELVA   You call that cowardly? It takes a *brave* man to say what he thinks, when every hand is against him.

JOE   (*Doggedly*)   He left of his own accord. I didn't send him.

BELVA   It takes real courage to fight prejudice on your own doorstep. (*With contempt*)   It's you and the rest of 'em that are cowards.

JOE   Every day of my life I have to listen to your craziness. If you want to go off lookin' for him, Belva, I'll give you the money.

Take the mornin' train. I'll even draw alone in the Lottery from now on. There—I couldn't offer more'n that, could I?

BELVA I'm not goin' anywhere. I'm goin' to stay right here and wait. (*Looks up and straight at him*) Because sooner or later your name might come up. I wouldn't want to miss that day.

(*Joe turns away abruptly and goes back to center. Belva stands motionless for a moment or two and then resumes her knitting.*)

JOE All right, Jack, that's good enough, I'm sure.

JACK Glad to do it, Mr. Summers.

JOE (*To nearby Women Villagers*) Think it's stirred enough, ladies?

MRS. WATSON (*Chuckling*) Don't worry, Joe. We trust you.

MRS. DUNBAR Oh, Joe knows what he's doin', all right.

(*General laughter from Women Villagers.*)

WARNER Hear those women hollerin' and cacklin'. They never would have stood for that in the old days.

DELACROIX Seen some changes, ain't you, Mr. Warner?

WARNER Bad enough to see Joe Summers up there crackin' jokes. Nobody shows respect for the ceremony. Just go through the motions nowadays.

(*Jack has crossed to where Warner is standing.*)

JACK How was it different, Mr. Warner?

WARNER Oh, it was *some* different. Everybody had to stand just so. And before the drawin', the head man spoke his piece real solemn-like. Had a regular recitation went with it.

HUTCHINSON (*Scanning Villagers*) Now where in tarnation is my wife?

(*Chuckle from those near him.*)

MARTIN Bill Hutchison lost his better half.

HUTCHISON (*To Mrs. Dunbar*) Janey, you seen her?

MRS. DUNBAR No, I ain't, Bill, and I been lookin', too.

MARTIN Guess she ain't gonna make it.

MISS BESSOM Late for the Lottery. Can you beat that?

HUTCHISON I don't know what's got into the woman.

DELACROIX That black box has seen a lot of service.

WARNER Yessir. That box was here afore I was born, and afore my father was.

JACK Just imagine.

WARNER Story goes it was made out of the pieces of the first box that ever was used.

DELACROIX   Makes you think, don't it?

WARNER   Goes way back to the days when they first settled down to make a village here.

JACK   Seems like we ought to be ready to build us a new one.

WARNER   (*Shocked*)   No, boy! Don't say that. Not even jokin'.

DELACROIX   No, Jack. We don't want to upset tradition more'n we have to. Long as it holds together, we ain't gonna change it.

WARNER   I can recollect when they used to use wooden chips 'stead of paper to write the names on.

JACK   What do you know? Wooden chips!

WARNER   (*Nodding*)   I was real little, but I remember.

(*Joe has been busy checking his list, looking about and making notations on the sheets of paper. Occasionally he consults with one of the Villagers close by him.*)

JOE   (*Raising voice*)   Now, folks, I'm just about ready to declare this Lottery open. But you know how I always got this last-minute fussin' to do. Want to make sure the list is accurate—with all the heads of families and members of each household in each family.

MRS. DUNBAR   You go right ahead, Mr. Summers.

MRS. WATSON   Joe never made a mistake yet.

(*Tessie Hutchison, wearing an apron over her housedress, enters.*)

MRS. DUNBAR   Why, Tessie! Where you been?

TESSIE   Clean forgot what day it was. (*Other women close by laugh softly.*)   Thought Bill was out back stackin' wood. But I looked out the window and seen little Davy was gone. Then I remembered it was the twenty-seventh—and come a-runnin'. (*She is drying her hands on her apron as she speaks.*)

MRS. DUNBAR   You made it all right, though. Joe is still checkin' his list.

TESSIE   Seems like there's no time at all between Lotteries any more. Seems like we barely got through with the last one.

MRS. DUNBAR   Time sure goes fast.

TESSIE   (*Glancing around*)   Where's Bill at? Oh, I see him. 'Scuse me, Janey.

(*Villagers make way for her as she moves to join Hutchison.*)

VILLAGERS   Hey, Hutchison! Here she comes! Here's your missus, Bill! Look, Bill! She made it after all!

TESSIE   (*Bending down, to Davy*)   Give Mama a kiss. (*Davy kisses her.*)   That's my good boy. (*Looks at Hutchison for a moment. He smiles faintly and takes her hand.*)

HUTCHISON   So you got here, did you?

JOE   (*Calling amiably*) Thought we were goin' to have to get on without you, Tessie.

TESSIE   (*With forced pleasantness*) Wouldn't have me leave my dishes in the sink, would you, Joe?

JOE   No, ma'am.

(*General ripple of laughter from Villagers.*)

HUTCHISON   You stay put, Dave, while I talk with your mother. (*Davy joins other children, as Hutchison brings Tessie to a spot where they talk somewhat apart from other Villagers. He is not angry, but seems deeply concerned and worried.*) What ever kept you?

TESSIE   I don't know, Bill. I just wasn't thinkin', I guess.

HUTCHISON   That story's all right for the women. I know better. You knew the Lottery was today.

TESSIE   Well, it don't matter now. So long as I'm here.

HUTCHISON   What about Davy? Why'd you try to hide him?

TESSIE   Hide him? I didn't hide him. What makes you say that?

HUTCHISON   I found him in the stable loft. He said you told him to wait there—

TESSIE   Yes, but I was goin' to get him, Bill. I was goin' to bring him— honest.

HUTCHISON   What reason did you have to put him there?

TESSIE   Oh, Bill, he's such a little boy! And his birthday just last month. I hate to see the children takin' part in grown-up ructions before they've even put aside their toys.

HUTCHISON   I went through it when I was little.

TESSIE   I know, Bill. I guess I was born and brought up with it, same as yourself.

HUTCHISON   Then how did you think you could get away with such a thing? You know Davy's name has to be there along with ours. And you know how careful Joe Summers is. Why, we'd have been a laughin' stock in front of everybody.

TESSIE   But I told you I intended to bring him. You got to believe me, Bill.

HUTCHISON   Talkin' a lot of sentimental tommyrot. I always gave you credit for more sense than some of these other females. What's come over you lately, anyway?

TESSIE   I told you—nothin'.

HUTCHISON   Next thing you'll be sayin' we ought to give up Lotteries altogether—like poor Joe Summers' sister.

TESSIE   Well, I've not come to that yet. But some places have given them up. Lots of little towns up to the north—

HUTCHISON   No good'll come of it, either. You wait and see.

TESSIE   I don't say it will. No, I reckon the Lottery serves its useful purpose. When a custom's been handed down from generation to generation, there must be good in it.

HUTCHISON   (*Wagging head, grinning*) Then you shouldn't be so cussed busy, findin' fault.

JOE   (*Clearing throat*) Well, now, guess we better get started—get this over with—so's we can get back to work. Anybody ain't here?

VILLAGERS   Dunbar! Clyde Dunbar! Dunbar ain't here!

JOE   (*Glancing at list*) Clyde Dunbar—that's right. He's broke his leg, hasn't he? Who's drawin' for him?

MRS. DUNBAR   Me, I guess.

JOE   Wife draws for husband. Don't have a grown boy to do it for you, Janey?

MRS. DUNBAR   Ralph's not but sixteen yet. Guess I got to fill in for the old man this year.

(*Mild chuckle from Villagers.*)

JOE   (*Making note*) Right. Jack Wilkins, you're drawin' this year?

JACK   (*Blinking nervously*) Yessir. I'm drawin' for my mother and me.

MARTIN   Good fellow, Jack. Glad to see your mother's got a man to do it.

JOE   Well, I guess that's everyone   (*With a wink.*)   Old Man Warner make it?

WARNER   (*Raising hand*) Here!

JOE   (*Nodding*) Knew you would. (*Raps on box*) All ready? (*Whisper runs through Villagers; then a hush follows. Everyone is quite serious now. There is no more laughter.*) Now, I'll read off the names—heads of families first—and the men come up and take a paper out of the box. Keep the paper folded in your hand without lookin' at it until everyone has had a turn. Everything clear? (*Villagers are silent, but nervous, wetting their lips, not looking around or moving. Joe reads from list.*) Adams. (*A man disengages himself from crowd, comes forward, reaches into black box and takes out a folded paper. Joe greets him.*) Hi, Steve. (*Holding paper firmly, the man goes back to his place and stands, not looking down at his hand. Joe calls next name.*) Allen. (*Another man comes to box, repeating same business.*) How are you, Mr. Allen? (*Now, as scene continues, Joe continues to call out names. Each time, someone comes forward, reaches into box, takes out folded piece of paper and returns to his place, not looking down at hand holding paper. As dialogue of Villagers breaks into scene, overlapping Joe's voice, calling of the names becomes less distinct, becoming sort of a muted background to Villagers' dialogue.*)   Appleby . . . Barrows . . .. Burgess . . . Caswell . . . Collins . . .

DELACROIX   They do say that over in the north village, they're talkin' of givin' up the Lottery.

WARNER   Pack of crazy fools! Listenin' to the young folks—nothin's good enough for *them*. Next thing you know, they'll want to go back to livin' in caves—nobody work any more—live *that* way for a while.

DELACROIX   That's right, Mr. Warner.

WARNER   First thing you know we'd all be eatin' stewed chickweed and acorns. There's *always* been a Lottery.

JOE   Dunbar . . .

MRS. WATSON   Go on, Janey. That's you.

MISS BESSOM   (*As Mrs. Dunbar crosses to draw*)   There she goes. . . .

JOE   Foster . . . Graves . . . Hutchison . . .

MRS. WATSON   Where do they keep the black box in between times?

MISS BESSOM   It varies. Sometimes one place—sometimes another.

MRS. WATSON   I heard it spent one whole winter in Mr. Graves's barn.

MISS BESSOM   Another year, Clem Martin put it on a shelf in his grocery and left it set there.

MRS. WATSON   Yep. I recall that time.

JOE   Tatum . . . Townsend . . . Tuttle . . . Vincent . . .

MRS. DUNBAR   (*To Tommy*)   I wish they'd hurry.

TOMMY   They're almost through, Ma.

MRS. DUNBAR   You get ready to run and tell Dad.

JOE   Warner . . . Howdy, Mr. Warner.

(*Warner takes slip and returns to his place.*)

WARNER   Got mine. Seventy-seventh year I been in the Lottery.

JOE   Watson . . . Hi, Stella.

MRS. WATSON   (*Drawing*)   Hi, Joe.

JOE   Wilkins . . .

MISS BESSOM   (*As Jack crosses to draw*)   Don't be nervous, Jack.

JOE   (*Kindly*)   Take your time, son.

JACK   (*Drawing*)   Thanks, Mr. Summers.

JOE   (*Checking off list*)   Now, that's all. (*A breathless pause. Joe draws and holds up his hand with his slip of paper in it.*)   All right, fellows. (*For a moment, no one moves; then there is a rustle as all the slips are opened.*)

VILLAGERS   (*Whispering*)   Who is it? Who's got it? Is it the Dunbars? Is it the Watsons? (*Then, louder ad libs are heard, building to an excited climax.*)   It's Hutchison! It's Bill! Bill Hutchison's got it! Hutchison!

(The Hutchisons break away from others and form a small group.)

MRS. DUNBAR   *(Excitedly)* Go tell your father!

(Tommy takes a last awestruck look at Bill Hutchison, where he stands quietly flanked by Tessie and Davy, then Tommy runs out. Hutchison is staring at bit of paper in his hand. Villagers are silent again, all eyes on Hutchison family.)

TESSIE   *(Shouting suddenly)* Joe Summers! You didn't give him time enough to take any paper he wanted. I saw you. It wasn't fair!

MRS. WATSON   Be a good sport, Tessie.

MISS BESSOM   All of us took the same chance.

HUTCHISON   You hush up, Tessie.

JOE   Well, everyone, that was done pretty fast, and now we've got to be hurryin' a little more to get done in time. *(Consulting list)* Bill, you draw for the Hutchison family. You got any other households in the Hutchisons?

TESSIE   *(Shrilly)* There's Don and Eva! Make *them* take their chance!

JOE   *(Gently)* Daughters draw with their husbands' families. You know that as well as anyone, Tessie.

TESSIE   It wasn't fair!

HUTCHISON   I guess there's just the three of us, Joe. Eva draws with her husband. That's only as it should be.

JOE   Then, as far as drawin' for families is concerned, it's you, and, as far as drawin' for households is concerned, that's you, too. Right?

HUTCHISON   Right.

JOE   How many kids, Bill?

HUTCHISON   Just the one. Little Davy here. Bill, Jr., he died when he was a baby.

JOE   All right, then. Jack, you got some blank tickets back? *(Jack holds up two blank slips of paper which he has taken from some of the Villagers.)* Put them in the box, then. Take Bill's and put it in. *(Jack does so.)*

TESSIE   *(Out of the ensuing silence)* I think we ought to start over. *(As quietly as she can)* I tell you, it wasn't fair! You didn't give him time enough to choose. Everybody saw that. *(Appealing)* Listen, everybody!

(Jack has stepped back from box. Other Villagers have crumpled their own slips and let them drop to ground.)

JOE Ready, Bill? (*Hutchison takes a quick glance at his wife and son and then nods.*) Remember, take the slips and keep them folded until each of you has taken one. Jack, you help little Davy. (*Jack takes Davy's hand and leads him to box.*) Take a paper out of the box, Dave. Take just *one* paper. (*Davy does so.*) That's right. Jack, you hold it for him. (*Jack takes paper and holds it carefully.*) Tessie next. (*Tessie hesitates for a moment, looking around defiantly, then she sets her lips and goes to box. She snatches out a paper and holds it behind her.*) Bill . . . (*Hutchison reaches into box and brings out last slip of paper. The Villagers are silent and tense.*)

MISS BESSOM (*Breaking silence*) I hope it isn't little Dave.

(*Villagers begin to whisper.*)

WARNER (*Clearly*) It's not the way it used to be. People ain't the same way they used to be.

JOE All right. Open the papers. Jack, you open little Dave's. (*Jack opens paper, holds it up, and a sigh of relief goes through Villagers as they see that it is blank. Joe turns to Tessie.*) Tessie . . . (*There is a pause. Tessie does not move to open her slip of paper. Joe turns to Hutchison, who unfolds his paper and shows it. It is blank. Joe speaks to Tessie in a hushed voice.*) It's Tessie. Show us her paper, Bill. (*Hutchison turns to Tessie and forces her slip of paper out of her hand. It has a black spot on it. He holds it up. A murmur goes through Villagers. Joe comes forward.*) All right, folks. Let's finish quickly.

(*Jack carries black box, paddle, and stool off and presently returns to rejoin Villagers.*)

MRS. WATSON (*Excitedly*) Come on, Janey. Hurry up! Come on, Miss Bessom.

MISS BESSOM I can't move as fast as I used to.

(*Villagers move toward front of stage, some of them picking up stones as they come. Dickie gives little Davy a fistful of stones. As Villagers shift about, Tessie backs away, like a trapped animal, until she is alone at the center of a cleared space at rear. Villagers are grouped at both sides of stage. Now Tessie holds out her hands in a desperate appeal, as Villagers turn to face her and begin slowly to close in.*)

TESSIE It isn't fair! It wasn't done fair!

HUTCHISON Be quiet, Tess. We got to do this. (*Throws a stone, and*

Tessie flinches, putting her hand to her brow.)   Come on. Come on, everyone.

(*Davy throws his fistful of stones. Tessie utters a cry and sinks to her knees. Villagers throw stones.*)

TESSIE   It isn't fair! It isn't right!   (*Shields her face as Villagers continue to throw stones at her.*)

(*Belva has crossed the stage, thrusting Joe aside in passing. She goes out without looking at spectacle on stage. By now, Villagers have hemmed in their victim, cutting her off from view. The clamor of voices builds, as does the ferocity of the stone-throwing.*)

VILLAGERS   Come on! Get it over with! Hit her! That's the way! Hit her, everybody! Get it over!   (*Lights dim out, and with darkness comes a low rumble of thunder. Voices of the Villagers stop abruptly. Silence.*)

Questions

1. What details of action and speech show that these townspeople are (as indicated in our headnote) friendly, easy-going, neighborly? What happens if you switch the names and comments of the male characters? Does it make any difference who says what? How about the female characters? With which ones of the males or females does it make a difference? What are we to infer about these people from the fact that such switching can be done?
2. When did you first sense that something extraordinary was going to happen? What dramatic preparation for the ending has the author given us? What psychological preparation?
3. The play is a shocker the first time one reads it (as is the short story it is based on), and, like "Sorry, Wrong Number," it's the kind of story no one ever forgets. But it isn't only a one-time shocker that loses its bite after the secret is revealed. It seems to get more shocking the more one reads it or thinks about it. Why do you suppose that this is so? (Or don't you have that response?)
4. What would you say to someone who argued that the play is symbolic of what can happen in a small, tightly knit community in which the

older generations have a great deal of authority, but that such a thing couldn't happen in a larger, more loosely knit community such as a suburban town or a city?

5. What do you think "The Lottery" is saying about human behavior? That we're all savages beneath our friendly exteriors? That some of us never question what we do? That progress toward human love and compassion can never come so long as we insist on using scapegoats? Can you think of other instances in history—or perhaps in your own experience—where innocent people have suffered outrage from communities or groups that couldn't or wouldn't change their ways?

6. We have included this play in a grouping called "Three Fantasies." Do you think it properly belongs under the heading, "Fantasy"? Why or why not?